THE LAST MANCHU

THE LAST MANCHU

The Autobiography of Henry Pu Yi,
Last Emperor of China

Henry Pu Yi and Paul Kramer

SKYHORSE PUBLISHING

*When the unreal is taken for the real, then
the real becomes unreal;
When non-existence is taken for existence, then
existence becomes non-existence.*

—DREAM OF THE RED CHAMBER *by Tsao Hsueh-chin,
Translated from the Chinese by Chi-Chen Wang*

Stripped of power but not of rank, Pu Yi lived in imperial opulence in the Forbidden City. When he went for a stroll, the boy Emperor was followed by eunuchs bearing umbrellas, chairs, cakes, tea, chamber pots and medicines. At age 17 he took two child-brides—one as empress and one as consort. But in 1924, Pu Yi fled before the armies of a Chinese warlord. After exile in the north of China, the Japanese installed him as the puppet Emperor of Manchuria. Virtually confined to his palace for years, Pu Yi terrorized his few remaining followers with beatings and torture.

As a Russian prisoner in Siberia, Pu Yi lived in luxury at a mineral springs spa. But in a Communist Chinese prison, the former Emperor was systematically brainwashed, forced to sleep on the floor and paste pencil boxes. After ten years his rehabilitation was branded a success and he was released. As a temporary guide, Pu Yi led a group of former prisoners on a tour of the Forbidden City, the palace that had been his childhood home. The fragrance of cypress trees in the Imperial Garden, he wrote, "brought back to me memories of my youth." Pu Yi died—an ordinary citizen of the People's Republic of China—in 1967.

Skyhorse Publishing books may be purchased in bulk at special
discounts for sales promotion, corporate gifts, fund-raising, or
educational purposes. Special editions can also be created to
specifications. For details, contact the Special Sales Department,
Skyhorse Publishing, 307 West 36th Street, 11th Floor, New York,
NY 10018 or info@skyhorsepublishing.com.

Skyhorse® and Skyhorse Publishing® are registered trademarks of
Skyhorse Publishing, Inc.®, a Delaware corporation.

Visit our website at www.skyhorsepublishing.com.

10 9 8 7 6 5 4

Library of Congress Cataloging-in-Publication Data
Puyi, 1906-1967.
[Wo de qian ban sheng. English]
The last Manchu : the autobiography of Henry Pu Yi, last
emperor of China / Henry Pu Yi and Paul Kramer.
p. cm.
ISBN 978-1-60239-732-3 (pbk.)
1. Puyi, 1906-1967. 2. Puyi, 1906-1967--Childhood
and youth. 3. Puyi, 1906-1967--Exile. 4. Emperors--
China--Biography. 5. China--Kings and rulers--Biography.
6. China--History--Republic, 1912-1949. 7. China--
History--1949-1976. I. Kramer, Paul, 1914-2008. II. Title.
DS773.C51513 2009
951.04092--dc22
[B]
2009024919

Printed in the United States of America

Contents

Contents

Preface

THIS BOOK IS THE STORY OF A MAN, HENRY PU YI, WHO always managed to survive. A brief chronology of major events in his life is proof of his perseverance in the face of continuing adversity:

1906 Born in Peking, China

1908 Crowned Emperor of China

1912 Abdicated, but continued to live as if he were still Emperor, within the Forbidden City in Peking

1924 Fled to the Peking Legation Quarter and then to Tientsin, an important seaport in North China

1931 Escaped Tientsin for Manchuria

1934 Proclaimed Emperor of Manchuria

1945 Captured by the Soviets and flown to Siberia

1950 Turned over to Maoist China for intense brainwashing as a war criminal

1959 Pardoned by the Maoist government of China and returned to Peking to become a member of the People's National Congress as representative of the Manchu people.

1966 Almost murdered by the Red Guards during the Cultural Revolution

1967 Died of natural causes.

From the chronology we can see that except for five years spent as a prisoner of the Soviets, Henry Pu Yi, the last Manchu Emperor of China, spent all his life in Northeast China and physically survived China's last eighty years of violence an achievement worth noting if one keeps in mind how near he always lived to the abyss of Chinese intrigue, war, massacre and revolution. The consequence is that his life itself forms a path of understanding between China's past and its future, in as much as every calamity that has overwhelmed China also overwhelmed Pu Yi and yet he, like China, survived.

Why? The reason seems to be his weak character in combination with the political importance of the Manchu tradition. By Western standards Pu Yi had more in common with the anti-heroes of Genet and Mailer than the heroes of Dickens and Anthony Hope. Indeed, his life suggests a historical justification for the appearance of the anti-hero of modern fiction. Pu Yi, by his own admission, was a liar, suspicious, tricky, a hypocrite and preoccupied with a fear of death. He also hinted that he might have been homosexual, and goes to some length to explain how these aspects of his character were developed as a result of his upbringing and the historic forces with which he had to contend. And it is these explorations into his vices that are such an important aspect of his life. For if Pu Yi had been able to rise above the corrupting influence of 1,200 eunuchs during his youth and the personality of an exotic English tutor, if he had been able to resist the blandishments of his courtiers and the pride of family and tradition, if he had been able to do without twelve-year-old boy pages and stand up to predatory Japanese militarists, then he clearly could never have been brainwashed as he was by the Red Chinese. The defects which were within him provided the suppleness necessary for survival. Without them he would either have been shot before he fell into Communist hands, died or gone insane during the thought-molding process, and his captors would have been without tools with which to work.

Although the facts of his life, which he describes with such charm and tells so well, could stand in themselves as illuminating and important vignettes of Chinese history, the book, over and above its *Gone with the Wind* fascination, confirms the significance of the Manchu tradition. Either the warlords in North China, or the Japanese, or the Soviets or the Maoist Communists could have executed him and extinguished the monarchy just as the Bolsheviks did the Czar of Russia and his immediate family. Yet they never did. On the contrary, they always accorded him some form of special treatment. At first, when the monarchy was overthrown, Pu Yi was allowed to live on, within the Forbidden City, and maintain the imperial traditions. Later, the Japanese made him the puppet Emperor of Manchuria. Then the Russians, who captured him from the Japanese, put him in a hot-springs resort. The Chinese Communists, to whom he was delivered, brainwashed him for ten years and then elected him to the People's National Congress as the representative of the Manchu people.

Even the Americans were ultimately forced by events to accord him special treatment. When he was brought to Tokyo in August 1946 to testify in the war-crimes trial of Japanese leaders, there was pressure to put Pu Yi himself on trial. But this, General MacArthur—the Supreme Commander of the Allied Powers, Japan—refused to do. To try Pu Yi as a war criminal might impair the position of the Emperor of Japan, whose mystique and cohesive force MacArthur was determined to preserve. Pu Yi had, as Emperor of Manchuria, close ties with the Japanese royal family. His brother and heir was married to a relative of the Empress. Their children were half-Japanese.

No other ousted ruler in modern history has exhibited the survival powers of Henry Pu Yi. To say that he led a charmed life is too easy an explanation. An ex-emperor can, perhaps, be lucky once, or even twice, but not six times! The explanation of this ability to survive is an underlying theme of his autobiography and, as such, becomes a key to understanding modern China.

The basis for this book originally appeared in three volumes in Peking in 1964. It was called to my attention in 1965 by Chinese living in the United States who read with interest and excitement a serialized version that was published in the popular press of Hong Kong. Their reaction led me to believe that an English edition might enjoy a similar response among American readers, and this conviction was substantiated when it became possible to obtain and read a copy of the original Peking version. In its original form, however, had it been literally translated, the autobiography would have come to over 1,000 printed pages, and would have suffered from a profusion of repetitious passages. Although Dr. Tsai translated the entire book on tape, it was necessary, in order to preserve reader interest, to make certain editorial changes. In all cases of excision and rearrangement, however, I have been as faithful as possible to the Chinese as a Westerner can possibly be. When the book dealt with specific events and detailed descriptions of imperial Chinese life this was not too difficult, although it was complicated by the fact that Pu Yi was a Manchu and his interests and preoccupations were without precedent in so far as the West was concerned. In addition, there was no basis for comparison of his account since no Chinese Emperor ever before revealed to the public the secrets of the Forbidden City. When it came to presenting Pu Yi's thoughts, ideas and reactions, however, the task was enormously difficult. An Oriental, and above all Pu Yi, simply did not think like a Westerner; the thoughts came out in a different and unaccustomed progression and passed through different convolutions. Superimposed on this, there was the Chinese Communist habit of equating events with ideology to the extent that an Occidental found himself so far removed from the actualities of daily life and the conflicts involved that it was difficult to grasp truth in terms of definable human emotions and reactions. It was therefore necessary to simplify and in some cases to rearrange Pu Yi's thoughts and conduct as described in the original Chinese version so that they became comprehensible. But in all cases, the book was as faithful an abridgment of the original Chinese as it was humanly possible to make it and, at the same time, create a readable and entertaining story for a Western reader.

Preceding the autobiography is a brief introduction designed to supply the reader with an overview of Chinese royal history during the years prior to the last Manchu's accession to the throne. Here again there were difficulties. No royal family in history guarded its secrets more zealously than the Manchus. What really went on within the Forbidden City was purposely withheld from those without. Genuine

source material was not published, and the official state-
ments that were released studiously avoided any revelations
as to the personal factors behind them. It was necessary to
puzzle things out, therefore, with the help of an occasional
foreigner who managed to penetrate some corner of the
Forbidden City on official business, the gossip of eunuchs
and an infrequent indiscretion by a palace official or royal
relative. Such sources were not always reliable, but were the
best available and I used them if only to help the reader
understand what would otherwise be an almost incomprehensible life-style on the part of Manchu royalty.

The first edition of this book was originally published by
Putnam's in 1967. Now, twenty years later, there is a demand for a second edition. Meanwhile, a major motion
picture is being made of Pu Yi's life story. The book's
substance and charm have stood the test of time. Also, and
perhaps more important, events of the past twenty years
have given an authenticity to the book it did not have for the
average Western reader in 1967. One reason for this is a shift
in attitudes. Relations with Communist China have been
resumed. Trade and tourism have been established. Hostili-
ties on both sides have subsided with the consequence that
Westerners can observe events and read books about China
with an objectivity that was heretofore difficult.

P. K.
Washington, D.C.

Introduction

AT 11 A.M. ON THE MORNING OF JULY 25, 1901, A BLUE-
eyed, prematurely graying young Scot, three years out of
Magdalen College, Oxford, stood on a pier at. Hong Kong.
From the German ship *Bayern* which had just docked, a shy,
boyish-looking man descended the gangplank. He stuttered
badly and was dressed in the rich silk costume of a Chinese
noble with the ruby button of a mandarin of the highest rank
on his hat.

It was the first time a Chinese prince had ever set foot on
British territory. Nevertheless, the reception, which had
been held to a minimum at the request of the prince, went
well. Within fifteen minutes of his welcome by the young
official, the prince was carried by four red-coated chair-
bearers from the pier to the entrance to Government House
where he was greeted by the Governor.

This nobleman, who had preferred to receive none of the
honors due him as a Manchu of the blood royal of China,
was Prince Chun and he was on his way to Germany to lay
the humble regrets and apologies of his brother, the Emperor, before the Kaiser for the murder in Peking on June
20, 1900, of the German minister during the Boxer Rebellion.
The young Scot who was at the pier to meet him was a
British civil servant named Reginald Johnston. These two
men were to have a profound influence on the events related
in this autobiography, for one was to become the father of
the author and the other his tutor and intimate friend. Within

the forces that led to this chance meeting are many of the strange, complex and fantastic elements that have resulted in the author becoming three times an Emperor, once a Chief Executive, an exile for eight years, a prisoner for fourteen years, a gardener, a scholar, a Communist propagandist, a member of the People's National Congress. And the tale is yet to be completed. For the man still lives. He is Henry Pu Yi—the last Manchu.

The first Manchus were a pastoral people who lived in the woodlands of Manchuria near what is now the city of Mukden. Through centuries of unrecorded history, their strength increased to the point where their leader, Nurhachi (1559–1626), while paying tribute to the Ming Dynasty rulers of China in Peking, began secretly to prepare his tribe for "the great deed" of piercing the Wall and conquering China itself. These preparations were continued by his son, Abahai (1592–1643), who made his rear safe for the venture by subjugating Korea, a Ming protectorate, and completing the conquest of Inner Mongolia.

When Abahai died in 1643, his brother Dorgon completed "the great deed" on behalf of his young nephew Shun-chih. He conquered China, overthrew the ruling Ming Dynasty and made Shun-chih Emperor, not of China, for that term no longer existed except in the minds of the barbarians (foreigners), but of the Great Ch'ing Country–Ch'ing being the dynastic name adopted by these new rulers who were not Chinese, but Manchus, people of Manchuria.

In contrast to other foreigners who had previously conquered and ruled China through naked military force, the Manchus based their rule on some form of popular support. In their administration of the area we call China, they also gave power and responsibility to the other four races of the land, the Hans (Chinese), the Mongols, the Tibetans and the Mohammedans. The Manchus also actively supported Chinese culture and the arts to the extent that their own written language became little more than a formality. Chinese scholars were invited to staff the Ch'ing bureaucracy and Chinese generals, once they had surrendered, were often given higher and better positions in the new government than they had held under the Mings. In fact, the Manchus became Sinicized. The rural-gentry class of the Great Ch'ing Country continued with the basic administration as it had under the Mings, and the population grew from 19,138,000 in 1661 to 438,425,000 in 1910.

The exception to this policy of Sinicization was the blood royal of the ruling family, which remained pure Manchu. The Emperor, who was absolute ruler, was thus a man who enjoyed consanguinity with less than 2 percent of the total population over which he ruled. Through the centuries, strange customs, traditions and forms developed within the Forbidden City in which the rulers of the five races of China lived and from which they governed not only their original motherland of Manchuria (the Northeast, which they regarded as crown property and into which they forbade Chinese, or Han, immigration), but the rest of the country as well.

Meanwhile, the dynastic succession of the Great Ch'ing continued from father to son much as it did among Western royalties until the reign of the seventh Emperor in dynastic succession, Hsien Feng, who lived from 1831 to 1861.

Hsien Feng, before his death at the age of thirty, had no sons until a Manchu palace concubine named Lady Yehonala gave birth to one in 1856. Originally promoted to the rank of Secondary Consort when her pregnancy was established, she became the Empress Dowager Tzu Hsi when her husband died and her son succeeded his father on the Dragon Throne at the age of five in 1861.

Although she was ostensibly the ruler of China on behalf of her young son, Tung Chih, who was yet a minor, power eluded her. For on his deathbed her husband, the Emperor, had created a Council of Regents headed by Su Shun, an Assistant Grand Secretary and President of the Board of Revenue. It was this Council that the Empress Dowager Tzu Hsi was determined to subvert so that she could rule in its place.

The true and detailed story of how the young Dowager Empress managed to defeat the Regency Council in her struggle for power is unknown to us. We do, however, know the result. Tzu Hsi won and one of her first edicts which ushered in her 47-year rule of China read:

As to Su Shun, his treasonable guilt far exceeds that of his accomplices and he fully deserves the punishment of dismemberment and the slicing process. But we cannot make up our mind to impose this extreme penalty and therefore, in our clemency, we sentence him to immediate decapitation.

While the dynasty was traversing the difficult course of this minority succession, the country was convulsed by disturbances from within and without. From 1856 to 1860, Britain and France fought the Second Opium War against China. Meanwhile, there was an internal revolt led by the Taipings which was suppressed with great difficulty. The Taiping Rebellion was the greatest social upheaval of nineteenth-century China. Led by a small farmer who claimed to be a son of God and Jesus' brother, the movement spread rapidly and its leader called for the overthrow of the Manchus, land reform, equality for women, and extermination of Buddhist and Taoist priests for worshipping "idols." Nanking was taken by the rebels in 1853 and not recaptured by the government until 1864.

The Emperor Hsien Feng had not done enough to secure his country against foreign invasion and domestic disorder. The mother of his son, however, with her lust for and skill in the use of power triumphed over every danger and, with her son, was able to return from Jehol Province, to which the court had fled because of the disturbances, and witness the elevation of her child to the Dragon Throne within the Forbidden City in Peking.

From this point on, Tzu Hsi lived in a world whose outward unrealities are only surpassed by the realities which surrounded her and which, to the present world, defeat the imagination. There can be no doubt, however, that she liked power and did not hesitate to murder and debauch people to keep it.

The death of the Dowager's son, in whose name she ruled from 1861 to 1874, has always been something of a mystery. Western historians have supposed he died of syphilis. Others, however, believe that the Empress Dowager, if she did not cause his death, most certainly hastened it along because of her violent temper.

One day, when the Emperor was ill with smallpox, his favorite wife went to visit him and burst into tears as she asked why her mother-in-law was always scolding her. The Emperor, Tung Chih, begged her to put up with it, saying that some time in the future she would have her day. When Tzu Hsi, who had never liked her daughter-in-law, heard that she had gone to visit her son, she stood outside his room to eavesdrop. Unaware of the disaster their few words of private conversation were to bring about, they saw Tzu Hsi rush into the room in a rage. She grabbed the Empress by the hair and started to beat her, shouting instructions to the palace eunuchs to prepare rods. In his weakened condition her son collapsed and died. Thus Tzu Hsi did not have to carry out the beating with rods. For once her son was dead, the Dowager put all the blame for his death on his wife and gave orders that her consumption of food and drink should be restricted. Two months later the Empress perished of starvation.

After the death of her son, the Dowager Empress was faced with the problem of preserving her own position. According to dynastic tradition, a close relation of the generation below the last Emperor should have been his heir. But this would have ended Tzu Hsi's regency since she would no longer have been the "Emperor's mother." She thus waived all precedent and appointed her nephew Kuang Hsu Emperor, although he was of the same generation as her son. He "reigned" from 1874 until 1908 and was succeeded by Pu Yi.

As the Empress Dowager grew older her temper became even more unpredictable. Once a palace eunuch, who was playing chess with her, forgot himself to the point of boasting about a particularly clever move he had just completed on the chessboard. The Empress Dowager flew into a rage, and, announcing that she would kill his whole family, had him dragged out and beaten to death.

She was very proud of her long hair. A eunuch who was combing it for her found a strand in the comb. In his panic the eunuch tried to conceal it but Tzu Hsi saw what he was doing in a mirror and he too was beaten. In later life she developed a facial tic and hated people to notice it. One day she asked a eunuch what he was staring at. When he could

give no answer she had him given several dozen strokes of
the heavy rod. Another eunuch who had heard about this
did not dare so much as to look up when he was on duty,
but she flared up at this too. "Why are you keeping your
head down?" she asked.

When he could think of nothing to say he was also punished. The palace women were often beaten as well.

Apologists of the Empress Dowager have claimed that her
excesses were the outbursts of a proud and patriotic woman
suffering from the frustrations of a ruler who was witnessing
the dismemberment of her kingdom by her enemies as well
as attempts by foreign powers to tamper with the dynasty.
And indeed it is true that during Tzu Hsi's lifetime China
was subject to continuing humiliations at the hands of the
Western powers and Japan. To list a few, in 1858 Russia took
all Chinese territory north of the Amur River and in 1860 the
present Maritime Territory of Siberia. In the same year,
Britain obtained a lease of Kowloon on the mainland opposite Hong Kong. In 1862 Portugal was confirmed in her
occupation of Macao. In 1879 Japan took the Liuchiu Is-
lands. In 1885 France was confirmed in the possession of all
of Indochina. In 1886 China recognized the British conquest
of Burma. And this was only the beginning.

But the Empress Dowager's courtiers were so frightened
of her and the continuing menace to their own lives that it
was difficult for them to give effect to sensible policies if
they thought such policies might, even in an indirect way,
remotely arouse the Dowager Empress's particular displeasure. Henry Pu Yi's grandfather, for example, was made
responsible for the founding of the Chinese Navy but felt
constrained to use a large part of the funds to build the
Summer Palace instead as a pleasure park for his sister-in-
law Tzu Hsi. It was therefore no surprise to him that four
years later the Navy came to a disastrous end in the Sino-
Japanese War and the marble boat in the Summer Palace
was the only one left of all the vessels on which so many
tens of millions of ounces of silver had been appropriated.

One of Tzu Hsi's most spectacular deeds was the destruc-
tion of the woman known to the West as the Pearl Concubine, who was, in fact, a wife of her nephew, the Emperor,
and thus Pu Yi's own aunt. It was the summer of 1900, just

six years before Pu Yi was born. The Empress Dowager was preparing to flee the Forbidden City because her armies, in cooperation with the Boxers, had failed to exterminate the foreign diplomatic corps assigned to her court. The Princess Pearl suggested that she and her husband, the Emperor, should not flee but remain in Peking to treat with the Western armies who at that moment were hammering at the gates of the city.

This suggestion made the Empress Dowager angry, for she saw in it a plot to tamper with her power and the succession to the throne itself once she was out of Peking. Indeed the Empress Dowager's decision to associate with the Boxers in the first place was derived from her suspicion that the Foreign Legations had been plotting to force her to hand real ruling power over to her nephew, the Emperor. Because of these fears money from the imperial treasury had been given to the Boxers, rewards were offered for the heads of foreigners, and those of her courtiers who had advocated an anti-Boxer policy were decapitated.

Thus, when the Princess Pearl had the temerity to suggest that she remain behind in Peking to deal with the foreigners, Tzu Hsi, despite the frantic pleas of her nephew, had the princess wrapped in a beautiful carpet by two eunuchs and slipped down a well within the Forbidden City. Immediately thereafter, disguised as a coolie, Tzu Hsi and her nephew, the Emperor, whom she had previously imprisoned because of his liberal views, fled in a horse cart. And yet it is a testimony to the resiliency of the Chinese, the cohesiveness and symbolism of the Manchu Court, the iron will of the Empress Dowager herself, that her power survived this flight. Months later, Tzu Hsi and her nephew returned to Peking with all the panoply and ceremony required of the Manchus on their return from a state visit to the provinces. During her flight to the Western part of her kingdom, her power and the glittering trappings of her office had survived.

Upon her return, the Empress Dowager ordered an accommodation with the West. This entailed the payment of an indemnity and the expiation, for their crimes, of many of her close advisers and relatives who had conspired with her to use the Boxers to drive the foreigners out of China. Some of these men were exiled by her orders. Others were beheaded or were commanded to commit suicide. Not one of all the leading statesmen who could have slipped away to a distant province and escape their fate did so. Chao Shu-chiao, for example, took poison when the Empress's edict was read to him. But he was strong and vigorous and the effect was negligible. He then swallowed arsenic, but this too failed, and it was only after his mouth and nose were stuffed with paper that he succumbed. Ying Nien choked himself to death by swallowing mud.

A short time after these events, Henry Pu Yi was born in Peking in the mansion of his paternal grandfather, Prince Chun, who was a brother of the Emperor Hsien Feng, Tzu Hsi's husband. Prince Chun's wife was Tzu Hsi's sister, so that the relationship was a double one. Prince Chun devoted his entire life to the service of Tzu Hsi and was one of her favorites.

Pu Yi's maternal grandfather, Jung Lu, was also devoted to the interests of Tzu Hsi. He was a close friend of her favorite eunuch and his wife ingratiated herself with the Dowager so successfully that she was often called to the palace to keep her company and chat with her. He and his wife were professional courtiers par excellence.

When the young Emperor had defied his aunt, the Dowager, and issued a series of liberal edicts in 1898 ordering political reforms, it was Jung Lu who worked out a plan for Tzu Hsi to defeat them. In the struggle against these reforms Jung Lu became head of the group known as the "Dowager's party" and the Emperor's former tutor headed the "Emperor's party," for it was through the tutor's privileged position that the reformers had been able to make contact with the Emperor in the first place. Following Jung Lu's advice, the Dowager forced the Emperor to send his tutor into retirement, and within a few days of his departure from Peking she gave the loyal Jung Lu a Grand Secretaryship and made him viceroy of the metropolitan province of Chihli with command over the armies around the capital.

The reformers and the Emperor had put their trust in a Han subordinate of Jung Lu named Yuan Shih-kai who was in control of the new modernized Imperial Army. They had told him of their plan to imprison the Dowager and execute Jung Lu. Yuan Shih-kai, who was later to become President of China, agreed to cooperate but then betrayed them by going straight to Jung Lu and revealing the whole plot. On hearing the news Jung Lu hastened to the Summer Palace to tell Tzu Hsi. The result was that the Emperor was "imprisoned," the leader of the plot fled to Japan, several other reformers were executed and the brief hundred days of liberalism were over. Jung Lu emerged from this crisis more powerful than ever.

During the calamitous events of the Boxer Rebellion, Jung Lu had followed a masterful policy of avoiding commitment. Taking his cue from Tzu Hsi's behavior, he never went against her wishes but at the same time he prepared a line of retreat for her. When obeying her command to send soldiers to attack the Foreign Legations in Peking he did not issue them artillery shells, and during the midst of the siege, he even discreetly sent fruit and melons to the Legations as a token of his concern, much to the surprise of the besieged diplomats who were subsisting on horse meat. After the troops of the foreign powers had entered Peking and relieved the Legations, Tzu Hsi fled, but it was Jung Lu who proposed the single principle to which officials responsible for negotiating the peace were to hold: any conditions from the West could be accepted *provided* Tzu Hsi was not held responsible for the affair and the Emperor, her nephew, was not returned to real power.

As a reward for this tortuous, but successful policy, the Dowager arranged the marriage between Jung Lu's daughter and Prince Chun's son, and it was they who became the parents of Henry Pu Yi.

The ultimate reasons for the selection of Henry Pu Yi by the Empress Dowager to rule China as the tenth Emperor of the Ch'ing House are derived from this affair and from the fact that her previous choice, Prince Tuan's son, became unacceptable as a result of the father's involvement with the Boxers and commitment to the policy of exterminating all foreigners living in China. In addition, she felt that Pu Yi's father, who was named Prince Regent until Pu Yi should become of age, was docile. And since she did not really expect to die she could thus continue to rule through him.

The Empress Dowager also seems to have felt that of all the princes of the blood royal Pu Yi's father was the best suited to deal with the growing threats to the throne within the country. For at the time of Tzu Hsi's and her nephew's death in 1908, Yuan Shih-kai was head of the Army and the Dowager Empress was most certainly aware of his questionable loyalty. It was common knowledge within the Forbidden City that Yuan Shih-kai's candidate for the throne, if not himself, was a Prince Ching, an ambitious Manchu who had started life as a low-ranking noble and had become a prince of the first rank and Grand Councillor. The Army connections of these two plotters, who were so well known and liked by the foreign diplomats in Peking, were a source of anxiety to the royal family. It was thought desirable to check them with another prince who was also held in esteem by foreigners. After all, it was not Yuan Shih-kai or Prince Ching but Pu Yi's father who had actually gone abroad and been graciously received by the Kaiser to whom he apologized for the murder of the German minister during the Boxer uprising. And although Tzu Hsi's interest in the West was severely limited, she was impressed by the Kaiser's statement—as it had been reported back to her—that the success of his own house was based on the continuing control of the Army by the royal family.

Thus, at the end, Tzu Hsi made her only dynastic gesture to what she supposed was the modernity of the West. By selecting the infant Pu Yi as Emperor she turned over power to the one member of the ruling family—Henry Pu Yi's father, the Prince Regent—who had actually met a real Western European potentate whose family had successfully coped with problems of army loyalties. And how was Tzu Hsi to know, surrounded as she was by the crenellated yellow tiled walls of the Forbidden City and waited upon by 3,000 eunuchs, that this model of Western dynastic skill and enlightenment sat on a throne that was only slightly more stable than her own? And how was she to understand that the Kaiser's own character and passions were as complex and distorted by family pride and jealousies as her own?

No sooner were Tzu Hsi and her nephew dead and Pu Yi on the throne, than many of the disruptive forces that she had so successfully suppressed for so long came to a head. Yuan Shih-kai, as commander of the Peiyang Army, the only modernized fighting force in North China, emerged as one of the most powerful men in the country. Pu Yi's father, aware of Yuan's questionable loyalty and remembering the Kaiser's advice about control of the Army, ordered him into retirement to "recuperate from a leg ailment." He then placed a Manchu prince in charge of the Palace Guard, founded a special army under the control of the royal family and put other Manchu relatives in charge of the Navy and General Staff.

But these reforms came too late to cope with Yuan's plots. The new commanders were unable to suppress a revolt that broke out in Wuchang in 1911 and the Prince Regent was forced to recall Yuan Shih-kai to resume command of the Peiyang Army whose officers would not fight without him as commander in chief. Yuan thus became the arbiter between the Manchu Government in the North and the revolutionaries who were ultimately led by Sun Yat-sen in the South.

On February 12, 1912, under Yuan's pressure, Pu Yi abdicated, although he continued to live the life of an emperor within the Forbidden City in accordance with agreements between the Ch'ing House and the new republican government. Yuan, meanwhile, was elected President of China and later became its personal dictator recognized by the foreign powers and supported by foreign loans.

PAUL KRAMER

I

MY CHILDHOOD

1

Coronation and Abdication

I WAS BORN ON THE 14TH DAY OF THE FIRST MOON OF THE 32nd year of Kuang Hsu's reign; on February 7, 1906, by the Western calendar.

On the evening of November 13, 1908, or the 20th day of the 10th moon, in the 34th year of Kuang Hsu's reign, the mansion of the Emperor's brother, in which I lived, was in turmoil. My grandmother had fainted and, while royal eunuchs and servants were trying to revive her, children and adults were weeping. All this because I, as Emperor apparent, of the Ch'ing Dynasty, had refused an imperial summons from the Forbidden City delivered by the Grand Councillor.

I would not let any of the eunuchs come near me to carry me to the palace. I cried so hard the eunuchs had to ask the Grand Councillor what to do. My father, meanwhile, rushed about from room to room—first entertaining the Grand Councillor and the eunuchs who had come with him from the palace, then ordering servants to get me dressed, then visiting my still-prostrate grandmother and forgetting that the Grand Councillor was waiting.

I have, of course, no impression or recollection of what my family thought of this situation, of the humiliation brought upon them by my refusal to obey the imperial edict. However, I was told several years later that in order to solve the impasse of my refusal to let the eunuchs come near me

3

it was finally agreed to waive all protocol and permit my wet nurse herself to carry me to the palace.

There was a great and unprecedented ceremony involved, within the palace, in my transfer from the arms of my wet nurse to those of the ranking eunuch who was to present me to the Empress Dowager, Tzu Hsi. All I remember of this first meeting with my great-aunt was my fright at finding myself suddenly plunged among so many strange people.

I stood in front of a dark heavy canopy. Sitting under it, I saw a very ugly, thin-faced and emaciated old woman. It was Tzu Hsi. According to what I have been told, my first sight of her brought on a tantrum. I screamed and cried and kicked and completely lost control of myself.

Tzu Hsi asked someone to give me a string of candy. Instead of eating it, I threw it on the floor and cried for my wet nurse. This displeased the Empress Dowager very much. She commented that I was stubborn and ordered my removal from her presence.

Two days after this, she died, and shortly thereafter her nephew the Emperor, Kuang Hsu, also died. On the 9th day of the 11th moon of the lunar calendar, or December 2, 1908, my ceremonial ascension to the Imperial Dragon Throne took place.

This ceremony was held in the Hall of Supreme Harmony in the Forbidden City which can accommodate several thousand courtiers. However, according to custom, before it began I had to receive the commanders of the palace guard and the ministers of the inner court in the Hall of Central Harmony where they performed their kowtows. It was only after this that I went to the throne in the Hall of Supreme Harmony to receive civil and military officials, viceroys and governors.

This pre-enthronement ceremony was very long and took up a good part of the day. Moreover, it was very cold and by the time I was finally placed on the high Imperial Throne my patience was exhausted. My father was privileged to kneel on one knee, with his face in profile, below me.

He had tried to help me ascend the throne by using his two hands to guide me and to protect me from making motions that were not part of the ceremonial tradition. But by this time I was so exhausted that all I could do was scream that I wished to go home. I wanted no more ceremony. I could stand it no longer.

My father became so nervous that his face was covered with perspiration despite the cold. All the hundreds and thousands of civil and military officials did their nine bows and three kowtows and while they were still doing them, I cried louder and louder. My father tried to appease me.

"Hush," he said. "Don't cry. Be patient. Everything will soon be over. It will soon be finished."

Some of the courtiers who were near the throne heard him and, after the ceremony, they talked with one another in whispers. "How could a Royal Highness say such a thing as 'it will soon be over'?" they asked. "This is a bad omen."

They felt that my father's remarks indicated that my reign would be an unlucky one.

Later, some of the diaries and articles on my coronation added more to this tale. One article mentioned that the gongs and drums of the ceremonial music had caused me to cry. Another said that my father had given me a little toy tiger to distract me from my crying. These stories were not true, but the annoyance of the high officials with my father's use of the words "it will soon be over" and my own cry of "I want to go home" was true. It was generally felt that these were very bad omens indeed.

However, the real premonitions of impending difficulties did not come from these two phrases. The historical record of the first year of my reign clearly shows the origin of the real worries of the Ch'ing officials. Take the following items for example:

A revolutionary group in Canton revolted and occupied part of Kwantung Province but was later defeated.

Sun Yat-sen led an attack in Kwangsi Province but was defeated.

An imperial edict was issued forbidding students to participate in politics or to gather and make speeches.

Officials in Kwangtung Province intercepted arms on a Japanese steamer en route to revolutionaries.

Sun Yat-sen ordered an attack in Yunan Province which was first successful, but later defeated.

5

These items are from the official history of the Ch'ing Dynasty. The word "defeat" occurs with striking regularity, and the more often it appears the more it serves as an indication of the intensity of the approaching storm. It was this that was the real focal point of worry among the high officials.

As my reign continued, the difficulties became more obvious. For when Yuan Shih-kai was recalled to serve my government there were many who realized that the Ch'ing House now had two hostile forces to contend with—the republican revolutionaries outside the government and Yuan inside.

I was Emperor for three years in such an atmosphere, without any real awareness of the political situation. I abdicated with a similar lack of comprehension of the true situation. An incident of my last days on the throne, however, stands out clearly in my mind.

One day, in one of the rooms of the Mind Nurture Palace, the Empress Dowager Lung Yu[1] was sitting on a *kang*[2] near the southern window and using a handkerchief to wipe the tears from her eyes. In front of her, kneeling on a red carpet, was a stout old man with tears streaming down his face. I sat to the right of the Empress Dowager feeling bewildered because I did not understand why these two adults were crying. There was no one else in the palace besides the three of us and it was very quiet. The fat man was sniffing so loudly when he talked I could not understand him. Later on I found out that it was Yuan Shih-kai. This was the only time I ever met him and it was the last time he paid his respects to the Empress Dowager. If what I have been told is correct, this was the occasion when Yuan directly raised the question of my abdication with Lung Yu. After this audience, Yuan used the pretext of an attempt that had been made on his life at one of the palace gates not to come to court again.

---

[1] Just prior to her death, Tzu Hsi had ordered that Pu Yi's father, as Prince Regent, should consult and ask for instructions from her niece and successor as Empress Dowager, Lung Yu, on all important matters.

[2] A sofa-like bed, commonly used in North China, which could be heated in winter.

The Wuchang uprising of October, 1911, had sparked off responses from revolutionaries all over the country, and when the Manchu commander in chief of the imperial forces proved incapable of directing the modernized Peiyang Army to resist the Republican forces, my father as Prince Regent had no choice but to recall Yuan Shih-kai from retirement. Yuan, who had been waiting to strike a political bargain, had been kept informed of developments in Peking by his friends in the Imperial Grand Council. Thus, he fully understood the situation and repeatedly refused Peking's offers of rein-statement until he was promised the premiership and supreme military command. Only then did he accept the imperial edict and order the Peiyang Army to attack the Republican revolutionary army. After recapturing Hanyang, he halted his troops and paid a visit to Peking where he was received by the Empress Dowager Lung Yu and the Prince Regent.

Yuan Shih-kai was no longer the Yuan Shih-kai of before. Not only did he enjoy supreme military and political power, but he also enjoyed something else even more valuable: foreigners, including the British Minister in Peking, acting under instructions from London, were interested in him and he also had friends on the Republican side who kept him well informed on developments in the revolutionary camp. In addition, some of the constitutional monarchists were beginning to feel well disposed toward him.

With all his new and old friends both inside and outside the Ch'ing Dynasty,[3] as well as his supporters and friends abroad, Yuan's position as the political favorite of all parties was stronger than ever. Within a month of his return to Peking he was able to force my father, the Prince Regent, into retirement. Immediately afterward, on the pretext of the need for money to meet military expenses, he took over the palace treasury from the Empress Dowager Lung Yu and, at the same time, he compelled the high officials and princes to contribute money for the support of the Army. Thus, political, military and financial power were concentrated in his hands alone. Once this was accomplished, Yuan suggested to the Chinese minister to Russia as well as to other Chinese

---

[3] Descriptive term for the Manchu ruling family.

7

diplomats abroad that they cable the Ch'ing court requesting my abdication. Meanwhile, he submitted a secret memorial in the name of the entire cabinet to the Empress Dowager saying that a republic was the only solution. He must have presented this memorial on the day I saw him and this would explain why Lung Yu wept so copiously. What frightened her the most were the following phrases in this memorial:

> The Navy has revolted entirely. . . . National protection is thus gone. . . . If the civil war reaches a stalemate, there might be intervention by some of the foreign powers. . . . In this case hostility toward the government on the part of the Republican armies will be heightened. . . . Delay in abdication might lead to a fate similar to that suffered by Louis XVI and his family during the French Revolution.

The terror-stricken Dowager immediately called a meeting of the Imperial Council to permit the members of the royal family an opportunity to reach a decision. When they learned of the contents of the secret memorial they were not so much shaken by the allusion to the fate of Louis XVI as they were by the sudden reversal of Yuan Shih-kai's loyalties. Heretofore Yuan had ostensibly been strongly anti-Republican and had favored a constitutional monarchy. "I will never betray the orphan son [Pu Yi] and widow [Empress Dowager Lung Yu]," he had written. Also, shortly after Yuan's return to Peking a decree was issued allowing officials to cut off their queues. On this day, after a court audience, a high palace official, while strolling down one of the streets of Peking, had asked Yuan, as he pointed to his queue, "What do you propose regarding this?"

"You can rest assured," Yuan had replied, "that I propose to keep it."

Because of remarks like these, even those who did not have complete faith in him were put at ease. Furthermore, the Ch'ing and Republican sides had reached agreement that the future structure of the state should be decided by a provisional national assembly. The suggestion of Yuan, therefore, that the dynasty should abdicate at a time when the structure of the state was still undecided, came as a shock to the royal family.

It was apparent, however, that Yuan Shih-kai by this time had foreign support and that his friends on the side of the Republican Army were sufficient to control its actions. Those revolutionaries who had originally been constitutional monarchists felt that Yuan was their only hope and this thinking had affected some of the Republicans as well. Thus the Republican side decided that if Yuan consented to a republic it could be achieved rapidly and, in this case, Yuan should be invited to become the first president. This was really exactly what Yuan had hoped for, especially since he knew that my father, the former Prince Regent, headed a group that was implacably hostile to him. He had decided to accept the Republican offer and was debating how to deal with the Ch'ing royal family when he learned that Sun Yat-sen had taken office as Provisional President in Nanking. An early solution of the problem of the dynasty was therefore all the more urgent for Yuan. If the Republicans in the South went on to set up a national assembly it would be difficult for him to get rid of it. He decided to frighten the royal family and the Empress Dowager Lung Yu so that she would consent voluntarily to my abdication and grant him full power to organize a provisional government. This was the real explanation for Yuan Shih-kai's sudden change in policy.

Those princes and nobles who had always been anti-Yuan and had felt he was a traitor were in favor of putting up a desperate last-ditch fight against both the Republicans and Yuan. Thus, when the Empress Dowager Lung Yu called the first meeting of the Imperial Council the atmosphere was charged with anger.

From various accounts of these meetings one can tell that they went approximately as follows. Having established that all present were in favor of a monarchy and opposed to a republic, the Dowager went on to say that she had been told by allies of Yuan that the imperial forces were incapable of defending the government and defeating the Republicans.

A leader of the anti-Yuan group among the nobility then stated that the rebels were nothing to be afraid of and reported that one of the generals of the new Peiyang Army insisted that three months' military funds would be enough to defeat them. But as the Dowager pointed out, Yuan Shih-kai had taken over all the funds of the palace treasury so that she had no money. "Besides," she added, "what if we lose? Surely in that case we will not be able to fall back on the Articles of Favorable Treatment."

One of the nobles then claimed that the Articles were only a trick, but when Lung Yu asked about the real state of the Army and its loyalty to the Ch'ing House there were only noncommittal replies.

As one inconclusive meeting of the Imperial Council followed another, the advocates of fighting it out became fewer and fewer. Telegrams began to arrive from Peiyang Army generals, heretofore considered loyal to the Ch'ing House, requesting abdication. Meanwhile two leaders of the war party in the royal family left Peking for German-occupied Tsingtao and Japanese-held Port Arthur where they sought to go abroad in order to plead the imperial cause. Local officials, however, blocked their departure.

On February 12, 1912, the Empress Dowager Lung Yu proclaimed my abdication. My father, who had not said a word during all the Imperial Council meetings, returned to his house to "hug his children." Yuan Shih-kai, meanwhile, was organizing a provisional republican government as he had been ordered to do by the Empress Dowager. At the same time, in accordance with an agreement with the revolutionaries, he changed his own position from premier of the cabinet of the Great Ch'ing Empire to Provisional President of the Republic of China. While all this was going on, I became the President's neighbor as I started my life in the "Little Court" according to the Articles providing for "The Favorable Treatment of the Great Ch'ing Emperor after his Abdication."

These Articles consisted of eight separate provisions. They provided for my retention of the title of Emperor and stated that the Republic of China was to pay me an annual allowance of $4,000,000. I was to be allowed to retain my usual bodyguard and to continue to live in the Imperial Palace. Also the Republic was to provide guards to insure the protection of my ancestral temples, and the imperial tombs; and the sacrifices at these places were to be continued forever. All persons employed in the Imperial Palace were to be continued to be employed as before, but no new eunuchs were to be engaged. All my existing private property was to receive the special protection of the Republic and the existing Palace Guard was to be incorporated into the Army of the Republic, its numbers and salary to be continued as before my abdication. The Republic of China was to permit the completion of the tomb of the Emperor Kuang Hsu according to the original plan and the funeral expenses were to be borne by the Republic.

2

Living as Emperor

"THE MOST FAVORABLE TREATMENT TREATY," WHICH WAS signed between the Republican Government and the Manchu Court, stipulated that I might continue to live in the Forbidden City and maintain the imperial traditions. There was in this agreement no definite time stipulated as to how long I might live in this manner. Except for three buildings that had been taken over by the Republican Government, the rest of the area of the Forbidden City remained my own little world.

From 1911 until 1924, when I was driven out by the soldiers of the National Army, I lived a most aimless and purposeless life. When I say that it was aimless and purposeless it is because, under the auspices of the Republic of China, people were entering the new life of the twentieth century while I still had to remain within the Forbidden City and live the life of an emperor, which was traditional and old-fashioned. Thus while others could enjoy modern ways, I continued to breathe the air of the nineteenth century and before. My life was an anachronism, a leftover of the type of life which had already become dust by that time.

Each time I think of my youth, my mind fills with a yellow mist of reminiscence. For the glazed tiles on the roofs were yellow, the sedan chairs were yellow, the cushions were yellow. The linings of my clothing and my hats were yellow. My belts, the porcelain dishes for my food and tea, including the cotton quilting with which they were covered to keep them warm, were yellow. The reins of my horse were yellow. This was the so-called "brilliant yellow" which was used exclusively by the Imperial Household and it gave me a feeling of difference and superiority.

When I was ten, my grandmother and mother began to come to the palace to see me, and they brought one of my brothers and one of my sisters to play with me for a few days. The first day of the visit nothing much happened, but on the second day, my grandmother and I sat on the *kang* and she watched me play Chinese dominoes while my brother and sister stood below us, motionless, like attendants on duty at court. Later on I took my brother and sister to my own living quarters where I asked my brother, "What games do you play at home?"

"Pu Chieh," he said, referring to himself, "knows how to play hide-and-seek."

My sister then said, respectfully addressing Pu Chieh, "Well then, Pu Chieh, you go and play hide-and-seek. That will be fun."

I had never played hide-and-seek before with other children, only with the eunuchs. We started off playing in the Mind Nurture Palace. The more we played the more fun we had, and my brother and sister soon forgot about court etiquette. Later on, we lowered the shades in one of the rooms and made it so dark that my sister, who was two years younger than I, became afraid. As soon as my brother and I became aware of this, we tried to scare her all the more. We were so happy that we laughed and screamed. Later, when we felt tired, we climbed up on the *kang* together to get back our breaths, and I told them to think of a new game to play.

Pu Chieh thought for a while, but said nothing. He was grinning at me with a sort of silly smile on his face.

"What are you thinking of?" I asked.

He simply kept on grinning and said nothing.

"Tell me, tell me," I urged. I thought he was thinking of some new game to play.

"I believe," he said finally. "Forgive me, Pu Chieh believes . . . Your Majesty the Emperor . . . would not . . . it's not like . . . Your Majesty is not like the long-bearded man on the stage," he giggled.

13

While he was talking he raised his hand and made a gesture of an old man stroking his beard. This was his undoing. For I noticed that his sleeve lining was of imperial yellow.

"Pu Chieh," I asked, "what are you doing with that color on? What makes you think you can use it?"

"But this is apricot yellow; it's not imperial yellow."

"Nonsense, it's bright yellow!"

"Yes, yes," he finally admitted. Then he put his hands to his sides and bowed while my sister ran behind him and began to tremble with fright.

"It is bright yellow. You shouldn't have worn it."

"Yes sire, yes Your Majesty," he replied.

With those bows and words, the rank of Emperor and servant was restored. The words "yes sire, yes Your Majesty" have today become a lost echo. Whenever I recall them now they seem laughable. But I was used to them when I was young. Those who did not use them I found offensive.

This same attitude applied toward kowtows. I was used to people kneeling before me and touching their heads on the ground. Many times the elder officials of the dynasty, my older relatives, men in Manchu court dress as well as those in the Western-style clothes of the Republic would kowtow. But I was used to it. It did not seem strange.

Young people today who read the classic *Dream of the Red Chamber* are surprised. They cannot understand why the grandmother in the story had so many people surrounding her that her passage from one room to another in her mansion was like the movement of a swarm of bees. Yet the retinue in the *Dream of the Red Chamber* was much smaller than the one I had in the Forbidden City.

The setting in the Red Chamber is similar to what my own was, but on a smaller scale. Every day, when I went to the Palace for the Cultivation of Happiness to study, or went to pay my respects to the High Consorts[1] or when I strolled in the palace garden, I was followed by a long retinue.

Each time when I went for a visit to the Summer Palace, outside the Forbidden City, not only did I need ten cars to

---

[1] Widows of previous Emperors.

form a retinue, but I had to ask the Republic police to post guard for me and line the road to protect me.

If I went for a visit within the Forbidden City, a eunuch from the Administrative Bureau walked in front of me. His function was essentially that of an automobile horn in that he made continuous bleating noises to warn people to avoid me. Behind him would follow two eunuchs walking crabwise on each side of the path; then ten paces behind them, myself or my mother. If I should ride in a sedan chair, two junior eunuchs would run on each side of me to attend my wants. If I were walking, their job was to support me. Behind me walked a eunuch holding a large silk canopy; behind him a large group holding all kinds of things. One, for example, carried a small chair should I care to sit; another carried a change of clothing, another a rain umbrella, another a sun umbrella. After these eunuchs of the Imperial Presence came the eunuchs of the Imperial Tea Bureau with boxes of cakes and pastries and, of course, a tea service and jugs of hot water. Behind these came the eunuchs of the Imperial Pharmacy bearing cases of medicines and first-aid equipment suspended from carrying poles. The medicine they carried always included potions and elixirs prepared from lampwick sedge, chrysanthemums, the roots of reeds, bamboo leaves and bamboo skins. In summer there were always Essence of Betony Pills for rectifying the vapors, Six Harmony Pills for stabilizing the central organs, Gold-coated Heat-dispensing Cinnabar, Fragrant Herb Pills, Omnipurpose Bars, colic medicines and antiplague powders. And throughout all the four seasons there would be the Three Immortals Beverage to aid the digestion as well as many other pills and powders. Bringing up the rear of the procession came the eunuchs bearing the chamber pots and commodes. If I was walking, a sedan chair would follow behind all these people with special summer or winter draperies depending on the season. This fantastic retinue proceeded in complete silence.

When I was very young, I was like any other child. When I felt good, I would start running. At first my retinue would try to follow me; it would run when I ran and walk when I walked. When I became a little older and had learned how to give orders, whenever I wanted to run I would first tell the eunuchs to stand aside and wait for me and then, except for the two junior eunuchs of the Imperial Presence, the rest would hold their boxes and poles and stand aside and wait until I had enough running. Then they would all fall into formation again and would follow me.

Later I learned how to ride a bicycle. Then I issued orders to saw off the thresholds of the palace doors so that I could ride my bicycle without any interference. But every day, when I paid my respects to the Imperial High Consorts and also when I went to my schoolroom, I still needed my retinue. Consequently, whenever I didn't have it, I felt peculiar. Thus, the story of the last Ming Emperor who had only one eunuch left with him when he died made me feel quite uncomfortable.

Perhaps the greatest extravagance in the palace involved the preparation and serving of food. There were special terms used to refer to the Emperor's eating, and it was forbidden to fail to use them. Food was not "food" but "viands." For example, I never said "eat food," but always "partake of the viands." When I wanted to send for the food, I had to say "transmit the viands." The "kitchen" was never the "kitchen" but always the "imperial viands room." There was no definite time of serving. It all depended on my decision. I would merely say, "Transmit the viands." The eunuchs near me would repeat the phrase, those guarding the palace in which I lived would pick it up from them, those outside would repeat it and so on into the distance where the word finally reached the imperial viands room on the Western Avenue of the Forbidden City.

Before the echoes of the order had died away, a procession issued forth from the viands room, like a wedding procession that used to take a bride's trousseau to her groom's house. It consisted of about 100 eunuchs in clean livery. They would carry about seven dining tables of various sizes and scores of bright red lacquered boxes. They walked in procession to the Mind Nurture Palace where the food would be received by young eunuchs with white sleeves who set it out on the tables in one of the eastern rooms. Usually the main dishes occupied two of the tables. But in the wintertime there would be an additional table for the chafing dishes. Also there were extra tables for the soups, another for the rice and another for the preserves and pastries. All the porcelain plates and bowls were yellow and the phrase *10,000 Long Lives without Limit* were painted on them as well as dragon designs. In winter I ate from silver dishes placed on top of porcelain bowls filled with hot water, and in summer there were strips of silver[2] on the porcelain dishes from which I ate as a precaution against poison; and, for the same reason, all the food was tasted by a eunuch before it was brought in. This was called "appraising the viands." When everything had been tasted and laid out, and before I took my place at the table, a young eunuch called out, "Remove the covers." This was the signal for four or five other junior eunuchs to take the silver lids off all the food dishes, put them in a large box and carry them out. It was only after this that I could begin to "use the viands."

What was in front of me? Each meal of the Dowager Empress Lung Yu would contain over 100 dishes and would require about six tables. She had inherited this extravagance from Tzu Hsi. I had over 25 at each meal. I still have one of my breakfast menus for March 1912. It reads as follows:

Imperial Mushrooms with Four Hour Steamed Whole Chicken
Duck of Triple Delight (duck, ham, chicken with mushrooms and a special sauce)
Sliced Chicken Meat with Garden Vegetables
Steamed Whole Ham
Slow Simmered Tripe and Lung
Sliced Beef with Hearts of Out-of-Season Cabbage
Spiced Stewed Mutton
Mutton with Young Spinach, Peas and Mushrooms
Sweet Fresh Southern Cherries with Potatoes
Steamed Meat and Vegetables in Chafing Dish
Sea Urchins in Duck Stock
Glazed Spiced Duck
Imperial Rice with Southern Potatoes
Fried Mushrooms
Cubed Pork with Broccoli

---

[2] It was presumed that poisons in the food would turn the silver black.

Thinly Sliced Lamb with Out-of-Season Spiced Vegetables
Fried Egg Rolls
Scallions with Sliced Meat
Cold Tripe Marinated in Spices and Wine
Bean Curds Sprinkled with Spices, Soya Sauce and Dried Vegetables
Smoked Dried Bean Curd with Bean Sprouts, Ginger and other Spices
Sautéed Out-of-Season Vegetables
Spiced Cabbage
Spiced Dried Game
Ancestor Meat Soup[3]

But all these dishes which were brought in with such ceremony were only for show. The reason why the food could be served almost as soon as I gave the word was that it had been prepared several hours or even a whole day in advance and was kept warm over the kitchen stoves. The cooks knew that since the time of the Emperor Kuang Hsu (1871–1908), this food had not been eaten by the Emperor. Actually the food which I ate was sent over by the Empress Dowager and, after her death, by the High Consorts. She and each of the High Consorts had kitchens of their own staffed by highly skilled chefs who produced twenty or more really delicious dishes for every meal. This was the food that was put in front of me, while that prepared in the imperial kitchens was set some distance away from me and it was only there for the sake of appearances.

The High Consorts, in order to show their concern and their love for me, sent these special dishes for me to eat. And they stipulated that after each meal a responsible eunuch was to report to them on the manner of my eating. But this too was only a formality. For no matter how I ate, the eunuch would always kneel down in front of the High Consorts and report the same thing: "Your slave reports that the Lord of 10,000 Years consumed one bowl of rice, one sesame bun and one bowl of *congee*.[4] He ate the viands with relish."

---

[3] A votive dish set out to show respect for one's ancestors.
[4] Rice soup.

At New Year and other festivals and on the birthdays of the High Consorts, in order to show my filial piety and appreciation my kitchen would prepare a special table of foods for them. Of these dishes I can only use four phrases to describe them: flowery without substance, showy without utility, elaborate without taste, no nutritional value.

But how much did this kind of ceremonial eating cost each month? I have found one volume of my menus showing the chicken, meat, etc., used during one month in the second year of my reign. The Empress Dowager, the four High Consorts and myself used over two tons of meat, 388 chickens and ducks of which roughly 1,000 pounds of meat was for myself as well as 240 chickens and ducks. In addition there was the monthly allocation for the numerous people in the palace who served us such as the members of the Grand Council, the imperial bodyguards, tutors, Hanlin academicians,[5] painters, men who drew the outlines of Chinese words for others to fill in, ranking eunuchs, priests who came every day to sacrifice to the spirits. Including the Dowager, the consorts and myself, the consumption of pork for the month was over eight tons and cost 2,342 ounces of silver.

On top of this were the extra dishes we had every day which often cost several times as much again. In the month in question, there were 20 tons of extra meat, 1,000 pounds of extra lard, 4,786 extra chickens and ducks, to say nothing of the fish, shrimp and eggs. All these extras cost 11,641 ounces of silver, and with the miscellaneous items added, the total expenditure came to 14,794 ounces of silver. This figure moreover does not include the cost of the cakes, fruit, sweets and drinks that were constantly being served.

Just as food was cooked in huge quantities and not eaten, so was a vast amount of clothing made which was never worn. I cannot remember details now, but I do know that the Dowager Empress and the High Consorts had no limitation on their expenditures for clothing. How many garments were made for them and for what purpose I have no recollection. Everything I wore was always new. I have before me an account from an unspecified year headed "list of materi-

---

[5] Savants and scholars serving the imperial household.

als actually used in making clothes for His Majesty's use from the sixth day of the tenth month to the fifth day of the eleventh month.'' According to this list the following garments were made for me: eleven fur jackets, six fur inner and outer gowns, two fur waistcoats, thirty cotton padded waistcoats and pairs of trousers. Leaving aside the cost of the main materials for these clothes and the cost of the labor, the bill for the minor items such as edgings, pockets, jeweled buttons and thread came to 2,137 silver dollars.

I also still have a list of materials used shortly after my marriage by my Empress, my secondary wife and the High Consorts. For the Empress:

16 bolts of crepe de chine
8 bolts of silk
23 bolts of satin
60 bolts of cotton cloth
20 pounds of woolen yarn
40 pounds of cotton thread
20 spools of gold thread
90 pelts of ermine and sable

For my secondary wife:

15 bolts of silk
21 bolts of satin
5 bolts of crepe de chine
30 bolts of cotton cloth
8 pounds of woolen yarn
20 pounds of cotton thread
10 spools of gold thread
30 pelts of ermine and sable

To this must be added what was used by the other four ladies of my household so that the total comes to:

136 bolts of satin
169 bolts of silk
81 bolts of crepe de chine
41 bolts of lining silk
234 bolts of cotton cloth

130 pounds of woolen yarn
250 pounds of cotton thread
106 spools of gold thread
400 pelts of fur

My changes of clothing were all laid down in regulations and were the responsibility of the eunuchs of the clothing storerooms. Even my everyday clothes came in 28 different styles, from the one in black with white inlaid fur that I started wearing on the 9th day of the first lunar month to the sable one I changed into on the first day of the 11th month. Needless to say, my clothes were far more complicated on festival days and for ceremonial occasions.

To manage all this there was of course a great proliferation of offices and personnel. The Household Department, which administered the domestic affairs of the Emperor, had under its control seven bureaus and 48 offices. The seven bureaus—the storage bureau, the guard bureau, the protocol, the treasury, the stock-raising bureau, the disciplinary bureau and the construction bureau—all had storerooms, workshops and so on under them. The storage bureau, for example, had stores for silver, fur, porcelain, satin, clothes and tea. According to a list of officials dating from 1909, the personnel of the Household Department numbered 1,023 (excluding the Palace Guard, the eunuchs and certain of the servants); in the early years of the Republic this was cut to something over 600 and at the time I left the Imperial Palace there were still more than 300. It is not hard to imagine an organization as large as this with so many people in it, but the triviality of some of the functions is difficult to realize.

One of the 48 offices, for example, was the As You Wish Lodge. Its only purpose was to paint pictures and do the calligraphy for the Empress Dowager and the High Consorts; if the Dowager wanted to paint something, the As You Wish Lodge would outline a design for her so that all she had to do was to fill in the colors and write a title on it. The calligraphy for large tablets was sketched out by experts from the Great Dilligence Hall or else done by the Hanlin academicians. Nearly all the late Ch'ing inscriptions that purport to be the brushwork of the Dowager or of an emperor were produced in this way.

The buildings all around me and the furniture of the palaces were all part of my indoctrination. Apart from the golden-glazed tiles that were for the exclusive use of the Emperor, the very height of the buildings was an imperial prerogative. It was said that the Emperor Chien Lung (1707–1799) once laid it down that nothing in the palace, not even a leaf from a weed, must be lost. To put this principle into practice he put some weed leaves on a table in the palace and gave orders that they were to be counted every day to see that not one single leaf was missing. Even in my time these 36 withered dried weed leaves were still preserved in a cloisonné box in the Mind Nurture Palace.

There is no longer any way of calculating exactly the enormous cost of the daily life of an emperor, but a record called "A comparison between the expenditure of the seventh year of Pu Yi (1915) and the past three years," compiled by a Household Department, shows that the expenditures in 1915 topped 2,790,000 ounces of silver and, while it dropped in each of the following three years, it was always over 1,890,000.

Some of the rules of the palace were originally not simply for the sake of show. The food dishes with strips of silver on them, the tasting of food before I ate it, and the large-scale security precautions whenever I went out were to protect me against any attempt on my life. It was said that the reason my ancestors had no outside toilets was that an early emperor had been assassinated while visiting one.

3

"Mothers" and Son

WHEN I ENTERED THE FORBIDDEN CITY AS THE ADOPTED son of the preceding Emperors Tung Chih and Kuang Hsu, all their wives became my "mothers." Although I was primarily the "son" of Tung Chih, and only secondarily the "son" of Kuang Hsu, the latter's Empress chose to ignore this distinction and used her authority as Empress Dowager to push the wives of Tung Chih into the background. As a result, they were not really treated as my "mothers." Thus, for example, when we all ate together, Lung Yu as Empress Dowager and I sat, while the others had to stand. After Lung Yu's death, however, the three consorts of Tung Chih combined with Kuang Hsu's consort to put their case before the princes and nobles, and succeeded in obtaining the title of High Consort. From then on, I addressed all of them as "august mother."

But even though I had so many "mothers" I never knew any motherly love. One day when I was five I ate too many chestnuts and developed stomach trouble. For over a month, Lung Yu allowed me to eat only a thick congee soup. Even though I cried for more solid food and said I was hungry, no one paid any attention.

Shortly after this I was walking beside one of the lakes at the Winter Palace, and Lung Yu asked someone to give me some stale bread rolls with which to feed the fish. I couldn't help but stuff one of them into my mouth, but the evidence that I gave of my hunger did not make Lung Yu change her mind about what I should eat.

Later, after I was restored to a regular diet, there were still times when I had to suffer. One day I ate six cakes at one sitting and the Chief Eunuch of the Presence found out about it. Afraid that I might have another attack of indigestion, he asked two eunuchs to pick me up by the arms, turn me upside down and bounce my head on the brick floor as if I were a sort of human pile driver.

Although this may seem unreasonable, there were many other things that were far more unreasonable. Before I was seven or eight, whenever I became angry or lost my temper and caused other people trouble, the chief eunuchs would seek to cure me by saying: "The Lord of Ten Thousand Years has fire in his heart. The best solution is for him to sing for a while to disperse the flames."

While saying this they would shove me into a small room and lock the door. No matter how much I kicked and banged and shouted no one would pay any attention until I stopped, or, as the eunuchs would say, until I "had dispersed the flames." Only then would they release me. This peculiar cure was not an invention of the eunuchs or of the Empress Dowager Lung Yu. It was a tradition in the royal family and my brothers and sisters also received similar treatment in my father's mansion.

The Empress Dowager Lung Yu died when I was seven years old, so that I actually lived longer with the remaining four High Consorts. I saw them very infrequently, however, and I never sat with them or talked with them in a family way. Each morning I would go to them to pay my respects. At this time of day the consorts were having their hair dressed and, while this was being done, they would ask: "Did the Emperor sleep well? How far have you read in your book?" It was always the same banal talk. Sometimes they would give me clay toys to play with, but they never failed to end the audience with the same final phrase: "Emperor, please go out now and play." This would be the end of the meeting and we would never see one another again for the whole day.

The High Consorts all addressed me as Emperor, as did my own parents and real grandmother. Everyone else called me "Your Majesty." Even though I had a name, as well as a childhood nickname, none of my mothers—real or by adoption—used them. I have heard others say that when they think of their childhood names they recall their youth and maternal love, but I have never felt such an association. Some people have told me that when they left their homes to go away to school and fell ill they would think of their mothers and of the times when they had been nursed by them through a sickness. I have often been ill as an adult and have, at these times, recalled illness as a child and the visits to my sickbed of the High Consorts. But these recollections have never aroused any feelings of maternal love in me.

As a child, whenever I was sick, the High Consorts would indeed come to see me one by one. But all they would do would be to say: "Is the Emperor getting better? Have you had a good sweat?" In two or three minutes they would be off, and, what was worse than their stilted and distant questions, was the swarm of eunuchs who accompanied each of them on their visits and packed themselves into my bedroom. Within several minutes, after one High Consort had left with her retinue, another would arrive and the room would be packed again. Every day there would be four entrances and four exits and the air in my room would be disturbed four times.

Whenever I was ill, the Imperial Dispensary in the palace of the High Consort Tuan Kang would prepare my herb medicines. This dispensary was better equipped than the others in the Forbidden City. She had inherited it from the Dowager Empress Lung Yu. In fact, Tuan Kang had more control over me than the other High Consorts. This was not in accordance with Ch'ing Dynasty precedent and it precipitated a tragic conflict within the family that had dire consequences for my real mother.

Tuan Kang's special position was derived from the interference of Yuan Shih-kai, for when Lung Yu died, Yuan had recommended to the Household Department that she should become the head of the High Consorts. I don't know why Yuan recommended this. Some people said that Tuan Kang's brother persuaded Yuan to make this recommendation;

whether this was true or not I do not know. But at any rate, Tuan Kang became my "mother" of the first rank.

It was under such an arrangement that I reached the age of twelve or thirteen under the care of my four "mothers." At that time, like any other child, I loved to play with new things and some of the Eunuchs of the Presence, in order to please me, bought me amusing things outside the Forbidden City. Once a eunuch bought me a uniform of an army officer of the Republic complete with a plume on the cap like a feather duster, and a sword and leather belt. When I put them on, I was pleased with myself and didn't anticipate that Tuan Kang would become enraged when she found out about it. But as a result of an investigation, she not only found out about the uniform but also that I was wearing some foreign socks that a eunuch had bought for me. She regarded this as intolerable and ordered the two eunuchs responsible to her palace and had each of them given 200 strokes of the heavy rod and sent to the cleaning department for hard labor. After she had punished them, she sent for me.

"The Emperor of the Great Ch'ing Dynasty has sought to wear the uniform of the Republic and foreign socks," she raged. "Where will this lead to?"

I thus had no alternative but to pack up the uniform and sword which I loved, take off my foreign socks and put on again my court clothes with the dragon designs.

If the High Consort Tuan Kang had limited her control of me to uniforms and socks, I would not later on have indulged in the disrespectful conduct I showed her. But Tuan Kang had set her heart on imitating the Empress Dowager Tzu Hsi even though it had been her own sister, the "Pearl Concubine," whom Tzu Hsi had ordered thrown down a well in the Forbidden City after the Boxer Rebellion. Still she wished to imitate her and thus she not only had the eunuchs severely beaten but she also sent a eunuch to the Mind Nurture Palace to spy on me. He would report to her in detail every day about me just as the Empress Dowager Tzu Hsi's eunuchs had reported on Emperor Kuang Hsu. All this hurt my self-respect. Also my tutor, Chen Pao-shen, was both indignant and disturbed about it and lectured me on the distinctions between the first wife and the secondary wives, which was the category into which Tuan Kang fell. As a result, I boiled with anger.

After this had been going on for a while, one of the physicians of the Imperial Medical Department was fired by Tuan Kang. It became the occasion for a big explosion. This particular doctor was one of those attendant upon Tuan Kang so that his dismissal had really nothing to do with me. Nevertheless, I discussed it in detail with my tutors, one of whom explained that "this kind of monopolizing of influence is really too much for a person who is only an imperial consort." Unexpectedly, too, the eunuch who had been the informer involved in the affair of the uniform and the socks now turned out to be on my side in the dispute over the physician. He adopted a similar point of view as my tutor.

"My Lord of Ten Thousand Years," he said, "aren't you becoming another Kuang Hsu? This affair of the Imperial College of Physicians requires a final word from you. Even your slave cannot bear to see such things happen."

These insinuations enraged me to the point where I rushed over to the palace of Tuan Kang and shouted at her: "For what reasons did you dismiss the physician? You are too dictatorial! Am I not the Emperor? Who has the final say around here, me or you? This is really too much!"

Tuan Kang's face turned white with anger but I did not wait for her answer. Instead, with a flick of my sleeve, I ran out of her palace.

The furious Tuan Kang did not call me back. Instead, she sent for my father and the other princes. With cries and shouts she asked them to support her decision. When I heard of this meeting, I asked all of them to come to the Imperial Study.

"Who is she?" I said. "She's only a consort. In all the generations of the Ch'ing Dynasty we have never had an emperor who had to call a consort of the previous generation 'august mother.' Are we to maintain no distinctions between the first wife and the secondary wives? If not, why does not my brother call his father's secondary wives 'mother'? Why should I have to listen to her at all?"

The princes, even after listening to my ranting, had nothing to say, but one of the other High Consorts who was also not on good terms with Tuan Kang came to see me after they had gone. "Take heed, Your Majesty," she warned. "I hear it said that Tuan Kang is planning to invite your real mother and grandmother to the palace to see her."

It was true! They were sent for by Tuan Kang, and although she had in fact got nothing by appealing to the princes, her shouting had an effect on my mother and grandmother. My grandmother, especially, became frightened and finally they both knelt before Tuan Kang and begged her to calm herself and promised to persuade me to say I was sorry.

When I reached the Lasting Peace Palace I found I could not resist the persuasion of my mother and grandmother, both of whom had tears in their eyes. I finally agreed to apologize to Tuan Kang.

But I resented having to make that apology. I walked up to her but did not look at her face. "Imperial August Mother," I mumbled, "I was wrong." Then I left. Although this saved Tuan Kang's face and she stopped her crying and shouting, it precipitated my real mother's suicide two days later.

In her whole life my mother had never been scolded by anyone. She had a strong personality and could not stand any form of correction, for she had been a favorite in her mother's house and continually indulged by my father. The terrible scene she had been through was too much for her. And so, after she had returned to my father's mansion from the Palace of Lasting Peace, she took an overdose of raw opium.

Tuan Kang, fearful lest I should order an official investigation of the circumstances of my mother's death, changed her attitude toward me completely. She not only stopped restricting my activities but also became very agreeable. As a result, the family in the Forbidden City was restored to the quiet of former days, and the mother-son relationship with all the High Consorts was restored. But for this, my own real mother had been sacrificed.

4

My Wet Nurse

IN THE JOURNAL OF MY LIFE, WRITTEN BY MY TUTOR, there is an entry dated February 21, 1913:

> His Majesty frequently quarrels with the eunuchs. He has already had about seventeen of them flogged for very minor offenses. His obedient servant, Chen Paoshen, and others have tried to persuade him to stop but he will not listen to them.

Often, when I became out of sorts, the eunuchs would receive punishment. And if I suddenly became happy and high-spirited, they would also be in for trouble. When I was a child, I not only enjoyed watching camels, feeding ants and worms and observing fights between dogs and cattle, I was also especially fond of practical jokes. Many of the eunuchs suffered as a result. One day, at the age of eight or nine, it suddenly dawned on me to find out if the eunuchs would really carry out an order of the "divine Son of Heaven" without question. And so I pointed to a lump of dirt on the floor. "Eat it up for me," I ordered. A eunuch knelt down and ate it without question. Once I was playing with a fire pump and, just then, an aged eunuch walked in front of me. I was seized with an irresistible urge to spray water on him. Instead of running away, he knelt down under the water and, as a result, received such a shock from the cold, for it was wintertime, that we later had to revive him with massage and artificial respiration.

The difficulty, of course, was that with everyone trying to please me and cater to my every wish, my propensity for practical jokes was increased rather than diminished. My tutors tried to use philosophy as a curb and talked to me about such abstract ideas as benevolence, humanity and forgiveness while, at the same time, they recognized my authority. But no matter how many times they reasoned with me in this way and told me of the heroic deeds and benevolence of the Emperors of the past, this sort of persuasion had no effect.

The only person, in the palace, who could control my practical jokes was my wet nurse, Mrs. Wang Chiao. She knew nothing of Chinese history and the heroic deeds of the great Ch'ing Emperors, but she could always persuade me and I felt I could not refuse her. Once there was a young eunuch who put on a special puppet show for me. I loved it and I decided to give him a piece of pound cake to eat. Then, all of a sudden, my fondness for practical jokes came over me. I decided to play a trick on him. I tore open the bag of little iron pellets that I used for my Chinese boxing lessons and put some of them in the cake. When my wet nurse saw what I was doing, she said:

"My own Master and Lord. How can you put pellets in that cake and let him eat it?"

"I just want to see his face after he bites into it," I said.

"But won't it break his teeth?" she asked. "If his teeth are broken he won't be able to eat."

I thought over what she had said for a minute. "Well," I explained, "I just want to see what he looks like after he cracks his teeth this once. I won't do it again."

"How about using green lentils instead? Biting on the lentils will be just as much fun for you to see as biting on the pellets."

In this way the little eunuch who played so well with the marionettes avoided disaster, and in the end I was happy for him.

Another time, I was playing with my air gun and pointing it at the windows of the eunuchs' rooms. I thought it fun to shoot little holes in their paper windows. Someone sent for my nurse.

"Oh Master," she said. "There are people in those rooms. You may hurt them."

Only then did I think that there were people behind the windows whom I could not see and that they might be injured by my shooting. My nurse was the only one who ever explained to me that other people were human beings as I was; not only did I have teeth, but other people had teeth as well; not only could I not bite into iron pellets without being injured, but other people could not as well; not only did I have to eat, but other people had to eat as well, otherwise they would go hungry. Other people also had feelings and could be hurt by the pellets from my air gun. Much of this was simply common sense which I knew as well as anyone. But in my peculiar environment, it was difficult to keep in mind because I tended not to think of other people and not to put myself in their shoes. In the Forbidden City in which I grew up, other people were all slaves—my subjects. In the palace, from my infancy until the time I grew up, only my wet nurse, because of her simple language, was able to make me grasp the idea that I was like other people.

I was fed on Mrs. Wang's milk until the age of eight. In these eight years we were inseparable. When I was eight, the High Consorts had her sent away without telling me. At that time I would rather have seen all of my four mothers expelled from the palace instead. I still wanted to keep my wet nurse, but no matter how I cried the High Consorts would not allow me to have her back.

After my marriage, I sent people to search for Mrs. Wang and sometimes I had her stay with me in the palace. During my Emperorship of Manchuria, I welcomed her to Changchun and supported her until I left the Northeast. She never sought anything for her own benefit because of her special position. She was, by nature, calm and mild and never quarreled with anyone. Her face always wore a smile. She did not talk much, and if no one took the initiative in conversation, she would remain silent, smiling quietly. When I was young I used to find her charming little smile rather strange. Her eyes seemed to be fixed on some far-distant place and often I wondered whether she had seen something in the sky outside the window or was looking at the scrolls on the wall. She never spoke about her own life or background.

In later years, I talked about her with her adopted son and for the first time I learned about the life of this person whose milk had fed me. She was born in 1887 to a poor farm family by the name of Chiao in a small village of Jenchiu County in what is now Hopei Province. She was one of a family of four, which included, besides herself, her mother, father and brother, who was six years older than she.

The father, who was about fifty, had a few acres of poor lowland which was parched when it did not rain and flooded when it did. Even in a good year there was not enough to feed them. When my nurse was about three, there was a severe flood and her whole family had to flee to avoid disaster. While en route, her father wanted to abandon her several times, but he always put her back into one of the broken baskets slung from his carrying pole. The other basket contained some tattered clothes and bedding which was all the property they had in the world. They did not have a single grain of rice to eat. When she later talked to her adopted son about how she had almost been abandoned as an infant, she had no word to say against her father. She only pitied him and thought of the hunger that had made him so weak he could hardly carry her along the road.

Finally the Chiaos reached Peking where they sought relief from one of their cousins who was a eunuch. But he refused to see them and they had to become beggars. Peking at this time was full of thousands of refugees who were sleeping on the streets and crying for food and clothing so that they had the greatest difficulty subsisting. At this point they tried to sell their daughter, but no one wanted to buy her. Later, the Prefecture set up a relief kitchen in order to feed the refugees and thus avoid rioting. Here the family found a temporary haven and also, at this time, the nine-year-old boy was finally accepted by a barber as an apprentice. Thus they managed to survive the winter and, when spring came, the Chiao family, along with the other refugees, began to think of their land. One by one, the refugees, the Chiao family among them, returned to their farms.

During the Boxer Rebellion of 1900, the troops of the Allied powers devastated their district. By this time the daughter of the family was thirteen, and she returned to Peking, a refugee again. She stayed with her brother, who was now a barber, but he could not support her and so, when she was sixteen, she was married to a tuberculous loose-living government messenger named Wang. After three years as a sort of slave, she gave birth to a daughter, and then her husband died, leaving her, her infant child and her in-laws destitute.

This is just about the time I was born and the household of Prince Chun was looking for a wet nurse for me. She was chosen from among twenty applicants because of her gentle personality and the quality and quantity of her milk. She was not allowed to return to her home to say good-bye to her child. Her pay was two ounces of silver each month and she was made to eat bowls of unsalted meat which, at the time, was felt to be beneficial for wet nurses.

Three years later her daughter died. The palace officials, however, kept the news from her in order to safeguard her milk. After she had been in the palace eight years, one of the women servants quarreled with a eunuch. As a result, the High Consorts decided to fire them, ordering them to take my wet nurse with them. It was then that this obedient, gentle, and humane woman found that her own daughter was no longer living.

5

Eunuchs

DURING MY CHILDHOOD, EUNUCHS WERE A VITAL PART OF my daily life. They served me when I ate, dressed me, and saw to it that I went to bed; they played with me and accompanied me to my lessons; they told me ghost stories and fairy tales and they had both rewards and beatings from me.

The eunuchs never left me. They were the main companions of my youth. They were my slaves and they were also my earliest teachers.

I do not know when the employment of court eunuchs began in Chinese history, but I do know exactly when it ended. It was at the end of World War II, when I lost my throne for the third time. At this time there were only about ten eunuchs left in the imperial entourage. It is said that the greatest number of eunuchs was recorded during the Ming Dynasty (1368–1644) when there were over 100,000. During my own Ch'ing Dynasty, however, there were certain limits on their functions and number. But even so, there were at least 3,000 during the time of the Empress Dowager Tzu Hsi. After the 1911 Revolution the majority of the eunuchs ran away, and although the Articles of Favorable Treatment specified that no more might be hired, the Household Department continued to take them on secretly. In 1922, there were still about 1,137 of them on the payroll. Two years later, after I had ordered their expulsion from the Forbidden City, their number was reduced to 200 of whom the great

34

majority were in the service of the High Consorts and my wives.

In the old days in the Forbidden City, after a certain hour, there were no true males allowed within the walls, apart from the guards on duty and men of the Emperor's own family. The duties of the eunuchs were very broad. Besides taking care of my food and daily wants, handling the umbrellas, carrying heaters and other such tasks, their duties, according to the Palace Regulations, included: transmitting imperial edicts; presenting high officials for audiences; receiving memorials; handling the documents of the various government departments; receiving money sent from treasuries outside the palace; managing fire prevention; filing my documents; tending antiques, scrolls, robes, belts, guns, bows and arrows; taking care of the ancient bronzes; guarding the awards to be presented to high officials and the yellow belts to be bestowed on meritorious functionaries; preserving the dried fruits and sweetmeats; fetching the imperial physicians for treatment of persons in the various palaces; obtaining construction materials to be used in the palace by outside builders; safekeeping the edicts handed down by my imperial ancestors; burning incense and candles in front of my ancestral portraits; checking the comings and goings of persons entering and leaving the various departments within the Forbidden City; keeping the rosters of the Palace Guards and the registers of the Hanlin academicians; safekeeping the imperial seals; recording the actions of my daily life; flogging offending eunuchs and maidservants; feeding the various living animals in the palace; tending the gardens; checking the accuracy of the clocks; cutting my hair; preparing the herb medicines; performing in palace shows; acting as Taoist monks in the City Temple; and substituting for the Emperor as lamas in the Yung Ho Kung, the temple reserved for visiting dignitaries and lamas from Tibet.

The eunuchs in the palace could be divided into two main categories: those in attendance on the Empress Dowager, the Emperor, the Empress and Imperial Consorts on the one hand, and all the others on the other. Both categories had very strict classifications and ranks. Roughly they could be divided into "general supervisors," "chiefs" and "ordinary eunuchs." The "general supervisors" served the Empress Dowager and the Empress as well as the Emperor; but the Imperial Consorts could only be served by "chief" eunuchs. The highest rank normally ever reached by a eunuch was the third grade; but the favorite eunuch of the Empress Dowager Tzu Hsi was accorded the even higher rank of second grade, so that the Chief Eunuch in my service was also given this rank, which meant he had the right to wear the peacock feather and headgear of the second rank. Other than my Chief Eunuch, the highest were those of the third rank and they could wear the peacock feather of this rank. These were in charge of the eunuchs of the 48 administrative sections of the Forbidden City, under whom were the "general supervisors" of the nine sub-sections and these were classified from the third to the fifth rank; below these were the "chief" eunuchs from the sixth to the ninth rank, and below these were those who did not rate a rank, or the "ordinary" eunuchs. The lowest of these were those who did the cleaning and sweeping. Eunuchs who committed a crime or misdemeanor or who made an error were reduced to this rank. The monthly pay of the eunuchs were eight taels of silver for the highest rank, plus eight catties of rice a month,[1] plus a monthly string of 300 iron coins. The lowest rank would receive two taels a month, one and a half catties of rice plus two strings of coins. In addition, however, the higher eunuchs enjoyed many legal and illegal fringe benefits. The result was that their real income exceeded by several times their official salaries. The Deputy Chief Eunuch of my entourage, for example was as rich as a prince. In the wintertime he could change his sable coat daily, and I never saw him in the same fur coat twice. The sea otter coat he wore on New Year's Day would have represented a lifetime's expenditure by a petty official. Nearly all of the general supervisors and many of the chiefs had their own private kitchens, "families," and were waited upon by young eunuchs. They also had their own households consisting of serving women and maidservants.

The life of the low-ranking eunuchs was very hard; they

---

[1] One catty is about 1¼ lbs. One tael equaled ¹⁄₁₆ catty, or a little over 1 ounce.

suffered the whole year round. They often received beatings and other punishments, and had no pensions or old age assistance. If they were driven from the palace for a mistake, they could only expect a future of begging and starvation.

The eunuchs with whom I was in the closest contact were those of the Mind Nurture Palace, especially the young Eunuchs of the Presence who dressed me and attended me at mealtimes. They lived in the east and west passageways behind the palace and each group had a chief eunuch. Those responsible for cleaning the palace also had a chief. All of these eunuchs came under the control of Chang Chien-ho, the Chief Eunuch and Inspector General of the eunuchs, and his deputy, Juan Chin-shou.

When the Empress Dowager Lung Yu was alive she sent one of her chief eunuchs to be my nursery tutor, a post in which his main duty was to look after my daily life and teach me palace etiquette. But I did not feel for him the affection and trust I did for Chang Chien-ho who was at that time about fifty years old and was a hunchback. Actually he was the one who taught me elementary reading. Before I entered the Palace for the Cultivation of Happiness to study, he taught me to recognize characters printed on cards and read with me through elementary texts including the *Three Character Classic* and the *Hundred Surnames*. After I started my formal schooling, he stood outside my bedroom and reviewed my lessons of the previous day and helped me to memorize them. Like the chief eunuch of any emperor, he would take every opportunity to show me his loyalty and affection. I could often tell from his face and from the tone of his voice, as he went over my lessons for me, the nature of the developments outside the Forbidden City which were affecting my prospects. He also lost no opportunity to tell me, before I entered my schoolroom, of the evil deeds of Yuan Shih-kai, the erosion of Ch'ing prerogatives by the Republic, and the unfriendly behavior of former Ch'ing officials serving the Republic.

Just as any other child, I loved being told stories. The tales that Chang Chien-ho and the other eunuchs told me always seemed to be of two types: ghost stories about the palace and myths about the spirits who helped the sacred son of Heaven. If I could recall now all the ghost stories I was told, I could write a book that would be thicker than the famous classic *Ghost Stories*. According to the eunuchs, everything in the palace—the bronze crane, the golden jars for fish, the trees, wells, rocks, each and every item—had at some time or other turned into a spirit and shown its magic powers. From these stories which I loved to hear, and of which I never tired, I came to believe that all the ghosts and spirits tried to flatter the Emperor, and although there were some who did not succeed, this only went to show that the Emperor was the most respected and exalted creature in the world.

The eunuchs especially liked to tell me the story of the bronze crane in the palace which had a dent on its left leg because it had once become a spirit and flew down to guard the Emperor Chien Lung (1707–1798) during a trip to the South. Unfortunately, however, it was accidentally struck by an arrow from the Emperor's own bow. Crestfallen and humiliated, the crane flew back to its original stand in the Forbidden City. The rusty dent on its left leg was supposed to be the arrow wound received during this unfortunate trip. The eunuchs also claimed that the ancient pine tree that grew by the Western Fish Pond in the Imperial Garden near the wall had once served as a shade umbrella for Emperor Chien Lung during one of his southern tours. When he returned to the palace he was supposed to have written a poem to thank it for its kindness and had it inscribed on a nearby wall.

Also, on the northwest corner of the terrace of one of the palaces in the Imperial Garden, there was a certain brick under which was said to be a fairy footprint. During Chien Lung's reign a fire had broken out and the fairy king stood on the terrace and pointed at it. Immediately the flames were extinguished and, for this reason, the footprint had been specially preserved at the order of the Emperor. Although I knew this story was nonsense, I loved to hear it.

There was also a fairy tale associated with the big pearl in the imperial hat. One day, Chien Lung was strolling along the stream in the Yuang Ming Yuan Palace outside the Forbidden City. He noticed a glittering light issuing from the water and shot at it with his fowling piece. The light vanished. He then asked a retainer to drag the stream and the man found a large mollusk in which there was a big pearl. After it was put on the imperial hat, the pearl would sometimes fly away by itself only to return just as mysteriously. Finally, after the priests ordered a hole to be drilled in the pearl and fastened it to the hat with a golden mount, it stayed put. I myself wore this particular hat several times. After I abdicated from my throne in Manchukuo it was lost in one of the northern rivers.

The impact of these ghost stories on me when I was a boy can be explained by the following story. Once when I was seven or eight, I wasn't feeling well, and Chang Chien-ho, my Chief Eunuch, brought me some purple pills and gave me one to take. I asked him what kind of medicine it was. "Your servant was sleeping," he explained, "and dreamed of a man with a white beard who held some pills in his hand. He said they were the pills of immortality which he had especially brought as a present for the Lord of Ten Thousand Years." After I heard this, I was happy and forgot about my illness. Then I remembered the famous twenty-four stories of filial piety. I immediately took the pills to the four High Consorts and asked them each to take some. Perhaps Chang Chien-ho had given them some previous information, for all of them laughed loudly and praised me for my filial piety. Some time later, I went to the Imperial Dispensary to get some medicine, and I discovered unintentionally some purple pills that looked just like my "pills of immortality." Even though I was a little disappointed I still believed the story of the old man with the white beard.

These fairy tales which the eunuchs told me made me feel very important, but at the same time they made me fearful of ghosts. According to the eunuchs, ghosts and spirits were everywhere in the Forbidden City. In the lane behind the Lasting Peace Palace, they claimed, ghosts strangled people, and in the well outside the Ching Ho Gate there lived a swarm of she-devils, but, fortunately, these were kept at bay by a piece of iron over the gate; otherwise they would come out every day. Every three years the bridge across the lake in the Summer Palace was supposed to witness the kidnapping of a passer-by by a ghost. The more I heard these stories the more frightened I became. But the more frightened I became the more I wanted to hear about these ghosts.

From the age of eleven, I became engrossed in books of ghost and fairy tales which the eunuchs bought for me, and these, combined with the continuous sacrifices to gods, plus the devil dances of the wizard, made me afraid of the dark, of thunder and lightning, and of being left alone in a room.

At sunset, the Forbidden City became truly mysterious. Those who had come into the palace for the day had gone; and, in the sudden quiet, from the Palace of Cloudless Heaven one heard the cries: "Shoot home the bolts, lock up, careful with fire and the candles." These chants would soon echo in ghostly response from all corners of the Forbidden City as the eunuchs from their various stations would take up the cries and repeat them. This routine, which had been started by the Emperor Kang Hsi (1654–1722) to keep the eunuchs alert, filled the Forbidden City with such an eerie atmosphere I did not dare go out of my room. I felt that all the ghosts and demons and spirits and immortals had gathered outside my window.

The eunuchs did not tell me all these ghost stories to frighten me. They themselves were very superstitious, Chang Chien-ho perhaps more than most. Whenever he was in doubt, he had to consult a book titled the *Record of the Jade Box* before he could make up his mind. In general, all the eunuchs dutifully worshipped the palace divinities—in the guise of snakes, foxes, weasels and hedgehogs. In fact, in the palace there were a great many different gods worshipped by the imperial house; but the palace divinities were not included in the offerings made by the royal family. According to the eunuchs, the palace gods had been made divinities of the second grade by some emperor. A eunuch once told me that one night, when he was climbing the steps outside the Palace of Cloudless Heaven, a man wearing a hat button, robes and insignia of the second grade had suddenly grabbed him and thrown him down the steps. This, he said, had been one of the palace gods. The eunuchs would not dare to eat beef because one of them said that if they violated this taboo the palace gods would punish them by making them rub their lips against the bark of a tree until they would bleed. Whenever a eunuch approached an empty hall of one of the palaces he would shout clearly and loudly "Open the palace" before daring to enter in order to avoid unintentionally colliding with a palace god. On the first and 15th of every month, at New Year and other festivals, the eunuchs would make offerings of eggs, dried bean curd, spirits and pastry to the palace gods, but on special occasions they would offer whole pigs and even sheep. The low-salaried eunuchs gladly paid for their share of these offerings because they hoped the palace gods would protect them from beatings or other forms of ill treatment and bring them good luck.

The eunuchs had many ways of augmenting their incomes. There are descriptions in plays and novels of how even Emperor Kuang Hsi (1871–1908) had to give money to the Chief Eunuch of the Empress Dowager Tzu Hsi, since he would otherwise delay reporting his presence to the Dowager. However, I do not really believe this happened. I have heard a lot of stories about how the eunuchs made money from the palace officials. At the wedding of Emperor Tung Chih (1856–1874) a Household Department official had neglected to distribute money to one of the sections of eunuchs. On the wedding day, the eunuchs of this section told an official of the Household Department that there was a crack in a pane of glass in one of the palace windows. According to regulations, a Household Department official could not dispatch a workman to the palace unless he was sent for. Thus, from a distance, the official stared at the palace and saw a big crack in the glass. He was terrified. He would be in dire trouble if Tzu Hsi heard there was anything so ill-omened as a cracked window on a wedding day. At that moment the eunuch said, "You don't need to find a workman to fix the window. We can do it for you." Although the official of the Household Department knew he was being taken, he willingly handed over a large sum of money to the eunuch for the immediate repair of the window. This was not difficult since the glass was not broken; the crack was simulated by a strand of hair pasted to the glass.

Once, when the Comptroller of the Household Department in Tzu Hsi's time failed to distribute enough presents on a special occasion, some of the eunuchs waylaid him when he was en route to pay a visit to the Empress Dowager by purposely throwing a pail of water from a window. The Comptroller's sable jacket was drenched. The eunuch apologized and begged for punishment, but the Comptroller, knowing that this was not the time to lose his temper, asked the eunuchs to think of some way to extricate him from his position since he could not wait upon the Empress in a wet jacket. The eunuch hastily produced another beautiful sable jacket saying: "This humble place of ours will be grateful to be able to share in your good fortune." The Comptroller had no recourse but to pay a handsome rental fee for the use of that particular sable jacket.

6

Studying in the Yu Ching Palace

WHEN I WAS FIVE YEARS OLD, AFTER THE EMPRESS DOWA-
ger Lung Yu had chosen tutors for me, the Imperial Astrol-
oger selected September 10, 1911, between the hours of
seven and nine in the morning, as an auspicious time for me
to begin my studies.

My first school was on an island in one of the lakes of the
Summer Palace, but it was later moved to the Yu Ching
Palace (Palace for the Cultivation of Happiness) in the Forbidden City. Only the two larger rooms on the western side
of the building were used for my schoolrooms; the rest
remained vacant. Under the southern window of one of the
two rooms was a long table on which stood hatstands and
flower vases. Along the west wall was a *kang* on which I
studied, at first with a low *kang* table serving as a desk.
Later I sat at a regular teakwood table-desk. There were two
more tables along the north wall for books and stationery
and there was also a row of chairs along the east wall. On
the east and west walls hung scrolls of poems and maxims
written by my grandfather, the first Prince Chun, for his son
the Emperor Kuang Hsu. On the north wall hung an enormous chiming clock 7½ feet in diameter with hands as long
as my arms. Its works were on the other side of the wall,
and something resembling a car crank was needed in order
to wind it. Where this object came from and why it was hung
there or what sort of chimes it had I cannot remember.

But even though this clock was colossal, the people in the

43

Yu Ching Palace had no concept of the passage of time in so far as the books I used were concerned. My principle texts were the *Thirteen Classics*[1] plus supplementary books such as the maxims and proverbs of the Ch'ing Dynasty, the history of China with commentaries by my imperial ancestors, and so on. When I was thirteen, English lessons were added. But besides my English reader, I had only two other books; one was *Alice in Wonderland* and the other was an English translation of the Chinese classical *Four Books*. Thus from 1911 until 1922, I learned nothing about mathematics, physics or chemistry. As for the modern history of my own country, I read only about such events as the unsuccessful struggles for power against the Empress Dowager Tzu Hsi by the two preceding Emperors, and my knowledge of foreign countries was limited to my trip with Alice in Wonderland. I had no idea about people such as George Washington, Napoleon, Watts or Newton. Insofar as geography was concerned all I knew was that "the great Pole produced the two Forms, the two Forms produced the four Symbols, and the four Symbols produced the Eight Trigrams." If it had not been for the willingness of my tutors to talk with me about things that were not in the texts, plus my own desire to read extensively, I would not even have known where Peking was or that rice grew out of the ground. In history, not even my tutors cared to expose the myths about the origins of the ancestors of the Ch'ing House. And in the matter of practical economics, no one ever told me how much a catty of rice cost. Thus, for a long time, I believed that my earliest ancestor was born after the fairy goddess Fokulun swallowed a red fruit and that everyone in China had a table covered with a variety of dishes at every meal.

Since I read a number of ancient books over a long period of time, I should theoretically have known the Chinese classics very well. But that was not the case. The truth was that I was not industrious and, up to the age of ten, I was far more interested in the big cypress tree that grew outside the Yu Ching Palace than in my books. In the summer there were always ants on this tree busy crawling up and down all

---

[1] Basic works of Confucianism.

day long. I became very interested in them and would often sit down to watch them and feed them crumbs of cake and help them move their food. Later I became interested in crickets and earthworms and had many antique porcelain bowls brought over for me to keep them in.

In my early teens I began to realize the importance of studies to my special position. I became interested in learning how to be a good emperor and in understanding the basic principles of rulership. My interest was centered in the content of the books rather than in the beauty and form of their language. But their content was usually devoted to the rights and privileges of an emperor and seldom to his duties. Even though some of the sages said, "If the emperor regards his subjects as so much grass, then the subjects will regard the monarch as the enemy," the books were more concerned with the relations between the emperor's ministers and the common people. My very first textbook, the *Classic of Filial Piety*,[2] stated that one should "start by serving one's parents and end by serving one's emperor."

My tutors never gave me any tests on my lessons nor did they require me to write any essays. I remember that once I wrote several couplets and poems, but my tutors never commented on them or sought to help me with my style. Actually when I was young I enjoyed writing this sort of thing, but since my tutors never encouraged me, I wrote them solely for my own amusement. After I was twelve or thirteen I read a lot of books besides the regular textbooks, such as diaries and unofficial histories of the Ming and Ch'ing Dynasties, historical romances, tales of knights and warriors with magic powers, detective stories, and current novels published by the commercial press. When I was a little older I also read English stories. I concocted and illustrated many imitations of these works, Chinese and Western, ancient and modern, drawn from my daydreams for my own amusement.

The subject at which I was worst in my studies was Manchu. Even after I had studied it for several years, the only word I knew was "yili," meaning arise, which was the

---

[2] Written in the third or second century B.C., a standard text used to indoctrinate children until the twentieth century.

word I used when my Manchu ministers knelt before me in audience.

When I was eight, I was provided with some fellow students. Each of them received 80 taels of silver a month as stipend and were also granted the special privilege of being allowed to ride a horse up to a certain point within the Forbidden City. This was regarded as a great honor among the young boys of the royal family. There were three recipients of these honors—my brother Pu Chieh, Yu Chung (a son of my cousin Pu Lun) and Pu Chia, the son of my uncle Tsai Tao. Another honor conferred on my companion students was to receive punishments in place of the Emperor. This was a 2,000-year-old tradition and, therefore, when I did not do well in my studies, my tutors would reprimand my companion students. Actually, however, Pu Chieh, my younger brother, was never called on to be "whipping boy," and the victim was nearly always Yu Chung. Pu Chieh was the best student because his own tutor at home prepared him specially for his lessons in the Yu Ching Palace, and Yu Chung was the worst because he was scolded whether he studied well or not and this made him lose interest. In other words, his studies suffered for occupational reasons.

When I had no fellow students, I was naughty. I once noticed the long eyebrows of one of my tutors and told him to come closer so that I could touch them. He obeyed me and bent his head, not anticipating that I would pull out a hair from his eyebrow. When he died a few months later the eunuchs said this was because I had pulled out his eyebrow of longevity. On another occasion, one of my tutors became so irritated with me that he forgot the distinction between Emperor and subject. On this occasion, I couldn't study because I wanted to watch the ants come in and out of their holes in the courtyard. At first the tutor tried to persuade me to sit quietly by explaining that "to be a gentleman one must be polite and grateful." But I continued to fidget and twist. Seeing that I was still unable to concentrate, he went on to cite another saying, "If a gentleman is not dignified, then he cannot show his prestige and his learning will not be well grounded." But instead of paying attention, all I wanted to do was stand up and go out. Suddenly he lost his temper and shouted at me, "Don't move!" I was frightened and quieted down a bit. But after a while, I thought again of my ants and started fidgeting once more.

But when I got some fellow students things went better and my tutors developed a way of warning me through them when I misbehaved. I remember once when I came skipping into the study I heard the tutor say to Yu Chung who was sitting like a good boy, "Look how undignified you are."

My daily study hours were from eight to eleven in the morning, and later when English was added, the hours were extended from one to three. At eight every morning, I sat in my yellow-canopied sedan chair to be carried to the Yu Ching Palace. Upon arrival I would say "Call," and a eunuch would then go and summon the tutors and my fellow students from a waiting room. They then entered the schoolroom in a set order; first a eunuch with the books, then the tutor of the first lesson and then my fellow students. Once in the study, the tutor would stand and look straight at me as a form of salutation. But I did not need to return this greeting since although he was my tutor he was also my subject. After this, Pu Chieh, Pu Chia and Yu Chung would kneel in front of me to pay their respects and when this was over we would all sit down. I sat in a chair on the north side of the desk, facing south; the tutor faced west and my fellow students sat beside him. As soon as the eunuchs had placed everyone's hats on the hatstands they filed out, and my lessons would begin.

Among my Chinese tutors, Chen Pao-shen exerted the deepest influence on me. Chen, a well-known scholar in Fukien, had passed the palace examination during the reign of Tung Chih and became a Hanlin academician at the age of eighteen. After entering the Grand Secretariat, he became known for strength of character as a result of having dared to reprove the Empress Dowager Tzu Hsi. But because he did not alter his political views to cater to her whims, in 1891 he was demoted five ranks and retired for twenty years. He was recalled on the eve of the 1911 Revolution and appointed governor of Shansi Province, but before he reached his post he was summoned to the palace to be my tutor. From this time on he never left me until I went to the Northeast. Of all the Ch'ing Dynasty officials he was considered one of the most stable and cautious, and in my eyes he was the most loyal man I knew. Until I decided that his caution was too much of a hindrance to me, he was my principal adviser and I sought his advice on all matters, whether trifling or important.

Tutor Chen would often smile and praise me with the following quotation: "Although the king is young he is really the Son of Heaven." When he smiled, his eyes became like small slits behind his glasses and he would stroke his long white straggly beard.

I always found his casual talk interesting, and when I grew a little older, almost every morning I would listen to his summaries of the latest news of the Republic—the tension between the North and South, civil strife among the war lords, the ill feelings between the presidency and the legislature. After these decriptions he would often go on to discuss the restoration of previous Emperors and the golden age of Kang Hsi (1654–1722) and Chien Lung (1707–1799). Naturally, he was fond of talking about the events surrounding his remonstrances with Tzu Hsi, and whenever he discussed Ch'ing officials who were serving the Republic, he became very angry. He believed that all these people should be considered traitors. In his eyes revolutions and republican governments were the source of all difficulties and disasters, and people who were involved in them were robbers and thieves. "Those who defy the sages have no law," he would say. "Those who defy filial piety have no parents. This is the cause of all disorders."

Tutor Chu Yi-fan, on the other hand, did not indulge in this kind of talk with me. He always seemed dispirited. Later on, I found that he enjoyed Mah-Jongg and used to play it all night. As a result, he suffered from lack of sleep. However, he did know the art of Chinese medicine and if I were ill I sometimes asked him to diagnose my illness. Tutor Liang was very talkative; the difference between him and Tutor Chen was that he talked principally about himself rather than events of interest to me.

At this time there were many things I did not understand and which were not explained to me. For instance, according to Confucius, a scholar should not talk about ghosts and spirits, but Tutor Chen really believed in fortune-tellers and even consulted the patron saint of fortune-tellers about the future of my dynasty. Tutor Liang believed in divining by a willow stick and sand writing. Tutor Chu even once recommended a soothsayer. They all knew how to fish for honorific awards, as well as scrolls and books of historic paintings, landscape paintings, and other valuables, which they selected for themselves.

After their deaths, all my tutors received posthumous awards that were the envy of other officials. It is fair to say that whatever they wanted to get from me, they got; and whatever they wanted to give me, they gave.

It was while studying in the Yu Ching Palace that I came to know my father, the Prince Regent, although not intimately. Whenever a eunuch would interrupt my studies to report that "His Royal Highness" was coming, my tutors would become very tense and would hastily tidy up the desk while they explained to me how I should behave. After this they would tell me to stand up and wait for him. A moment later a clean-shaven stranger wearing a peacock feather in his hat would appear in the door of the schoolroom and stand stiffly in front of me. This was my father. After greeting him I would pick up my book and start to read aloud as I had been instructed to do by my tutor.

In a few moments, I would get stuck, being unable to remember how to pronounce a character. This would make me flustered, but fortunately my father would appear more nervous than I and would keep nodding his head and mumbling "Good . . . good . . . very good indeed, Your Majesty. Study hard. Study hard."

Then he would nod his head a few more times, get up from the table and leave. He had only spent two minutes with me.

Thus I came to know what my father looked like. He had no beard and his face was unwrinkled. The peacock feather on the back of his hat was always bobbing up and down. He used to make these visits every two months and he never stayed longer than two minutes. It was his stutter that made him shake his head as he groped for words, causing the peacock feather on his hat to bob about more than ever.

7

Reginald Johnston— My British Tutor

THE FIRST TIME I SAW FOREIGNERS WAS AT A RECEPTION given by the Empress Dowager Lung Yu for the wives of the chiefs of mission accredited to Peking. Their strange clothing and the various colors of their eyes and hair made them seem to me both undignified and alarming. I had not yet seen any foreign men. My knowledge of them was limited to the magazine pictures printed at that time in which they all seemed to have moustaches like a Chinese figure eight on their lips, creases in their pants and walking sticks. The eunuchs claimed that foreigners' moustaches were so stiff that one could hang a lantern on them and also that their legs would not bend. This latter belief led a high official in 1900 to recommend to the Empress Dowager Tzu Hsi that the easiest way to fight foreign soldiers was to push them down with a bamboo stick, since, once they fell, they could not stand up again.

My tutor Chen Pao-shen had once been in Southeast Asia where he had actually met foreigners, and he passed on his knowledge of them to me. What he told me gradually replaced what I had learned from the eunuchs, but when I heard that I was to have a foreigner as a tutor, I had some strange and uneasy feelings for a youth of fourteen.

It was on March 4, 1919, that my father and my Chinese tutors introduced me to Mr. Reginald Fleming Johnston in the Yu Ching Palace. First, in accordance with protocol, I sat on my throne and he bowed to me. I then stood up and shook hands with him. Then he bowed again and withdrew. Later, he re-entered and I bowed to him in order to demonstrate my respect for him as my teacher. After this ceremony was over, he began to give me lessons in the company of one of my Chinese tutors.

I soon discovered that Johnston was not so alarming after all. His Chinese was very fluent and much easier to understand than the Fukinese and the Kiangsi dialects of my other tutors. Johnston at that time was a little over forty and although he seemed to be much older than my father his movements were much more nimble. His back was so stiff and straight that I thought he might have it encased in a cast concealed beneath his clothes, and even though he did not have a moustache and could bend his legs he gave me a feeling of being stiff. I found the clarity of his blue eyes and the yellowish gray of his hair frightening.

Also within about two or three months, I discovered that this Scottish tutor with so many alien characteristics was really much like my other tutors. He not only respectfully called me Emperor but also, when I became tired during my studies, he would push aside my books and talk to me about everything under the sun. Based on his recommendation, a companion student was provided for my English class.

Johnston had received an M.A. degree from Oxford University in England. He had been a secretary to the Governor of Hong Kong and, before he came to me, he was a Commissioner of the British Leased Territory of Wei-hai-wei. He said he had been in Asia for over twenty years, had visited almost every corner of China, and had admired its famous mountains and rivers, its ancient monuments and scenic views. He knew Chinese history and was well acquainted with the customs and habits of the interior of China. He had done research in Confucianism, Mohism,[1] Buddhism and Taoism and was especially fond and appreciative of Chinese poetry. I do not know how many Chinese classics he had

---

[1] A philosophy of universal love and nonmilitarism that challenged Confucianism as a leading system of thought in the fourth century B.C.

read, but I noticed that he, like my other Chinese tutors, would move his body and shake his head according to the rhythm when he recited Tang poems.

Just as with my other tutors, he felt honored when I bestowed titles on him. After he had received the hat button of the highest grade, he had a full set of court clothes and headgear made. He posed for a photo in these in front of his summer home outside of Peking in the Western Hills and sent prints of it to many of his friends and relatives. The Household Department rented a house for him in the city and he had it decorated as a court official would have done. Upon entering the gate one could see four red tablets on which were written in black ink: *Companion of the Yu Ching Palace; Privileged to Be Carried in a Sedan Chair with Two Bearers; Awarded the Hat Button and Robes of the First Rank; Endowed with the Right to Wear a Sable Jacket* Whenever he received a special honor he would have a formal memorial written to thank me.

He was very fond of Chinese tea and peonies and liked to talk with the veteran Ch'ing Dynasty officials. When he retired to England he set aside a room in his house for displaying the things I had given him and also his formal Ch'ing robes. He also flew the flag of Manchukuo over a small island he had purchased in order to show his loyalty to the Emperor. When I think back, I realize that the cordial relationship that developed between us was due to his patience. It could not have been an easy task for such an easily aroused Scot to adopt the attitude he did toward me. Once he showed me some foreign magazines filled with World War I pictures of aircraft, tanks and artillery and explained them to me: the functions of the tanks, which country's airplanes were the best, the bravery of the Allied soldiers, etc. Although fascinated at first, I eventually became bored as usual and emptied the contents of a snuff bottle on the table and started drawing flowers in the powder. Without a word, Johnston put away the magazine and waited patiently while I played, until it was time to close the class.

On another occasion he brought me some foreign candies, and I was delighted with the tin box, the foil wrapping paper and the different fruit flavors of the candies themselves. He then told me that the different flavors were derived from chemicals and explained how the candy box had been shaped by machine. I didn't understand anything of what he told me and I did not want to understand. After I had eaten two pieces, I thought only of the ants in the pine trees outside and I wanted them to taste the chemicals contained in the machine-made box. I therefore went out to the courtyard while Johnston waited patiently until the time for the class to end had come.

As I gradually came to understand his patience I became interested and obedient. He not only taught me English; he also sought to educate me to be a gentleman in the British tradition. When I was fifteen years old, I decided to follow his advice about being an English gentleman and sent some eunuchs out to buy a complete foreign outfit for me. Later I put on the suit, which was too big for me, and then tied my necktie in a knot, as if it were a piece of rope, outside my collar. When Johnston saw me he became so furious he nearly burst. He told me to take off my foreign clothes immediately and, the following day, he came back with a tailor to take my measurements and had a suit made for me. "If you cannot wear foreign suits made to order," he explained, "it would be better for you to wear Chinese gowns. A person who wears a ready-made suit bought in a shop is not a gentleman. You'll be . . ." But what I would be he did not go on to say.

"If Your Majesty ever visits London," he told me, "you will be invited to tea parties which, although comparatively casual, can be important occasions. The time will usually be on Wednesdays. At these teas, you will be required to meet many of the aristocrats, scholars, philosophers and other prominent people. Your clothes need not be too formal but your manners will be very important. It would be a disaster for you to drink your tea as if it were hot water, to eat the refreshments as if they were a real meal, and to make too much noise with your fork or spoon. In England tea and cakes are refreshment [he used the English word] to restore your spirits, not a meal."

Even though I could not remember all of Johnston's tea party instructions and threw the caution with which I had eaten the first cake to the winds by the time I ate the second, Western civilization as represented by airplanes in the mag-

azines, candies produced by chemistry, and the etiquette of
tea parties made a deep impression on my mind. From the
time I first saw the World War I magazines I became interested in foreign periodicals. I was especially struck by the
advertisements and immediately ordered the Household Department to order foreign-bred dogs and diamonds from
abroad like the ones in the magazines. I also bought some
foreign-style furniture and had the red sandalwood table
with brass fittings used on the *kang* for the support of the
elbows changed for a small painted desk with porcelain
fittings. Imitating Johnston, I also ordered a pocket watch
with chain, rings, tie pins, cuff links, neckties, etc., etc. I
also asked him to give me a foreign name as well as ones for
my younger brothers and sisters and "empress," and "consort." I was called "Henry" and my "empress," "Eliza-
beth." I even imitated his way of talking in a mixture of
Chinese and English with my fellow students:

"William [Pu Chieh], hurry up and give me a *pencil* [pencil
in English], sharpen it and put it on the *desk* [in English]."

"Joseph [Pu Chia], ask *Lily* [my third sister] to come
around this *afternoon* to *hear* some foreign military music."

I felt very proud when I talked like this, but when Chen
Pao-shen heard this jargon he would lift his eyebrows and
close his eyes as if he had a toothache.

In my eyes, everything Johnston did was the best. He
made me feel that foreigners were the wisest and most
civilized people and he the most learned man of all Westerners. I don't think he fully realized how deep his influence
was; that the woolen cloth of his suit made me question the
value of Chinese silks and brocades; and that the fountain
pen in his pocket made me ashamed of my writing brushes
and Chinese writing paper.

Because Johnston spoke disparagingly of Chinese queues
and said they looked like pigtails, I had mine cut off. Since
1913, the second year of the Republic, the Minister of
Interior of the Republic had sent several letters to the
Household Department requesting that the Ch'ing officials
persuade the Manchu bannermen to cut off their queues.
They also had expressed the hope that the queues in the
Forbidden City would go. The tone of these letters was very
polite and they never referred to the queues on my own head

or those of the high officials. The Household Department used many reasons to defend the use of queues and even went so far as to say that queues were a useful way of distinguishing who should be allowed in and out of the palace. Several years after the matter was first brought up the Forbidden City was still a world of queues. But now, after Johnston's remark, and within a few days of cutting off my own queue, at least 1,000 disappeared. Only my three Chinese tutors and a few senior functionaries kept theirs.

The High Consorts wept over the loss of my queue and my tutors wore gloomy expressions on their faces. Later Pu Chieh and Yu Chung had theirs cut off.

The people who disliked Johnston the most were the staff of the Household Department. At that time, expenditures in the palace were still enormous yet the payments under the Articles of Favorable Treatment from the Republic had been in arrears year after year. In order to meet operating expenses, the Household Department had to sell or mortgage antiques, paintings, calligraphy, gold and silver objects and porcelain from the palace every year. I learned from what Johnston said that there were some questionable practices involved in all this. On one occasion the Household Department wished to sell a golden pagoda as tall as a man, and I recalled that Johnston had told me that the Household Department, when it wished to sell gold and silver objects, should treat them as art objects, and thus receive much more money for them. According to what Johnston had said, only a fool would sell these objects by weight. I then called in a Household official and asked him how he planned to sell the golden pagoda. When he said he planned to sell it by weight, I blew up.

"Only fools would do such a thing," I said. "Haven't you any sense?"

The Household officials realized that Johnston was really calling their hand so they thought up a new method to forestall him. They had the golden pagoda sent to Johnston's house and asked him to sell it, saying that I had requested this. Johnston saw through the trick right away and exploded with anger. "If you don't take it away," he ordered, "I'll report this to the Emperor immediately." The result was that the officials dutifully removed the golden pagoda and made no more trouble for Johnston because they came to appreciate his position within the royal family and knew that he had my full trust.

In the last year of my studying in the Yu Ching Palace, Johnston had become the most important part of my soul. Our discussion of extracurricular topics occupied more and more of my class time and the area of our discussions broadened. He told me about the life of the British royal family, about the conditions and political systems of the various countries, the strength of the powers after World War I, about conditions all over the world, about the customs of the British Empire "on which the sun never set," about China's civil wars, about the vernacular language movement in China (the May 4th, 1919, New Civilization Movement, as he called it) and the relationships of the various Western civilizations with one another. He even talked about the possibility of my restoration and the unreliable attitude of the war lords.

"Judging from the newspapers," he said one day, "the Chinese people are longing for the Great Ch'ing Dynasty. They are tired of the Republic. I do not think Your Majesty need worry about the war lords; nor need Your Imperial Majesty try to find out their position by spending so much time reading the newspapers, nor by concerning yourself with their varying attitudes about supporting your restoration or defending the Republic. What Tutor Chen says is true. The most important thing is for Your Majesty to improve himself. But in order to develop your sage virtue you should not always stay in the Forbidden City. Your Majesty can broaden your horizons in Europe, especially in Britain at Oxford University where the Prince of Wales is studying."

At times, my intoxication with Western life and my imitation of Johnston did not give him complete satisfaction. For instance, our ideas on Western clothes differed. On my wedding day, after I had appeared at a reception for foreign guests and drank a toast, I returned to the Mind Nurture Palace and took off my dragon robe and changed into a Chinese long gown on top of which I put on a Western-style jacket. Also I put a peaked tweed cap on my head. Just then Johnston came in with some friends. A sharp-eyed foreign lady noticed me standing in the corridor and asked, "Who is that young man?"

Johnston looked at me and when he saw what I had on his face turned red. His appearance frightened me and the expression on the faces of the foreigners further mystified me. I did not understand what was wrong.

After they had left, Johnston was still in a temper. In fact he was so worked up, he looked as if he would explode with anger.

"What kind of style is that?" he asked furiously. "Your Majesty the Emperor—for the Emperor of China to wear a hunting cap! Good God!"

II

MY YOUTH

8

A Brief Restoration

IT WAS A PECULIARITY OF EARLY MORNING IN THE FORBID-den City that sometimes, even in the heart of the palace, one could hear city noises from afar. There were clear cries of the peddlers, rumbling sounds of the wooden wheels of the heavy Peking carts, and occasionally, soldiers singing. The eunuchs called this phenomenon the "city of sounds." After I left the palace, I often recalled this "city of sounds" which has so frequently stirred in me many strange dreams and visions.

But there was another "city of sounds" which aroused in me very deep interest while I still lived in the Forbidden City. This was derived from the talk of my tutors and consisted of rumors regarding my restoration.

Restoration, in the language of the court, was also called "recovery of the ancestral heritage" and "the glorious return of the old order" or "returning the government to the Ch'ing." Activity toward this end did not begin with my brief restoration in 1917 and did not stop with my flight to the Japanese Legation in 1924. It would be safe to say that it did not cease from the day of my abdication in 1912 until the establishment of the Manchu Imperial Regime in Manchuria (Manchukuo) in 1934 under the "protection" of the Japanese.

At first I acted out my part under the direction of my tutors. Behind them in the background were the officials of the Household Department and behind them, in turn, was my father, the former Prince Regent. Eventually I came to understand that real power, from the standpoint of achieving a restoration, was not vested in them. And in fairness to them, it must be admitted that they understood this. Comical as it may now seem, the hopes of the Forbidden City were based on the new politicians and officials who ruled in place of the great Ch'ing. The first object of these illusions was President Yuan Shih-kai himself.

The death of the Dowager Empress Lung Yu in 1913 was an occasion when the splendor of the good old days was fully restored. Yuan Shih-kai put a black band on his sleeve and ordered flags at half-mast throughout the country. He also decreed a period of mourning for 27 days for all military and civil officials and even sent the members of the National Assembly to attend the funeral. Within the Forbidden City and amidst the wailing of the eunuchs, the black court robes of the Ch'ing Dynasty and the Western formal dress of the Republic were intermingled.

Soon after this, Yuan Shih-kai surrounded the National Assembly with military and police forces and compelled it to elect him President in place of his previous position as acting president. He then wrote me a most deferential memorial in which he spoke of the gratitude of the five races of China[1] for my virtues which, as he explained, compared with "the sun and moon, and also the mountains and the rivers that nurture all life in the country."

Later, however, there was a slight change in the political wind. An official of the Republic's Inspectorate General proposed an investigation of reports of a Ch'ing restoration and Yuan ordered this investigation referred to the Home Ministry for handling. As a result, a high Republican official, who had once lectured on the subject of returning government to the Ch'ing, was sent back to his home town under army escort. But even this could not be regarded as completely definitive in so far as Yuan's views were concerned since he gave the exiled official 3,000 Mexican dollars[2] as a

---

[1] The five races of China are the Hans, Manchus, Mongolians, Huis (Mohammedans of Turkestan, etc.) and Tibetans.

[2] Mexican dollar was worth about 40c U.S.

farewell gift and permitted the various government departments to tend the official innumerable farewell parties.

This vague situation continued until 1916 when Frank J. Goodnow, an ex-Columbia University professor and American adviser to President Yuan, published an article saying that a republican form of government was not suitable for China. At the same time, a Society for the Preservation of Peace was organized which recommended that Yuan Shih-kai himself be elected Emperor. It was not until these two events that people began to understand what kind of restoration Yuan Shih-kai really had in mind. As a result, the atmosphere in the Forbidden City changed markedly.

One day, soon after this, Chen Pao-shen looked furtively out of the window of the Yu Ching Palace to make sure that there was no one listening. Then he pulled a note out of his sleeve and said to me: "This is a divination made according to the *Book of Changes*.³ Please look at it, Your Majesty."

When I took it, I saw the following words: "Since my enemy is ill, he is not able to approach me. Auspicious!"

Chen explained that it meant that my enemy's future was evil and unlucky and that he would be unable to endanger me. He also told me that besides consulting the *Book of Changes* he had scorched a tortoiseshell and consulted the milfoil⁴ and they had both given favorable indications too. As a result, Chen concluded, he was sure Yuan Shih-kai could not escape his fate and "would come to a bad end."

However, activity by my tutors, as well as my father and the Household Department, to protect my position under the Articles of Favorable Treatment was not confined to consulting the oracles and making divinations. Although I was told nothing about it officially, I was not completely in the dark. To put it crudely, they made a deal with Yuan Shih-kai by which the Ch'ing House would support Yuan as Emperor if he would observe the Articles. Documents to this effect were exchanged, including an assurance in Yuan's handwriting that he would incorporate the Articles of Favor-

---

³ *Book of Changes*, one of the Chinese classics, revered by Confucius, written in 800 B.C. by the first Emperor of the Chou Dynasty, set forth methods of divination.

⁴ Grass from a particular plant used in making divinations.

63

able Treatment in his new constitution. It was even arranged that I would take one of his daughters as my Empress, but before any of these arrangements could be put into effect, Yuan died in June, 1916, after only 83 days as Emperor.

The news of Yuan Shih-kai's death was received with great rejoicing in the Forbidden City. The eunuchs rushed about spreading the news, the High Consorts burned incense before the tutelary god, there were no lessons that day in the Yu Ching Palace, and new voices could be heard in the "city of sounds."

"Yuan Shih-kai failed because he wanted to usurp the throne."

"It's not that monarchy cannot be restored; the fact is the people want their old sovereign."

"Yuan Shih-kai was not like Napoleon III; he had no ancestry to rely upon."

"Instead of having a Mr. Yuan as Emperor, it would be better to return to the old master."

After Yuan's death, Li Yuan-hung, who had previously been Vice-President, succeeded him as President with General Tuan Chi-jui[5] as Premier. The palace sent a representative to congratulate President Li and he, in turn, returned to the palace some imperial processional weapons that Yuan had taken. Some of the Ch'ing princes and senior officials who, during the Yuan Shih-kai period, had tried to hide away were now given Republican decorations which they wore at social functions. At New Year and my birthday, the President even dispatched high officials to greet me and my father sent special foods to President Li Yuan-hung. The Household Department became very busy preparing rescripts that bestowed posthumous titles, the right to be transported in a sedan chair carried by two persons and the right to wear peacock feathers and ruby buttons.

In short, the Forbidden City became lively again and, with

---

[5] Tuan Chi-jui was a member of the Peiyang clique, a term used to describe army officers who were the personal followers of Yuan Shih-kai.

Chang Hsun's[6] audience with me in 1917, this particular restoration movement reached a climax.

On June 16 of this year, Chen Pao-shen, who had only recently been promoted to Grand Guardian, and Liang Ting-fen, a newly appointed tutor, arrived at the palace together. Even before they sat down, Tutor Chen said: "Today Your Majesty need not study. There will be a high official come to pay his respects to Your Majesty, and a eunuch will be here to receive your permission for this audience very shortly."

"Who is he?"

"Chang Hsun, the former Viceroy of Kiangsi, Kiangsu and Anhwei and Governor of Kiangsu."

"Chang Hsun? Is he the Chang Hsun who refuses to cut off his queue?"

"Yes, yes," said Liang Ting-fen, nodding in approval. "Your Majesty's memory is truly excellent." Tutor Liang never missed a chance to flatter me.

According to Ch'ing Dynasty custom, no one else could be present when a high official was received by the Emperor. Therefore my tutors instructed me beforehand in what to say. Tutor Chen told me that I should praise the loyalty of

---

[6] General Chang Hsun ushered in the war-lord period in Chinese history. Upon the death of Yuan Shih-kai, he moved his troops to Peking, dissolved Parliament, restored the Ch'ing Dynasty and vested real power in himself. General Tuan Chi-jui, however, who was headquartered in nearby Tientsin where he cast himself as the savior of the Republic, soon defeated Chang Hsun and forced Pu Yi to abdicate again.

Within a short time there were dozens, if not hundreds, of war lords. Small war lords attached themselves to big war lords but declared their independence as soon as they were strong enough. China became completely divided.

By the early 1920's, the power struggles of the war lords evolved around three principals: Tuan Chi-jui in Peking and its environs, Wu Pei-fu in the middle Yangtze valley, and Chang Tso-lin in Manchuria. Tuan Chi-jui, as Premier, was challenged by Wu Pei-fu, who defeated him. Chang Tso-lin fought Wu but was eventually driven back to Manchuria where he continued to rule. In South China there were even more war lords.

Chang Hsun and should remember that Chang Hsun was High Inspecting Commissioner for the Yangtze River and had 60 battalions of troops in the region of Hsuchow and Yenchow. He said that I should ask him about the military situation and wound up his advice by repeating twice: "Chang Hsun will unavoidably praise Your Majesty. Your Majesty should remember to reply to him in a very humble way in order to show your divine virtue."

"When a thing is too full, it cannot be filled. When one is humble, one immediately receives benefits," added Tutor Liang.

Soon after I arrived at the Yu Ching Palace in my court robes, Chang Hsun came in. I sat on the throne and he knelt before me and kowtowed.

"Your servant Chang Hsun kneels to greet Your Majesty's sacred feet."

I pointed to a chair and asked him to sit down. At this time the palace had abandoned the custom of having high officials report while in a kneeling position. He kowtowed once more to thank me, and then sat down. I followed my tutors' instructions in asking about the situation of the army in the areas of Hsuchow and Yenchow, but I did not pay much attention to his reply. I was somewhat disappointed in his looks. He wore a lightweight summer costume, his face was ruddy, he had very thick eyebrows and was fat. Had he not worn a moustache he could have passed for one of the eunuchs in charge of the imperial kitchens. I noticed, however, that he did in fact have a queue.

"Your Majesty is really gifted by the heavens," he said, talking just as Tutor Chen had anticipated.

"I am far from being so," I replied. "I am too young. What I know is very limited."

"In our dynasty, the Emperor Kang Hsi [1654–1722] also ascended the throne at a very young age. He was only five."

"How can I be compared with my ancestor? He was, after all . . ."

The following day, when Chen Pao-shen and Liang Ting-fen saw me, they told me that Chang Hsun had praised me as being wise and humble. I didn't stop to wonder why he had come to pay me his respects or why my tutors were so elated over this audience.

Two weeks later, however, on July 1, Chen Pao-shen and Liang Ting-fen again appeared together at the Yu Ching Palace with grave expressions on their faces. It was Chen who spoke first: "Chang Hsun came early this morning. . . ."

"Has he come to pay his respects again?"

"No, it is not for that. Everything is ready, everything is arranged. He has come to bring Your Majesty back to your throne, to rule. It is the restoration of the Great Ch'ing Dynasty!"

Seeing that I was taken by surprise, Chen immediately said: "I beg Your Majesty to allow Chang Hsun to do this. He is asking for a mandate on behalf of the people; heaven has complied with the wishes of the people."

I was stunned and confused by the startling suddenness of this happy event. In a sort of dumbfounded way, I looked at Tutor Chen hopefully so that he would say a bit more and let me know how I might be a "real emperor."

"You need not talk too much to Chang Hsun. All you have to do is accept."

Tutor Chen seemed to have everything well planned. "But you don't need to promise him right away," he continued. "At first, decline; then, later on, you can say, 'Since it is this way, I will try to do my best.'"

This time, when I received Chang Hsun in audience, he explained that it had only been because the Empress Dowager Lung Yu had not wished to see the common people suffer that she had proclaimed my abdication. But, as he said, events had demonstrated that a republic was not compatible with the condition of China. "The people can achieve deliverance from their suffering only through Your Majesty the Emperor's restoration."

"But my age is too young and I have neither virtue nor ability," I replied. "I don't think I could shoulder such a great responsibility."

Chang Hsun then began to praise me and, while listening to him mumble on, I began to think of President Li Yuan-hung. "What will we do with the President?" I asked him. "Will we give him some sort of favorable treatment too?"

"Li Yuan-hung has memorialized for permission to resign.

67

Your Majesty the Emperor should permit him to resign according to his memorial."

Even though I did not fully comprehend the situation, I felt sure my tutors must have completed all the arrangements so that all I need do was terminate the audience quickly. "Since things are this way" I said, "then I must do my best to take care of the situation." With this I felt that I was again Emperor of the Great Ch'ing Empire.

After Chang Hsun left, groups of people came continuously to kowtow to me and pay their respects. Later a eunuch of the presence brought in a whole pile of imperial edicts that had already been prepared. The first of these proclaimed my return to the throne and another created a Board of Regents including Chen Pao-shen and Chang Hsun.

Old Pekingese recall how on that day the police asked all the households to hang out imperial dragon flags. The citizens who did not have any handy made them out of paste and paper. Ch'ing court robes which had disappeared for a few years appeared on the streets. It was as if the dead had stepped from their coffins in their burial robes. The press brought out extras about the restoration.

Outside of the Chien Men Gate some of the stores did a boom business. Tailors made and sold dragon flags; secondhand clothing shops found that the Ch'ing court dress became their bestselling items since the newly appointed officials all wanted them; and theatrical supply houses were besieged with requests for artificial queues made out of horsehair.

Tutor Chen was normally a very stable and studious man, and I would never have anticipated that this experienced old scholar would change so completely on the day of my restoration. His attitude regarding the treatment of ex-President Li Yuan-hung was drastic. At first, one of my other tutors, not anticipating that he would meet with a refusal, had volunteered to go and see President Li to persuade him to move out of the presidential mansion. Upon his return, he angrily told Chen that the President had refused.

Chen Pao-shen, on hearing this news, became livid with anger. He seemed to have lost control of himself. "Li Yuan-hung has dared to refuse to accept the order," he raged. "I request Your Majesty the Emperor to bestow upon him instructions to commit suicide!''

I was startled to hear him talk this way and felt his methods were too extreme. "It is beyond my imagination why I should command Li Yuan-hung to die just after I have been restored to my throne," I said. "After all, didn't the Republic give me favorable treatment?''

This was the first time that Chen Pao-shen had ever received a public rebuff from me. But he was so carried away by his hatred for the President that, oblivious of everything, he raged on: "Li Yuan-hung has not only refused to resign, but he is also hanging on to the presidential residence and refuses to move! He is like a rebel or a bandit who has commited a high crime against his sovereign. How can we talk about him in the same breath as Your Majesty?''

Later, however, when he noticed that I was determined to refuse to follow his advice, he agreed to let Tutor Liang go back to the presidential palace once more in order, at least, to persuade the President's relatives to move, but before he arrived Li Yuan-hung had already fled to the Japanese Legation with the seal of Office of President.

During this brief restoration period, Chen made a deep impression on me as a man of action. Just before the end, an imperial edict was prepared to send to Chang Tso-lin appointing him viceroy and commander of the three eastern provinces (Manchuria) and ordering him to come to my aid as soon as possible. At this time, Chang Tso-lin, who was already military governor of Fengtien (Mukden, in Manchuria), was utterly dissatisfied with Chang Hsun, who had only named him viceroy of Fengtien Province. Tutor Chen had great hopes in Chang Tso-lin's ability to save my position. But when a search was made for the "imperial seal," after the decree had been prepared, it was found that the key to the box containing it was in the hands of my father. If it had been necessary to send someone to fetch the key, we would have lost too much time, so Tutor Chen immediately decided to have the chain that locked the seal box broken. Actually, however, this imperial decree never reached Chang Tso-lin since the official messenger who carried it was intercepted before he reached the Manchurian border.

During the first few days of the restoration, I spent half of my time in the Yu Ching Palace. Although my studies were suspended, I was obliged to see my tutors and listen to their instructions and guidance on all state affairs. The rest of the time I read over the imperial edicts that were to be issued and the cabinet gazette, and I received the homage and kowtows of many people. There was still an opportunity, however, to watch the ants in the courtyard move from hole to hole and to ask the Imperial Stables to send round a camel for my entertainment. But it all lasted no more than four or five days. Everything changed when an airplane from Tuan Chi-jui's Army to Punish the Rebels dropped some bombs into the palace. Then there were no longer people who came to pay their respects or kowtow to me and there were no more imperial edicts to read. Furthermore, most of the high officials who had a hand in state affairs disappeared.

On the day of the air raid I was talking to my tutor in the Imperial Study when I heard an airplane overhead and the unfamiliar sound of an explosion. I was so frightened that I began to tremble and my tutors became terrified. In the confusion, the eunuchs rushed me to the Mind Nurture Palace, as if my bedroom would be the only safe place. The High Consorts were in an even worse state—some of them hid in the corner of their bedrooms and others under tables. The whole palace was in confusion. This was the first air raid in the history of China and the first time a Chinese air force was used in the civil wars. Fortunately, the pilot did not really mean business and gave us no more than a scare with three small bombs about a foot long. One fell outside the Gate of Ancestral Veneration injuring a sedan-chair carrier; another fell into the Imperial Garden and destroyed a corner of a pond; the third fell on a roof of one of the gates along the Western Avenue and, even though it failed to explode, scared the daylights out of some eunuchs who were gambling there.

The day after my dispatch of the edict to Manchuria we could hear gunfire approaching the Forbidden City. Even Chen Pao-shen failed to show up and the palace was cut off from contact with the outside world. The next morning, however, the Household Department brought me the news of Chang Hsun's flight to the Dutch Legation and, later in the day, my father and Tutor Chen appeared, their faces gray and drooping. When I saw the abdication decree they had prepared I was both frightened and saddened, and I wept openly.

But this abdication edict was never issued. As is so often the case, history was rewritten and all that was published was an announcement of the Household Department which was incorporated into a decree of the new President:

The Home Ministry reports that it has received the following communication from the Household Department of the Ch'ing House:

This day the Household Department received an Edict:

Formerly on the twenty-fifth day of the twelfth month of the third year of Hsuan Tung[7] a Decree was issued by the August Empress Dowager Lung Yu in which, recognizing that the whole people were inclined toward a republic, she and the Emperor returned sovereign power to the whole country. She ordained that there should be a republic and settled that the Articles of Favorable Treatment for the Ch'ing House should be adhered to forever; for the past six years the Ch'ing House has been very well treated and has never had any intention of using the political power for its own ends; what cause could it have had for going back on its word?

But contrary to expectation Chang Hsun led his soldiery to occupy the palace on July 1. He fraudulently issued edicts and decrees and altered the state structure, thus disobeying the instructions of the Empress Dowager of the former dynasty. I, a child living deep in the Forbidden City, had no choice in the matter; in these circumstances I should have allowances made for me by the whole world. The Household Department has been instructed to request the Government of the Republic to make this generally known both within the country and abroad.

---

[7] Reign title of Pu Yi.

When the Ministry received this letter they thought it right to report this matter.

As it is common knowledge that Chang Hsun the traitor and usurper was the originator of the disturbances, let the details of this document be speedily proclaimed.

For general information,

Issued by the Prime Minister, July 17, 6th year of the Republic of China.

The original abdication decree, as first prepared, had recognized that I myself had "assumed power," but in this announcement it was said that "Chang Hsun had occupied the palace and I, a minor" had been unable to do anything about it. This change in the facts was the result of collaboration between the Forbidden City and three leaders of the Peiyang clique and was executed by the new President, Feng Kuo-chang, and Premier Tuan Chi-jui. The role of the Forbidden City in the restoration was thus obliterated and new restoration activities were given little public attention.

One day, as I was riding my bicycle in the Imperial Gardens, I nearly collided with someone. For such a thing to happen in the palace could only mean that the person involved was being deliberately impolite to his sovereign, but I didn't pay any attention. Instead, I circled around and was about to ride off when I saw the man kneel down and heard him say: "Your humble servant pays his respects to the Lord of Ten Thousand Years."

He was wearing a purple vest of the type the eunuchs wore but, as I looked at him more carefully, I saw he had a moustache and I therefore knew he was not a eunuch. Riding in circles around him, I asked what he was doing.

"Your servant is in charge of the electricity," he replied.

"Oh, you are in charge of that kind of thing. You were lucky I didn't knock you over a minute ago. Why do you continue to kneel?"

"Your servant is really lucky today! I have been able to see the true dragon, the Son of Heaven. I beg the Lord of Ten Thousand Years in his celestial bounty to grant his humble servant a title."

I could not help but laugh at his request and recalled the nickname the eunuchs had told me was reserved for the beggars at the ends of the bridges in the Peking streets.

"Very well," I said, "I give you the title of the 'Marquis Guarding the Bridge.' "[8]

I did not expect that my practical joke would really cause this man to go to the Household Department and ask for his "patent of nobility." When they told him it was only a joke, he became very excited. "The saying of His Majesty the Emperor is like gold and jade," he stormed. "How dare you people say it is a joke! This won't do!"

Even as late as 1920, eight years after the founding of the Republic, there were still people infatuated by monarchy. There was a merchant named Wang Chiu-cheng who had made a fortune out of supplying uniforms to the Chihli clique.[9] His ambition was to obtain the privilege of wearing a yellow riding jacket and he spent a considerable amount of money to achieve this. The eunuchs called him the "money scatterer." I do not know how he arranged it, but at New Year and at every important festival he would come in with the retired officials who came to pay their respects to me and kowtow. He always brought with him thick wads of bank notes which he scattered about liberally. The eunuchs were always pleased to see him come, for it did not matter whether they merely showed him in, announced him, raised the door curtain for him, poured tea for him or just spoke a few words to him—they always got a roll of bank notes. And this is not to mention the money he spent to get into the palace itself. Later he finally achieved his goal and was granted the honor of being allowed to wear a yellow riding jacket.

Men came to the Forbidden City every day or submitted memorials from distant places for the sake of a yellow riding jacket, the right to say in their family registers that they had held a Ch'ing office, or for a posthumous title. There was even one man, known as "Lunatic Liang," who threw himself into a pond in Peking in order to show his loyalty

---

[8] Marquis in Chinese has the same pronunciation as the word "monkey."

[9] A war-lord group.

and win with his sodden body a posthumous memorial as "true and upright." Later there were so many requests for posthumous titles that in order to avoid diminishing their value we had to stipulate that they would only be given to people above a certain rank. Even tighter limitations were placed on the bestowal of the right to ride a horse in the Forbidden City and the right to be carried in a two-man sedan chair as well as the granting of scrolls in my handwriting. The result was that not only the Manchu nobility but even military commanders of the Republic regarded obtaining one of these as a "signal honor." Those of lower rank, merchants and local gentry, as well as those with neither titles nor wealth, had to be content with tablets in memory of deceased relatives, obituary cemetery stones from retired Ch'ing officials or attendance at their children's weddings by these same officials.

Despite this sort of thing, as well as articles in the foreign-language press suggesting that a reversion to monarchy was not unlikely, the fact was that it was the war lords themselves, with guns in their hands, who directly controlled the fate of the Little Court. As the *North China Daily Mail* pointed out, "The comings and goings to places where military officials are known to congregate are not devoid of significance."

I remember how in the second half of 1919 the Little Court had close relations with war lords other than those of the old Peiyang clique. The first of these was High Inspecting Commissioner Chang Tso-lin, the head of the Fengtien (Mukden) clique.

The palace's dealings with Chang Tso-lin started when my father received a large sum of money from Fengtien, in northeast China where Chang Tso-lin's power was centered, as payment for some land that had been my property. My father wrote a letter of thanks and the Household Department dispatched a high-ranking official with some antique vases and a picture from the palace collection as a present for Chang Tso-lin. Chang sent his sworn brother Chang Ching-hui, then the second in command of the Fengtien Army and later premier of Manchukuo, to accompany our envoy back to Peking and convey his gratitude.

In 1920 the Fengtien clique aligned itself with the Chihli

clique (a northeast province of China proper) to defeat the Anhwei clique (East China Province) and when the Chihli chief and Chang Tso-lin entered Peking the Little Court sent an official of the Household Department to welcome them. A rumor that Chang Tso-lin was going to come to the palace for an audience precipitated a special meeting of the senior officials of the Household Department in my father's house to discuss what presents he should be given. But Chang Tso-lin went back to Fengtien (Mukden) without visiting the palace.

In 1923 the head of the Chihli clique, Tsao Kun, bought the votes of the members of Parliament for 5,000 dollars apiece and had himself elected President. The court had only just stopped being frightened of him when another rising Chihli commander, Wu Pei-fu, attracted attention. That same year I sent lavish presents to Wu to congratulate him on his fiftieth birthday. But, as it turned out, Wu Pei-fu's success was short-lived since, the year after his birthday, his subordinate Feng Yu-hsiang[10] changed sides in the fighting between the Chihli and Fengtien cliques. And so it went, politically.

---

[10] Feng Yu-hsiang, also known as the "Christian General," changed sides again a number of years later when he switched from Chiang Kai-shek to the Communists. Subsequently he was said to have burned to death while watching a movie aboard a Soviet passenger ship. His outstanding collection of Ch'ing art treasures was left to the Soviet Government.

9

My Wedding

DESPITE THE CONFUSION OUTSIDE THE FORBIDDEN CITY, and notwithstanding my restoration and second abdication, my personal life as Emperor continued as before. Thus, if I entertained any interest in the proposal that I had reached the age for my Grand Nuptials, it was because it meant that my wedding would mark my coming of age. After this, no one could control me any more as if I were a child.

It was the older ladies of the court who were most concerned about this affair. Early in the tenth year of the Republic, in 1921, when I reached fifteen years of age, the High Consorts summoned my father for a number of consultations on the matter and then called a meeting of about ten royal princes to discuss it. Two years elapsed from the time these discussions started until my wedding actually took place. There were a number of reasons for this. First of all, there was the death of the High Consort Chuang Ho, and then of my own mother. Second, my tutors advised me to delay my wedding owing to the unstable political conditions. Third, there were a number of complicated disputes over the choice of a bride so that my engagement had several ups and downs before a conclusion could be reached.

Two of the High Consorts, Tuan Kang and Ching Yi, each wished to choose as empress someone who would be partial to them. This was not because of love or prejudice on their part, but because of the fact that the selection might affect their future positions. Ching Yi had been an imperial consort of the Emperor Tung Chih (1856–1874) and she had never forgotten that the Empress Dowager Tzu Hsi had declared in her will that I was the heir of Tung Chih and only concurrently the heir of Kuang Hsu (1871–1908). But Yuan Shih-kai had interfered in our "internal affairs" and designated the High Consort Tuan Kang as administrator of the palace. As a result Ching Yi felt she had not received the respect due her and Tzu Hsi's will had not been fulfilled. She was therefore a rival of Tuan Kang and had her own candidate for my hand. Neither could agree.

My two uncles were also divided in their choice. In the last resort, however, the Emperor had the final say. During the two previous reigns the maidens were all lined up in a row and the future bridegroom had personally selected one of them. He then immediately gave a token to the girl of his choice. I have heard two versions of the kind of tokens that were used. One was that the future bridegroom gave the girl of his choice a jade mushroom. The other was that he put a pouch on the buckle of the girl. But when it came to my time, and after due consideration by the royal princes and officials, it was felt that it would no longer be appropriate to line up the maidens of the noble families in a row for selection in this manner. A method of selection by photographs was devised and I was to take a pencil and make a mark on the picture of the one I liked best.

Four photos were sent to me at the Mind Nurture Palace. But the four girls looked so much alike, and their figures looked so much like paper tubes, that it was difficult for me to decide. Besides, their faces in the photos were so small that it was hard for me to see if they were beautiful or not. In fact, all I could distinguish was the designs on their Mandarin dresses. It did not occur to me that this was one of the great events of my life, and I had no real standard to guide me.

Without hesitation, I drew a circle on one of the pictures which seemed the more agreeable to me. She was of the Manchu Ordet clan and was named Wen Hsiu. She was three years younger than I and thus only twelve when I saw her picture. Since she was the favorite of the High Consort Ching Yi, Tuan Kang was utterly dissatisfied with my selection and, disregarding the opposition of Ching Yi, insisted on summoning the princes and officials to persuade me to make another selection and choose her candidate. She claimed that Wen Hsiu came from a rather humble family and was not very beautiful, whereas the one she recommended was of a rich family and much prettier. The one she had chosen was Wan Jung, and she was of my age. On the photo it said sixteen. I followed the advice of the princes and high officials and wondered why they had not explained all this to me before. But anyway, it did not disturb me too much, and I therefore drew a circle on the photo of Wan Jung.

This second selection, of course, greatly displeased Ching Yi. After a long series of arguments among the High Consorts and princes, Jung Hui, another of the consorts, finally came up with this suggestion: "Since your Majesty has already circled Wen Hsiu she can never marry one of your subjects. Therefore Your Majesty should take her as your secondary consort." But since in my own mind I did not feel an urgent need for one wife, how could I choose two at the same time? I therefore did not wish to accept her advice. Finally, however, I gave in as a result of the pressure of the princes and officials who argued that according to ancestral custom "the Emperor must have an empress *and* a consort."

I have, as a matter of fact, rather simplified the process of choosing an empress and secondary consort. Actually it took over a year before a decision could be reached. And after the decision, the civil war between the Chihli and Fengtien war lords caused my wedding to be postponed until December 1, 1922. Although by this time China had a new President and it was feared that he would be more apt to interfere with the arrangements than his predecessor, the preparations had developed to such an extent that it was too late to stop them. But as it turned out, the government of the new President supported the wedding far beyond expectations. A letter was sent by the Minister of Finance of the Republic to the Household Department, written in an apologetic tone, saying that because of financial difficulties in the past, the government had fallen behind in the payments due under the Articles of Favorable Treatment. Nevertheless, in order to help out with the cost of the Grand Nuptials, the government had set aside $100,000 from customs revenues of which $20,000 was to be regarded as a gift of the Republic. Meanwhile the Army, National Guard and Police of the Republic presented their own plans for affording protection to the double wedding ceremony which involved the deployment of thousands of men along the processional routes in Peking and the use of several military bands. Furthermore, the Republic allowed the Empress's Phoenix Chair[1] to enter the Forbidden City through the Glorious Eastern Gate, an entry which had previously been denied the Ch'ing House.

The actual wedding ceremonies were scheduled over a period of five days. On November 29, between 9 and 11 A.M., the trousseau of the secondary consort would enter the palace. On November 30, between 11 A.M. and 1 P.M., the trousseau of the Empress would enter the palace. Between 9 and 11 A.M. on the same day the Rite of the Golden Seal and Scroll would be performed,[2] and between 1 and 3 A.M. the secondary consort entered the palace. On December 1, between 3 and 5 A.M., the ceremony of welcoming the Empress would be held and this would be followed by the Grand Nuptial Ceremony to be followed on December 2 by the worship of the bridegroom's imperial ancestors. On December 3, the Emperor would receive the greetings of the Manchu and Mongol princes, the officers of the court and household and ex-ministers of state in the Cloudless Heaven Palace.

In addition to this there were other functions including three days of opera commencing on the second day of the wedding ceremonies. Also before the actual wedding there were quite a few ceremonies which had to be performed— the granting of the right to send wedding gifts to the bride, the promotion of the four High Consorts to Grand Imperial

---

[1] A great bridal sedan chair, draped in scarlet and gold, carried by 22 bearers and adorned with mythological emblematic devices, the most conspicuous of which were four silver birds perched upon the corners of the roof—hence, Phoenix Chair.

[2] Imperial symbols of rank as Empress, sent from the Forbidden City to the mansion of the Empress and then brought back with her into the palace.

High Consorts, and the granting of many honorific titles to the princes and high palace officials.

There was some surprise and indignation over the fact that the Manchu court, after its unsuccessful attempt at restoration in 1917, presumed to show off its pomp outside the walls of the Forbidden City under the respectful protection of such a large number of Republican soldiers and police. The ceremonial emblems of the Ch'ing House had been paraded with great majesty on the streets of Peking. On the actual day of the wedding ceremony, two princes, in court robes, with staffs of office in their hands, had ridden behind two Republican military bands and had been followed by two more bands as well as the Republican cavalry, mounted police and mounted security guard. Farther behind had come the dragon-and-phoenix flags and umbrellas, 72 pairs of imperial emblems, 4 yellow pavillions (in which were contained the golden seal and scroll and the robes of the Empress) and 30 pairs of palace lanterns. With much pomp, this procession had set out for the mansion of the Empress. In front of her house there had been a company of soldiers and police for the protection of her father and brothers. All of them had knelt to welcome the princes from the Forbidden City who had brought with them the "imperial edict."

The rich gifts from the leading figures of the Republic also attracted considerable attention. The President sent the following: a red gift card along with four pieces of cloisonné, two kinds of silk and satin, one curtain and one pair of scrolls on which were greetings wishing me longevity, prosperity, and happiness. The ex-President sent $20,000 and many other valuable gifts including 28 pieces of porcelain and a majestic rug with a dragon-and-phoenix design. Many politicians sent important gifts as did such war lords as Chang Tso-lin and Wu Pei-fu.

The personal representative of the Republic at the ceremony was Yin Chang who was chief aide-de-camp in the Office of the President. He congratulated me formally as he would have done if I were a foreign sovereign. But when he had finished bowing to me, he suddenly declared: "A moment ago I was representing the Republic. Now your slave will greet Your Majesty." With this he knelt on the floor and kowtowed.

At the time, many of the newspapers published stern editorials on these strange occurrences, but this did not restrain the gaiety and enthusiasm of the princes and high court officials. Many of the former Ch'ing veterans came to Peking in groups, like swarms of insects after the spring rains. With them they brought their gifts including money and antiques. But what counted most for them was not the money and presents, but the style and pomp. This was far greater than they had expected. It made them feel that something might be done for the future.

What caused the most excitement for the retired officials, their sons and daughters, and the Grand Imperial High Consorts were the guests from the Legation Quarter. This was the first time that the foreign diplomats had appeared in the Forbidden City since the Revolution of 1911. Even though they came in their personal capacities, they were still foreign officials. In order to show gratitude for their attendance, at the suggestion of my tutor Johnston, a reception was arranged especially for them in the Cloudless Heaven Palace. I read them a short message in English:

> Today I come to meet many noble and respectful guests from all the countries of the world. I, the Emperor, feel honored and I thank all of you for your coming and I wish you good health and good luck.

In the midst of all the hustle and hubbub of the wedding ceremonies I kept repeating to myself this question: "Now that I have an empress and a consort and I'm married, what is the difference between now and before?" The answer that I gave myself was: "I'm of age now. If it were not for the Revolution this would be the time for me to start ruling without regents."

I gave no thought to the relations between husband and wife, and of raising a family. And it was only when the Empress, whose face was hidden by a red scarf embroidered with dragon-and-phoenix design, came into my field of vision that I began to wonder what she really looked like.

We spent our wedding night in the Palace of Earthly Peace. The bridal chamber was about 33 feet square. There was little furniture save for the bed which occupied one quarter of the room. Everything in it was red. After we had gone through the rites of "drinking the nuptial cup" and had eaten "sons and grandsons cake," we entered this dark red chamber together. Suddenly I felt cooped up and stifled. My bride sat on the bed with her head bowed low. I stood at her side and stared about the room while feeling engulfed by the red bed curtains, the red quilt, the red pillows, a red dress, a red flower, a red face. It was as if all had melted into a blob of red wax from a melted red candle.

I became very uneasy and did not know whether to stand or sit. I suddenly felt that I should prefer to be in the Mind Nurture Palace, and so I opened the door and went back there.

Immediately upon my return I caught sight of a long list of officials from many places in China which had been placed on the wall. The question came to my mind again: "Now I have an empress and a consort. I am married and of age. What is the main difference between now and before?"

What were the sentiments and emotions of Wan Jung who had been left alone, all by herself, in the Palace of Earthly Peace? What was the young girl, my consort Wen Hsiu, who was not yet fourteen thinking? At the time these questions never occurred to me.

What I was thinking was: If it were not for the Revolution I would have commenced to rule by myself without regents. I would recover my great ancestral heritage.

10

Family Clashes

From the time Johnston entered the palace, I became more and more difficult for the princes and high officials to deal with. As the month of my wedding approached, my conduct must have seemed very erratic. One day, I would ask the Household Department to spend $30,000 on a diamond, and the next day I would berate it for not being able to make ends meet and accuse it of corruption and waste. In the morning I might call in the high officials to order a thorough inspection of the antiques, paintings and scrolls and ask for a written report on the same day; and yet by afternoon I would ask for motor transportation to Fragrance Hill outside Peking. I had become tired of traditional ceremonies and had reached the point where I hated to ride in the gold-canopied yellow sedan chair. Sometimes I would accuse the eunuchs of disloyalty for some minor reason and would have them sent to the Administrative Bureau for flogging. What made the princes and high officials most uncomfortable, however, was that at one moment I would plan a reorganization of the internal affairs of the palace and a thorough investigation of its financial affairs and the next moment I would announce that I wanted to leave the Forbidden City to study abroad. They were in fear and trembling all day and their queues almost went white with worry.

Some of the princes and high officials had even considered my going abroad before I did and this was why Johnston had been sent for to teach me English. After my marriage, I received many memorials from retired Ch'ing officials proposing that I go abroad. Yet when I started to raise the question, almost everyone opposed it and the reason given most frequently was: "If Your Majesty, the Emperor, leaves the Forbidden City it will mean that you have abrogated the Articles of Favorable Treatment. Since the Republic has not revoked the Articles, why should you give them up?"

None of them, whether they sympathized with my wish to go abroad or whether they basically opposed it, whether they had already despaired of "restoring the ancestral heritage" or whether they still had hopes for it, wished to give up the Articles of Favorable Treatment. Even though the $4,000,000 annual subsidy provided for in the Articles had been shown to be an empty promise, the clause stipulating that the Emperor's "title of dignity is to be retained and not abolished" still held good. For those who had not given up hope of a restoration it was very important that I stay on in the Forbidden City and keep the Little Court intact. For those who had lost all hope my continued presence meant a rice bowl and status.

But my way of thinking was different from theirs. First of all I did not believe that the Articles of Favorable Treatment would continue forever and I was more conscious than anyone else of the precariousness of my position. The new outbreak of civil war, the retreat of the war lord Chang Tso-lin to the Northeast, the fall of President Hsu Shih-chang and the assumption of the Presidency by Li Yuan-hung made me feel that the danger was imminent. A real question in my mind was whether these new political figures would kill me. I was not thinking of favorable or unfavorable treatment. Even though the status quo might be maintained, who could predict amidst the ever-changing political and military environment which war lord or politician would come out on top? Who could know what kind of military man would come to power tomorrow or what kind of politician would form a cabinet the following day? I gathered from many people, especially from Johnston, that there was not a single case in which there wasn't some foreign power behind these changes. Instead of depending on favorable treatment from the latest Republican authorities, why didn't I establish contact with the foreigners directly? Might it not be too late if I waited until some man who was implacably hostile to me got on top? In addition, I felt that I knew more about the final fate of each Chinese dynasty than anyone else. For 25 centuries the last Emperor of each dynasty had usually been murdered, and the last Ming Emperor (of the dynasty preceding my own) had hanged himself on Coal Hill outside the Forbidden City.

Of course, I did not relate these fears to the princes and high officials. The only argument I used with them was:

"I don't care for 'favorable treatment.' I want the people of China and the world to understand that I do not expect the Republic to treat me favorably. To do this is better than waiting for them to abrogate the Articles of Favorable Treatment."

"But the Articles were agreed upon between us and are recognized internationally. If the Republic were to abolish them, the foreign countries will come to our aid."

"If the foreigners will help us, then why don't you people let me go abroad? Do you mean to say they would not help me if they met me in person?"

No matter how I argued, they still did not wish to agree. The only result of several arguments with my father, tutors, princes and high officials was that the preparations for my Grand Nuptials were speeded up.

Another reason why I wanted to go, although I didn't dare say it, was that I had become very tired of my whole environment. Ever since Johnston had entered the palace and introduced me to Western civilization and had stimulated my youthful curiosity I had become dissatisfied with my surroundings. I felt I was being controlled. I agreed thoroughly with the analysis made by Johnston that the root of the trouble lay in the conservatism of the princes and high officials.

In their eyes all new things were terrifying. When I was fifteen, Johnston discovered that I might be nearsighted. He therefore recommended that a foreign optician be invited to examine my eyes. If his guess was correct, I should have to wear glasses. Unexpectedly this recommendation created an uproar throughout the whole Forbidden City. "This is impossible. How can we let foreigners look at the eyes of the Emperor? The Emperor is at the height of his vigor. How can he put on spectacles like an old man?" From the Grand Imperial High Consorts—thunder! They all refused. It was only due to the convincing arguments of Johnston and my own strong persistence that it was finally accomplished.

One day when I was fifteen I learned from Johnston about the function of telephones. Later I heard from Pu Chieh that the Northern Mansion, where my father lived, had one of these novelties. I therefore asked the Household Department to install one in the Mind Nurture Palace. When the head of the Household Department heard of my command his face turned white. Yet in front of me, he did not dare to oppose me. "Yes, yes," he answered and withdrew. But the following day all my tutors tried to dissuade me:

"There is nothing in our ancestral regulations to provide for this. If there should be a telephone in the palace anyone could talk to Your Majesty directly. Our ancestors never used this kind of Western novelty."

"In the palace the chiming clocks, pianos and electric lights are all Western novelties that have no place in our ancestral system. Did my ancestors use them?" I asked.

"If outsiders can call you up by telephone," they replied, "it may offend the Celestial Countenance. Will this not damage the imperial dignity?"

At that time perhaps even my tutors did not understand the real reason behind the efforts of the Household Department to dissuade me. What really frightened the Household Department was not the fear of offending the "Celestial Countenance" but that I might have more contact with the outside world through the telephone.

It was bad enough for them that I should have a talkative Johnston at my side and take forty newspapers. Almost every month in the papers there was at least one denial issued by the Household Department saying that the Ch'ing Court was not in contact with a particular provincial authority or refuting the rumor of the sale of some antiques.

Nine out of ten of these rumors, although denied, were true and at least half of them were things that they did not wish me to know. The combination of the newspapers plus Johnston kept them busy enough. If a telephone should be added, forming the third link between me and the outside world, their position would be impossible. Therefore they tried their utmost to oppose my proposal.

When they found that my tutors could not dissuade me, they invited my father into the dispute. But he only repeated what my tutors had already said. He had no new reasons, and, furthermore, he had no valid reply. I asked him if there had not already been a telephone installed in his mansion.

"But . . . but . . . but it's dif . . . different with an Emperor. You would do . . . do . . . do better to postpone it for a few days," he repeated again and again in his stuttering fashion.

I explained to him that his queue had been cut off before mine; that he had a telephone before me; that he had not wanted me to buy an auto, but he already had one. All this made me very dissatisfied.

"Why should the Emperor be different?" I asked. "Can I not have any freedom at all? No, it won't work. I want a telephone right away." I then turned to a eunuch. "Send my orders to the Household Department right away," I said. "Install a telephone for me today!"

"Very well . . . very well." My father nodded his head. "Very well, very well."

The telephone was installed. Then new complications ensued.

The telephone company sent over a directory along with the apparatus. I became really happy when I turned the pages of the directory and I wanted to have some fun with my new telephone. I happened to notice the telephone number of a famous Peking opera actor and called his number into the phone. When I heard a voice at the other end, I said: "Could this be the famous opera actor of Peking?" The voice answered laughingly: "Yes, this is the famous opera actor of Peking. Who are you?" I hung up right away. I was utterly happy and amused.

Next I called a famous vaudeville actor and did the same thing. Then I called a well-known restaurant and asked them to send a first-class meal to a false address. After amusing myself like this for a while, I recalled that Johnston had recently talked to me about Dr. Hu Shih, the author of *Picnic by the River*. I therefore called his number. By coincidence, he answered the phone himself.

"Is that Dr. Hu Shih?" I asked. "Well, well, can you guess who this is?"

"Who are you? How come I cannot place who you are?"

"Ha, ha, you don't need to guess. Let me tell you. I'm Hsuan Tung."

"Hsuan Tung? Are you the Emperor?"

"Yes, I am the Emperor. I've heard your voice now, but I don't know what you look like. I wish you would come to my palace when you have time and let me look at you.

This joke really brought him around. From what Johnston told me, Hu Shih, in order to verify the phone message, called on him because he was not sure it was the Emperor who had really telephoned him. When he found out from Johnston that I did not want him to kowtow to me and that I had an equable temperament, he came to see me. But I had forgotten about his proposed visit and had failed to tell the eunuchs to inform the Imperial Guard. Thus when Dr. Hu arrived at the Gate of Divine Valor, they would not let him pass. Not knowing whether to believe him or not, the guards referred the matter to me and only then was he let in.

This meeting lasted for more than twenty minutes. I asked Dr. Hu about the uses of vernacular writing, and about the places he had visited in foreign lands. Later on, in order to gain his confidence, I explained that I did not care about the so-called favorable treatment or lack of it; so long as I could devote more time to studies so that I might become a "promising young man" of the sort one read about in the papers. Thus he couldn't help but shower me with compliments by saying, "Your Majesty is most enlightened. If Your Majesty studies hard your future will be very hopeful!"

After he left, I thought no more of this affair and didn't realize that the princes and high officials, especially my tutors, after they learned of my private meeting with this "modern figure," were thrown into an uproar like the explosion of a hot, burning oil pot.

As I grew up the princes and high officials saw that I was becoming more and more dissatisfied and that I found them increasingly unbearable. By this time I had already been outside the Forbidden City twice, a small freedom I had won on the pretext that I wished to pay my respects to the tomb of my mother after her death. This was gained only after overcoming many protests and it whetted my appetite for more. I was thoroughly dissatisfied with these conservative people who got excited over nothing. In the summer of the eleventh year of the Republic, in 1922, all my accumulated anguish reinforced my determination to go abroad. The conflict with the princes and high officials reached a climax when I formally proposed going to England to further my studies.

They were determined not to give in. Even my uncle Duke Tsai Tao, who had previously been most sympathetic, would only go so far as to give permission for a house to be got ready for me in the British concession in Tientsin in the event of an emergency. Knowing that it would be impossible for me to leave the Forbidden City openly, I sought the help of Johnston, but he felt that the time was not opportune and would not agree to my going. Forced to bide my time, I made secret preparations for an escape from the palace. At this time I had a very loyal and willing helper—my younger brother, Pu Chieh.

Pu Chieh and I were a really well-matched pair of brothers who shared the same distress and ambitions. Our feelings and illusions were even more alike than our appearance. He was determined to escape from his family circle and fly high so that he could find his own way; he believed that all his wishes would be fulfilled once he went abroad. The difference between his environment and mine was the same as our bodies; his was one size smaller.

Pu Chieh was a year younger than I but he had more knowledge of the outside world. He could also move freely in and out of the palace. Our first need was to raise some money. I used the pretext of bestowing on Pu Chieh valuable palace scrolls and antiques so that he could store them in the big house in the British concession in Tientsin. Every day, at five o'clock when he would return home, Pu Chieh would take a big bundle of things with him. This went on without interruption for over a half year. At this time the officials of the Household Department and my tutors were making an inventory of the scrolls of paintings and calligraphy so that it was easy for me to take the best of their selections and give them to Pu Chieh. The total number amounted to about 1,000 hand scrolls, 400 bound volumes and pages from albums, and 200 different types of Sung Dynasty printed books. All of these were taken to Tientsin. Less than 100 were sold. After the foundation of Manchukuo, the Chief of Staff of the Japanese Kwantung Army transported them for me to the Northeast, but after the Japanese surrender, they disappeared.

The second stage of our plan was to make a secret escape from the Forbidden City. Once I was out of the palace and inside a foreign Legation, it would be impossible for either the high palace officials and princes or the Republican government to do anything. Johnston at this point entered into the plot. He suggested that we get in touch with the doyen of the diplomatic corps, the Dutch Minister, W. J. Oudendijk, and ask him to make appropriate preparations. Why he felt that the time had now come, I did not know.

At first I asked Johnston to inform the Dutch Minister, but later I called him up by telephone myself. I also sent Pu Chieh to call on the Dutch legation. Everything seemed to be satisfactory. Oudendijk personally made arrangements with Pu Chieh. Even though he could not send an automobile into the palace, he agreed to wait for me outside the Gate of Divine Valor. Once I had passed through the gate there would be no problems. He would take care of everything from my first night's room and board to my entry into an English university. We fixed the day and hour of my departure from the palace.

The day was set for March 25. The only remaining problem was how to pass through the Gate of Divine Valor. The situation in the Forbidden City was such that I had to reckon with my entourage of personal eunuchs as well as the special eunuchs guarding the palace gate. Outside the Gate of Divine Valor were guards under the control of the Republican Army. I believed that the most important thing was to take care of the eunuchs attending me personally and those guarding the palace gate. If I could handle them, the problem would not be serious. But my solution was really too simple. I gave them some money and thought that everything was set.

But one hour before my scheduled flight, one of the eunuchs who had taken my money notified the Household

Department. Even before I had left the Mind Nurture Palace I learned that my father had issued an order shutting off all traffic in and out of the palace and had placed the entire Forbidden City under curfew and martial law.

When Pu Chieh and I heard the news we sat in the Mind Nurture Palace stupefied.

Before long my father arrived.

"I . . . I . . . hear . . . that Your Majesty wa . . . wan . . . wants to go away. . . ."

He looked so desperate and ill at ease that one might have thought he was the wrongdoer, and I could not help laughing.

"No such thing," I replied, after suppressing my laughter.

"It's not good. Wha . . . what should we do about it?"

"But I don't want to go," I lied.

My father glared suspiciously at Pu Chieh, who was so frightened that he bowed his head.

"But I don't want to go," I repeated. My father muttered a few more words before leaving, taking my "accomplice" with him. After they left I called in the eunuchs of the presence to question them in order to find out who had given out the information. I wanted to have the culprit flogged to death but I had no way of finding out. And this affair naturally could not be referred to the Administrative Bureau for investigation. I could only suffer alone.

From this time on, I hated the sight of the high palace walls. "Prison! Prison! Prison!" I muttered to myself as I stood on the artificial hill looking at the palace walls. "It is understandable that the Republic should not be on good terms with me," I said to myself, "but for the princes and palace officials to be so hostile is really unreasonable. It is only for the sake of my ancestral heritage of mountains and rivers outside the Forbidden City that I want to run away. Why should you people do this to me? The worst are the people in the Household Department! I'm sure it is they who dragged my father into this."

The following day, when I saw Johnston I unloaded my sorrow on him. He tried to comfort me and advised me to put the matter out of my mind for the time being. He said it would be more realistic if I started to reorganize the Forbidden City.

A new hope was kindled in my mind. Since I could not recover my ancestral heritage outside the palace walls, at least I could reform my property within the Forbidden City.

11

Dispersal of the Eunuchs

ON THE SURFACE, THE FORBIDDEN CITY APPEARED TO BE calm and peaceful, yet underneath, it was in complete confusion. From my earliest years I had heard stories of burglary, arson and criminal assault, not to mention opium smoking and gambling. At the time of my wedding, theft had developed to such an extent, for example, that right after the ceremony it was discovered that fakes had been substituted for the pearls and jade in the Empress's crown.

From my tutors I learned that the treasures of the Ch'ing House were known throughout the world and that the amount and value of the antiques, the calligraphy and paintings were tremendous. The treasure collected by the Ming and Ch'ing Dynasties for several hundred years, with the exception of the items taken by foreign troops in 1860 and 1900, were still in the palaces in the Forbidden City. But since most of these items were uncatalogued it was impossible to tell if anything was missing. This made it easy for thieves.

When I was sixteen, out of curiosity, I asked the eunuchs one day to open up a storeroom adjacent to the Palace of Established Happiness. The doors were sealed with tape and had clearly not been used in several decades. Inside were a large number of chests piled to the ceiling. Each chest was also sealed with tape from the reign of Chia Ching (1760–1820). I had a eunuch open one of them. Inside were famous calligraphy and paintings, scrolls and many beautifully carved antique jade pieces. Later on, it became clear to me that these items were those especially enjoyed by the Emperor Chien Lung (1707–1799) and after his death, Chia Ching, who had succeeded him on the throne, had decreed that they should be sealed and stored. The treasures I had discovered were in but one of the many storage rooms set aside for this purpose.

Some of the storage rooms were for bronze pieces, some for porcelains, some for famous paintings, including many done by an Italian painter especially for the Emperor. In the rooms behind the Mind Nurture Palace I also found many "hundred treasure boxes" that were also said to be part of the art treasury of Chien Lung.

These "hundred treasure boxes" were made of beautiful purple teakwood. Outside they looked like a book box, but when opened there were a series of partitions on ascending levels and each level contained several compartments within which was an art treasure, such as Sung porcelain, a hand-written book 1½ inches in size, a beautifully carved ivory ball, several ivories the size of watermelon seeds with carvings of poetry or paintings, an old Egyptian coin, and so on. In any one of the "hundred treasure boxes" there were paintings, calligraphy, gold, gems, jade work, bronze work, porcelains, carvings of ivory. Even the smallest boxes contained more than several hundred items, and the larger ones contained more than a thousand. I found over 40 or 50 of these boxes and I took them all to the Palace of the Cultivation of Happiness.

The discovery of all this art, stored away and not used, made me wonder how many treasures I owned. Those I found stored away I had taken to the palace where I did my studies. But how many were there that I had not seen? What should I do about all the storage rooms scattered about the Forbidden City? How many items had been stolen from them? How could I prevent theft?

My tutor Johnston had told me that many new antique shops had been opened in Ti An Men Street in Peking. According to Johnston some of them were run by eunuchs and by relatives of high officials of the Household Department. My Manchu tutors as well as Johnston felt I should take adequate measures to prevent further theft. Eventually

I received a recommendation from them suggesting that I should order an inventory. But this led to even more trouble.

First of all the number of thefts increased. The lock to the storeroom in the Yu Ching Palace was broken and one of the windows in the Cloudless Heaven Palace was smashed. Later, a big diamond that I had recently purchased disappeared. In order to trace its theft the High Consorts ordered the head of the Administrative Bureau to form a committee to question the eunuchs on duty and to use beatings and third-degree methods if necessary, but neither this nor the offer of big rewards produced any results. And this was not all. On the night of June 27, 1923, soon after starting an inventory of the storerooms behind the Palace of Established Happiness, a fire broke out and everything, whether it had been inventoried or not, was destroyed.

This fire, which was fought all night by fire brigades of all sorts, from both within and without the Forbidden City, reduced the whole area around the palace to ashes. This was the location where most of the treasures of the Ch'ing House were stored. What was lost in the fire remains a mystery. Later the Household Department drew up a makeshift inventory which estimated that 2,665 gold Buddhas were lost, 1,157 scrolls, 435 curios, and also several thousand ancient books. But heaven only knows what these figures were based on.

The best way to describe the damage done by this fire is to tell the story of the disposal of the heap of ashes that remained. At that time I had been looking for a cleared space for a tennis court where Johnston could teach me to play. According to him it was a game played by all British aristocrats. The space left by the fire would, I thought, suit this purpose perfectly, so I ordered the Household Department to clean it up. Although there were no scrolls, porcelain, or art objects in the ashes, there was plenty of melted metal including gold, silver, bronze, and pewter. The Household Department asked the various bullion dealers in Peking to submit bids for the ashes and the successful bidder paid $500,000 for the right of disposal. He gathered 17,000 ounces of melted gold from them. After this was done the Household Department had the remaining ashes put in burlap sacks for distribution among its members. Later, an employee of the

Department told me that his uncle contributed two gold altars, each one foot in height, to the Peking Lama Temple and the Cypress Grove Temple from the ashes he had received.

There was no real way of investigating the cause of the fire. I suspected that it had been set by thieves in order to cover up evidence, for a few days later another fire broke out above one of the windows of the No Idleness Study in the eastern wing of the Mind Nurture Palace. Fortunately, this one was discovered early and extinguished right away. The fact that someone had started it with a wad of kerosene-soaked cotton aroused my suspicions even more. I came to feel that there were not only arsonists about but that there were also people who were trying to murder me.

That there had been thefts and fires set to destroy evidence was proved. My tutors talked about it openly. But my fears of being murdered may well have been derived from my supersensitivity. My suspicious nature had already become apparent. According to the ancestral regulations of the Ch'ing House, the Emperor, no matter how busy with his daily duties, had to read a page from the sacred scripts of his ancestors which were placed in his bedroom every day. I especially admired the "Vermilion rescripts, edicts and decrees" of Emperor Yung Cheng (1678–1733) who once wrote:

> Man is to be trusted, and yet never to be trusted completely.
> If this is not understood it is impossible to make use of the right people correctly.

Emperor Yung Cheng also once made a notation on a memorial submitted by his most trusted official:

> One can only have faith in the deeds of the past.
> One must watch out for the future.

These impressed me deeply and made me recall the sayings of Kang Hsi (1654–1722), who had especially warned against eunuchs.

"I have observed," he wrote, "that from ancient times to

the present there have been very few good eunuchs. It is up to the Emperor to avoid any errors in judgment from the beginning so that one can guard against the future.''

I decided that in order to disperse the eunuchs from the Forbidden City, one supreme effort to win ''eternal ease'' was required. I knew that my decision would arouse a storm of opposition and that if I could not cope with the inevitable objections of my father it would never be carried out. I felt that it was essential not to give him time to negotiate or to discuss this issue with the officials of the Household Department and my tutors, and so I went to see him, unannounced, in his mansion outside the Forbidden City.

When he was confronted with the problem so suddenly it made him stutter even more than ever. He spoke with great effort and stammered out many unconnected and miscellaneous reasons why the eunuchs should be retained. He begged me to reconsider.

"You . . . Your Highness, Emperor should go . . . back . . . to the palace first. After a couple of days . . .''

I ignored his pleas and used only one phrase in reply. "If the Prince does not agree, I shall not return to the palace from this moment on.''

When he heard this he became so excited that he didn't know whether to sit or to stand. He scratched his head and cheeks and began to whirl about the room in his excitement. In doing so he knocked over a bottle of soda water with his sleeve and it made a big crash as it struck the floor. As I looked at his face and saw his anxiety I could not help but laugh out loud. Then I opened a book on his desk and pretended to read in order to demonstrate my intention of not returning to the palace unless he acceded to my demand.

My father was finally convinced and it was decided that, except for a few attendants on the High Consorts, all the eunuchs were to leave the Forbidden City.

12

Reorganizing the Household Department

MY EXPULSION OF THE EUNUCHS WAS VERY WELL RECEIVED by public opinion, and, under Johnston's guidance, I made the reform of the Household Department the next item on my list.

It will suffice to cite only two examples of the Department's graft and embezzlement. One was the alarming size of the annual expenditures which could not have been met by income even if the $4,000,000 annuity under the Articles of Favorable Treatment had been paid. The other was the way in which the Department sold large amounts of gold and jewelry at a fraction of their real value.

Although I did not have detailed evidence of the Department's corruption while I was still living in the palace, I knew one thing from the rate of annual expenditures: they were far higher than they had been under the Empress Dowager Tzu Hsi. In obedience to an edict of mine ordering that the finances be put in order, the Household Department had prepared a comparison, and according to it, the annual expenditures at the beginning of Tzu Hsi's rule had only been about 300,000 taels and, even in the year in which her seventieth birthday was celebrated, they had only gone up to 700,000 taels. In contrast to this, mine had been 2,640,000 in 1915; 2,380,000 in 1919; 1,890,000 in 1920 and 1,710,000 in 1921.

At the same time I saw reports in the public press that some members of the noble families and the families of former high officials had become very poor and that a few had died of starvation. It was also reported that princesses and daughters of noble families had become prostitutes. Meanwhile, many of the Household Department people were opening antique shops, banks, pawnshops, construction firms, and other businesses. Even my tutors, though they had joined the Household Department in opposing my purchase of a car and installing a telephone, had nothing good to say for the Household Department.

My Manchu tutor, Yi Ko Tan, a year before my wedding, claimed that my tutor Chen Pao-shen had been guilty of "deceiving the sovereign" because he had not been willing to expose the corruption of the Household Department to me and for this reason argued that he was not worthy of receiving the title of Grand Tutor. Needless to say, Johnston regarded the Household Department as a "bloodsucking monster."

"The Household Department and the servants of the royal princes are all rich," Johnston told me. "Their masters know nothing about finance so that they are completely dependent on them. Without them they cannot even lay their hands on a farthing. Quite apart from getting back what is already lost, if their masters don't put their financial affairs in order, they won't be rich for long!"

"The motto of the Household Department," Johnston said on another occasion, "is to preserve the status quo at all costs. It makes no difference whether the change involved is a minor reform or a major overhaul. Whatever runs into this obstacle has to *stop*." He emphasized the last word by putting it in English.

After my wedding, I utilized my new power as head of the family to choose several retired officials who came to the wedding and were known for their capability and loyalty to advise me in this undertaking. They in turn recommended their friends, and in this way, a total of twelve or thirteen new officials were added to the Forbidden City. I made each of them either a Companion of the Southern Study or a Companion of the Great Diligence Hall.

The specific recommendations of these people are no

longer in existence, but I do have a general recommendation
of one of them which can be summarized as follows:

"In your servant's opinion, the important thing today is
secretly to plan a restoration of your dynasty. In order to
restore your regime and gain control of the whole country,
priority must be given to the consolidation of your base and
the protection of your court. The next most important thing
is to put your property in order so as to secure your finances.
For it is necessary to have the wherewithal in order both to
protect your present position and to plan a restoration." He
went on to suggest in more detail how these principles could
be carried out, and one of his proposals with which I
thoroughly agreed was that we should begin by reforming
the Household Department.

Even the most apathetic retired officials were not opposed
to the protection of the court by means of administrative
reforms. There was, however, a small minority, led by my
tutor, Chen Pao-shen, who would shake their heads over the
suggestion of reform. Although this group acknowledged the
corruption and weaknesses of the Department, they felt it
had become so deep-rooted as to be impossible to clean up
and pointed out that Emperor Chia Ching's previous attempts at reform, as far back as 1800, had ended in failure.
They thought it would be better to leave the Department
alone and argued that the time was not opportune. But even
they, including tutor Chen, had nothing good to say for it.

At the urging of Johnston I had tried unsuccessfully, even
before my wedding, to put my property in order and had
chosen a veteran diplomat and friend of his to take charge of
the task. But he had proven unwilling to take up the job and
had recommended a relative. At that time the Household
Department had tried to get my father to block this appointment, but I had insisted. However, after he had been at work
less than three months, he asked for a long leave of absence
and returned to Shanghai.

Notwithstanding this incident, I did not detect the super-
natural power of the Household Department and only
blamed my failure on the selection of the wrong man and on
the fact that I had not yet come of age and had thus not
personally assumed power. I now felt that the situation was
different. First, I had come of age and was master of my

family and no one else could stop me. I now had a group of my own people around me and I felt that my strength was greatly augmented. With high spirits and keen interest I selected Cheng Hsiao-hsu to take charge of the reform.

Cheng Hsiao-hsu came from the same province as my tutor, Chen Pao-shen. He had served as consul in Japan and later as a border commissioner in Kwangsi Province. Chen Pao-shen and Johnston both recommended him to me, especially Johnston, who said that he was the one he admired most in all his twenty years in China and that his character and learning were without equal in the whole country. My tutor Chen further stated that Cheng had refused many times to serve the President of the Republic, that he was one of the best poets in the country and that his calligraphy was superb. His income from his calligraphy was said to be very large and since he was willing to give this income up to volunteer to work for me, I felt sure he would be loyal.

As a first step, Cheng Hsiao-hsu was named a Companion of the Great Diligence Hall in order to study the problem of the Household Department. Later, he came to see me several times to explain his ideas. He thought that four sections would be quite enough to do the work and believed that great numbers of its staff could be dismissed and enormous economies made. In this way the drain on my resources could be stopped and my financial position strengthened. He felt that if his plan were carried out, the financial basis for a restoration would be assured. I was so struck by his plan that I broke all precedent and appointed him Comptroller of the Household Department and Keeper of the Keys and Seals even though he was a Han and not a Manchu. He became the leading official of the Household (in place of its former comptroller, Shao Ying) and was so pleased with his appointment that he composed two poems to celebrate the occasion.

But to suppose that the uneducated and ignorant Household Department could be defeated by Cheng Hsiao-hsu was to underestimate this organization which had over 200 years of running the palace behind it. For all Cheng's eloquence which was "like flowers falling from the heavens" and the support and confidence I gave him, he lasted only three months.

I have never fully understood how the Department got rid of him.

The first thing that Cheng encountered on entering office was a backlog of files dating back to the Revolution of 1911. His method of coping with this problem was to dismiss the holder of a key job and give it to a friend. The Household's response to this was to behave as if it had been paralyzed. If Cheng asked for money, there was no money and there were accounts to prove it. If he wanted some object or file, no one knew where it was, and this too was clearly stated in the records.

In order to win over his subordinates, Cheng made a great show of listening to their opinions and holding weekly staff meetings at which he asked for suggestions. One of the staff suggested that the expenditures on fresh fruits and cakes used for offerings at the various shrines in the palace were too high. He explained that since these offerings were only symbolic, it would be better to use wooden or clay replicas. Cheng agreed with the proposal, ordered it into effect and promoted the man who had made the suggestion one grade. The eunuchs, however (there were only 100 left after the dispersal), felt that these offerings were a source of legitimate income for them and hated Cheng bitterly for his decision. Within a few days of taking office, Cheng became the most hated man in the Forbidden City.

Because Cheng would not retreat, he immediately received a number of threatening letters. One accused him of starving people to death and warned that he had better watch out if he wished to stay alive. Johnston, who had been commissioned by me to reorganize the Summer Palace outside Peking, also received threatening letters. Later Johnston proudly told me that he did not ride to the Summer Palace in an automobile, but went out on horseback for the express purpose of daring his enemies to kill him. As a result, he explained, "I am still alive and I look through them."

The final act in all this reform program was really performed by me. Soon after I had appointed Cheng to office, I received some painful news: two members of the Republic's congress were going to introduce a bill asking for the abolition of the Articles of Favorable Treatment. A similar bill had been presented two years previously both because of the brief restoration of 1917 and on the grounds that the Ch'ing House was bestowing titles and posthumous awards on Republican officials, but this had been tabled. Now it was being revived and to the old charges had been added the accusation that I had acted illegally in appointing a Han, Cheng Hsiao-hsu, Comptroller of the Household Department and extending to him the privilege of riding a horse in the Forbidden City.

The appearance of this news in the press was a signal for a series of attacks on the Household Department; various forms of corruption that had previously gone unnoticed came up for public criticism. In the meantime the inventory of the scrolls and paintings and other objects of art that my new advisers were making came under attack. Who would have thought that this inventory would have created a veritable wind of gossip that blew through the entire Forbidden City? I had never anticipated that it would have been better not to have asked for an inventory at all since the photographic prints of the treasures, painting and calligraphy (which formed the inventory and copies of which were sold) attracted attention both in China and abroad. But what concerned me most was that the Republic's Ministry of Interior suddenly promulgated a Provisional Bill for the Preservation of Ancient Scrolls, Ancient Treasures and Ancient Objects which appeared to be designed to prevent the sale of palace objects of art.

Shortly afterward, Cheng, as a fund-raising measure, proposed that the encyclopedia of China, which included the four divisions of all the important literature, be shipped to Shanghai for photographing and publication by the commercial press. Transport for this project was stopped by order of the Republic. At this time my father came to see me, and in a very roundabout way said that the measures of Cheng Hsiao-hsu should be carefully reconsidered and explained that if the Republic did not approve of what he had already done, there might be worse trouble later on.

Soon after this Shao Ying, the former Household Comptroller, appeared before me to say that the Commander of the Republican Army was deeply dissatisfied with Cheng Hsiao-hsu's actions and that if Cheng persisted with his measures and the Republic took action, he would be able to do nothing to help me. I became frightened by this news and then on top of it Cheng memorialized me asking to be relieved of his duties. The result of it all was that Cheng reverted to being a Companion of the Great Diligence Hall and Shao Ying resumed control of the Household Department.

III

MY EXILE

13

From the Forbidden City to the Legation Quarter

ALTHOUGH THE REORGANIZATION OF THE HOUSEHOLD DEpartment was declared a failure, it did not make me "stop the car" insofar as my efforts to improve my situation were concerned, and there were plenty of people to offer me advice.

After my marriage, there were many retired Ch'ing officials who secretly presented plans for my restoration. One group operated in China and abroad through an organization called the Imperial Chinese Constitutional Monarchist Party, which in a memorial claimed 100,000 members abroad and five newspapers and suggested that I support it with my personal wealth. Reports on its activities were transmitted to me in the palace via Reginald Johnston.

I also gave money to charity. I have forgotten which of my tutors suggested the idea to me. At that time the social pages of the Peking papers would carry items almost every day about the gifts to the poor by the Emperor. My gifts usually were of two types. Sometimes I would send money to a newspaper office to distribute when the paper carried items about poor people, and at other times I would send Ch'ing officials with gifts of money direct to destitute families. Whichever method I used, the newspapers would carry an item about it within the next day or two.

My biggest donation was made after the Japanese earthquake of September, 1923. Japan's losses from this disaster had shocked the world, and I thought I would take this opportunity to display my benevolence. My tutor Chen Pao-shen showed foresight in advising this. After praising "the magnificence of the imperial bounty and the humanity of the celestial mind," he told me that "this action will make its influence felt in the future." Since I was short of ready cash I sent antiques, paintings and calligraphy that were valued at about 300,000 U.S. dollars. The Japanese Minister Yoshi-zawa came with a delegation from the Japanese Diet to thank me, and the excitement in the palace was similar to that created by the presence of foreign envoys at my wedding.

This relatively placid life went on until November 5, 1924, when the struggles between the various war lords around Peking reached a climax and the army of General Feng Yu-hsiang drove me out of the Forbidden City. September, 1924, had marked the beginning of the second Chihli-Fengtien war, a renewal of the convulsive struggle between the North Chinese and Manchurian war lords. At first the war lord Wu Pei-fu was on top, but in October while attacking the forces of Chang Tso-lin on the Manchurian border, his subordinate Feng Yu-hsiang deserted him, marched his troops back to Peking and issued a peace telegram. Under the combined pressure of Feng Yu-hsiang and Chang Tso-lin, Wu's troops collapsed and Wu himself fled. (Two years later he made a comeback.) Even before the news of Wu's defeat came through, Feng's army occupied Peking, put the President of China under house arrest and dissolved Parliament.

When the news of this *coup d'état* reached the palace, I immediately felt that the situation was dangerous. The Pal-ace Guard had already been disarmed by Feng's army and moved out of the inner city. His troops had taken over their barracks and posts at the Gate of Divine Valor. From the Imperial Garden, I looked at Coal Hill through a telescope and saw that it was swarming with soldiers. The Household Department sent them tea and food which they accepted, and although there was nothing alarming about their behav-ior, everyone in the Forbidden City was worried. We all remembered that previously Feng had published telegrams demanding that the court be expelled from the Forbidden City and this made us realize that the *coup d'état*, and the replacement of the Palace Guards boded ill for the future. I sent for Johnston and asked him to go to the Foreign Legations, find out the latest news, and arrange for me to take refuge somewhere.

All the princes and high officials were concerned. Some had already made reservations for themselves in the Wagon-Lits Hotel in the Legation Quarter, but when they heard that I wished to leave the Forbidden City they said it was not yet necessary. They argued that since all the foreign powers recognized the Articles of Favorable Treatment nothing serious could happen to me.

But the inevitable at last did happen. At a little after nine o'clock on the morning of November 5, I was eating fruit in the Palace of Accumulated Elegance and conversing with my wife, Wan Jung, when the high officials of the Household Department suddenly entered in great disorder. Shao Ying, the head of the Department, was in the lead with a document in his hand.

"Your Majesty . . . Your Majesty," he panted, for he was out of breath, "Feng Yu-hsiang has sent soldiers with an envoy who has told us that the Republic is going to abolish the Articles of Favorable Treatment. They have sent us this document and they want you to sign it."

I jumped up at once, dropped my half-eaten apple on the floor, and grabbed the document from him. It was a "revision" of the Articles of Favorable Treatment which abolished my position as Emperor and made me an ordinary citizen, reduced the size of the annual subsidy from $4,000,000 a year to $500,000, required me to abandon the Forbidden City, provided for the protection of my ancestral temples and mausoleums and guaranteed the retention of my private property.

Actually, these Revised Articles were not nearly as bad as I had originally anticipated. What startled me the most was a remark of Shao Ying's—"They said that in three hours' time, we must move out of the Forbidden City."

"But what shall I do about my property? What about the High Consorts?" I was so nervous that I paced back and forth.

"Telephone Johnston," I said after a moment.

"The wires have been cut . . . cut . . . cut," my father-in-law interjected.

"Send someone to fetch the Prince Regent. I always said that something would happen, but you people wouldn't let me go away. Look for the Prince Regent, look for the Prince Regent!"

"But we can't get out; there are people on guard at the gate and they won't let anyone out."

"Then go and negotiate for me."

"Yes, Your Majesty."

The High Consort Tuan Kang had died a few days before and there were only two High Consorts left in the palace. They absolutely refused to move. Using this as an excuse, Shao Ying finally went to negotiate with Feng's envoy and succeeded in getting an extension of the time limit until 3 P.M. After midday it was arranged that my father should be allowed into the palace along with my tutors Chu Yi-fan and Chen Pao-shen; only Johnston was kept out.

When I learned that my father had come, I went out to meet him and as soon as I caught sight of him coming through the gate I shouted, "Your Highness, what are we going to do?"

At the sound of my voice he stood stock-still, as if a spell had been cast upon him. He neither came any closer nor answered my question; his lips quivered and then he got out a completely useless sentence: "I . . . I . . . obey the e . . . edict. I obey the edict. . . ."

Now angry as well as worried, I spun around and went back into my room. Later I heard from a eunuch that when my father had learned that I had put my signature on the Revised Articles, he had pulled his hat with a peacock feather off and thrown it on the floor, muttering, "It's all over, it's all over. I won't need this again."

Subsequently Shao Ying returned to my room, his face an even more dreadful sight than it had been earlier. He was shaking as he said, "Their envoy is pushing us. He says we can only have another twenty minutes, and that if we aren't out by then . . . they'll open fire with artillery from Coal Hill."

Although Feng's envoy had only brought twenty soldiers armed with pistols, his threat was effective. My father-in-law became so frightened that he rushed into the Imperial Garden to find someplace to hide from the threatened artillery fire and refused to come out again. Seeing the terror of the princes, I decided to accept the demands for my immediate departure and go to my father's house.

The Army had five cars ready for us. Feng's envoy rode in the front car, I followed in the second, my wives Wan Jung and Wen Hsiu, and Shao Ying and others came behind.

When I got out of the car at the main gate of the Northern Mansion (my father's house), Feng's envoy came up and shook hands with me. "Mr. Pu Yi," he asked, "do you intend to be Emperor in future or will you be an ordinary citizen?"

"From today onward I wish to be an ordinary citizen."

"Good," he said with a smile, "then we shall protect you."

"I have felt for some time," I explained, "that I did not need the Articles of Favorable Treatment and I am pleased to see them annulled. I had no freedom as Emperor, and now I have found my freedom."

When I finished this little speech the soldiers of Feng's army who were standing nearby applauded. My last sentence was not entirely untrue. I was sick of the restrictions with which the princes and high officials had surrounded me. I wanted my freedom and also "freedom" with which to realize my ambition of regaining my ancestral heritage in my own way.

After speaking these words I hurried past Feng's army guard and through the gate of the Northern Mansion. But as I sat in my father's study, I came to realize that it was more like a tiger's mouth than a princely mansion. The first thing I had to do was find out how dangerous my situation really was.

My father was a big disappointment to me. He was even more flustered than I was. From the time I entered the Northern Mansion he never stood still for a moment. When he was not walking up and down muttering to himself, he was rushing in and out in a panic, making the atmosphere even more tense. When I could not bear it any longer, I said to him:

"Your Highness, sit down and talk it over. We must decide

what to do, and before we do that we must get some news from the outside."

"Decide what to do? Very well." He sat down, but before two minutes were up, he leapt to his feet, made some meaningless remarks, and started pacing up and down again.

"We must get some news," I repeated.

"Get some news? Very good, very good." Then he went out of the room and came back a moment later. "They . . . won't let us out," he stammered. "There are soldiers at the main gate."

"Use the telephone."

"Telephone, yes, yes, the telephone," But before he had gone many steps, he came back. "Whom shall I telephone?" he asked.

I saw that the only thing to do was have the eunuchs summon the senior officials of the Household Department. But of these, Jung Yuan, my father-in-law, had already entered a foreign hospital with a nervous disorder (he stayed two months) and the others were either moving out my clothing and personal effects, dealing with the eunuchs and palace maids, or looking after the two High Consorts who had stayed behind. Only Shao Ying was with me. He was in much the same state as my father and incapable of making a single phone call.

Fortunately other princes and officials soon came as did my tutors; otherwise I do not know how bad the confusion in the Northern Mansion would have become. The best news was that brought by Johnston, who said that the Dutch Minister Oudendijk, as doyen of the Diplomatic Corps, along with the British and Japanese Ministers had already protested my treatment to the new Foreign Minister who had guaranteed the safety of my life and possessions. This news calmed everyone in the Northern Mansion except my father.

Next day the restrictions at the gates were tightened and people were allowed in but not out. Later they were relaxed a little, but still only my tutors Chen Pao-shen and Chu Yi-fan and the senior officials of the Household Department were allowed in and out; foreigners were absolutely barred. This really alarmed everyone in the Northern Mansion; if the Army had no respect for foreigners there was no guarantee for the future at all.

The storm of November 5, 1924, that had blown me out of the Forbidden City had dropped me at the crossroads. Three roads of action stretched out before me. One was to do what the Revised Articles suggested: to abandon the imperial title and my old ambitions and become an enormously wealthy private citizen. Another was to try to get the help of my "sympathizers" to cancel the new Articles and restore the old Articles in their entirety, to regain my title and return to the Forbidden City to continue to live my old life. The third possible course was the most tortuous: first to go abroad and then to come back to the Forbidden City, the Forbidden City as it had been before 1911. In the words of that time, this course was "using foreign power to plan a restoration."

As I faced the problem of which decision to make I was surrounded by men who argued endlessly over the merits of the different choices. They regarded the first possibility as not worthy of serious consideration, but fought stubbornly over the other two; and even the advocates of the same course would differ over their specific proposals.

Meanwhile the situation in Peking continued to deteriorate and warnings of violence began to drift into the Northern Mansion. My tutor Lo Chen-yu insisted that Feng planned action against me any day and stated, "Your Majesty must leave here as soon as possible and take refuge in the Legation Quarter." After the withdrawal of Feng's troops from the gate, Johnston turned up with news that Feng was going to make a new move against Peking, and my tutor Chen Pao-shen pointed out that since Feng's troops were not at the gate it was imperative for me to seek refuge in the Legation Quarter. He suggested that on arrival in the Quarter I first enter the German Hospital where there was a doctor who was an acquaintance of mine. Once there, arrangements could be made for me to seek refuge in a foreign legation. He and Johnston and I discussed these plans secretly, since they not only had to be kept from Feng's people but also from my father who was bitterly opposed to my leaving his mansion.

We acted according to secret plans and carried out the first step. I went with my tutor Chen Pao-shen to visit the two High Consorts, who had finally moved out of the palace a few days after me and were now living in Chilinpei Lane, and then came back to the Northern Mansion. This was to make those in the Northern Mansion believe that I was trustworthy and had no intention of leaving. We decided to carry out step two the following day. I was to say that I was going to inspect a house that I intended to rent in Piaopei Lane and, once out of my father's house and en route, slip into the Legation Quarter and enter the German Hospital. The third step would be to go to a legation. Once I was in the Legation Quarter, this third step and the fourth step of having Wan Jung and Wen Hsiu rejoin me would be easy. But when we were about to start out on step two, my father ordered his Chief Steward to accompany us. I rode in the first car with Johnston and the steward sat behind Chen Pao-shen in another.

"That's a bit awkward," Johnston said in English, frowning as he got in the car and motioning toward the steward.

"Never mind him." I was furious. I told the driver to start and we drove out of the Northern Mansion. I never wanted to enter its gates again in my life.

Johnston felt that we could not ignore the steward and would have to think of some way of shaking him off. As we drove along, he decided that we should stop at a shop to buy something and send him back.

There was a foreign store selling watches, clocks and cameras situated at the entrance of the Legation Quarter. When we reached it, I went in with Johnston, and after looking around, I chose a French pocket watch. But although I delayed for a long time the steward waited outside and obviously had no intention of leaving. Johnston therefore had to fall back on a last resort and told the steward that I did not feel well and was going to visit a doctor at the German Hospital. The steward became suspicious and followed us there. Johnston explained to Dr. Dipper why I had come and he ushered me into an empty sickroom to rest. The steward, seeing that something was up, disappeared at once. Since we knew that he would be bound to go back to the Northern Mansion to report to my father, Johnston lost no time in going to negotiate with the British Legation. But as hours passed and I had no news from him, I became very anxious. While I was worrying, fearing that the steward would bring my father, Chen Pao-shen turned up, followed by Cheng Hsiao-hsu, who recommended that, rather than wait for Johnston, I go to the Japanese Legation. I sent him there to negotiate for my refuge, which he arranged. Immediately upon his return, we left the hospital by the back door and quickly traveled the quarter mile to the Japanese Legation.

In those days the Legation Quarter and the foreign concessions were definitely hospitable places. Seven years earlier the then President of China had been driven to take shelter in a legation when I was briefly restored as Emperor, and then the war lord Chang Hsun himself, after I had abdicated for the second time, had become a "guest" of the Netherlands Legation a few days later. Whenever a legation was going to receive some "guests," the hotels and hospitals in the Legation Quarter would also become very busy since many nervous people whose status was too low to get into a legation would pack these places so full that some would even be willing to pay for space under the stairs in order to gain admission.

My reception was the first and probably the last of its kind. Later, when I sent for my wives from the Northern Mansion, Feng's police would not let them out, so the Japanese Legation delegated a secretary to arrange the matter. And when he too failed, the Japanese Minister personally went to see the Chief Executive of the new government, Tuan Chi-jui, and, as a result, Wan Jung and Wen Hsiu with their eunuchs and ladies-in-waiting rejoined me.

When the Minister saw the size of my entourage he realized that the three rooms he had set aside for me were inadequate to accommodate us, and he cleared a whole building in the Legation Compound for us to live in. There was thus room for everyone, from Companions of the Southern Study and senior officials of the Household Department to the dozens of attendants, eunuchs, ladies-in-waiting, maids and kitchen help. In this way the essential administrative offices of the Great Ch'ing Emperor functioned once more within the Japanese Legation.

A group of princes led by my father came to try to persuade me to return to the Northern Mansion. They said it was now safe. But I refused to go.

Upon seeing the enthusiasm with which the Japanese Legation looked after me, many Ch'ing veterans who were previously unknown to me were stirred into action. They sent telegrams from all over the country asking the Chief Executive, Tuan Chi-jui, to restore the original Articles of Favorable Treatment; they sent me contributions to cover my expenses and some of them even came to Peking to pay their respects and offer me advice. Meanwhile the Ch'ing princes and high officials refused to take part in the meetings of the Committee for the Readjustment of the Affairs of the Ch'ing House. This committee, which had been formed to take an inventory of Ch'ing property and divide it into my public and private possessions in accordance with the Revised Articles, held no real meetings. Shao Ying, the head of the Household Department, and the three other Ch'ing members of the committee followed up their refusal to attend its meetings with a public announcement that they did not recognize it.

As time went on, more and more former Ch'ing officials, both young and old, came to the Japanese Legation every day to show their loyalty, pay their respects, present money and explain their "grand strategies for restoration." On Chinese New Year's Day my small living room was filled with queues. I sat facing south in imperial style on a Western-type chair that substituted for a throne and received congratulations.

Many of the retired officials were full of gratitude for my Japanese hosts. They saw grounds for hope in the reception I received from the Legation or at least drew psychological satisfaction from it. Thirteen days after Chinese New Year came my twentieth birthday, by Chinese reckoning.[1]

Since I was in a stranger's house I had not intended to celebrate my birthday, but my host was determined to please me and offered me the main hall of the Legation in which to receive congratulations. The hall was specially furnished for the occasion with expensive carpets, and behind an armchair with imperial yellow cushions that served as a throne stood

---

[1] Nineteenth by Western calculations since, in the Orient, one is a year old at birth. In China, the tenth, twentieth, thirtieth, etc., birthdays are occasions for special celebrations.

a glass screen covered with imperial yellow paper. All the servants and attendants wore Ch'ing hats with red tassels. Over a hundred former Ch'ing officials came from Tientsin, Shanghai, Kwangtung and Fukien for the birthday celebrations which were also attended by members of the Diplomatic Corps, princes, high officials and local Ch'ing veterans, making a total of over 500 people.

I wore a blue silk robe and a black satin jacket for the occasion, and all the princes, court officials and Ch'ing veterans wore the same attire. Apart from this, the ceremonial procedures were much as they had been in the Forbidden City. Imperial yellow, queues and ninefold kowtows were all employed and they created an atmosphere that gave me a feeling of anguish and melancholy. Afterward, I made an impromptu speech of thanks.

An unusual incident occurred on that day. While the third group of Ch'ing officials were performing their nine-kowtow ceremony, I heard a strange shrieking and crying from one of them. Immediately thereafter I saw a man cover his face with his sleeve. He cried aloud as he walked out and I thought perhaps he had injured his eye. He was recognized as a high official of the Household Department, Chin Liang, but no one seemed to know why he had cried aloud.

The following day, however, when an item appeared in the press containing one of his poems, we realized that the reason he had made the scene on the previous day was to prepare us for the publication of his poetry.

About the time of my birthday celebration the press was full of attacks on me and my group. Disapproval expressed itself in various ways: small satirical items, direct accusations regarding my pro-Japanese tendencies, well-meaning advice, and criticism of the pomp and show of my court. The newspapers also printed many revelations regarding my selling and mortgaging of palace antiquities. When I look at them today I realize how different my life would have been if I had accepted a single one of these criticisms.

While living in the Japanese Legation I went for several bicycle rides at night out of curiosity, taking one or two servants with me. On one of these trips I rode as far as the moat outside the Forbidden City and as I looked at the silhouette of the turrets and battlements I thought of the

Mind Nurture Palace and the Cloudless Heaven Palace that I had so recently left and of my throne and of imperial yellow. A desire for revenge and restoration welled up in my heart. My eyes filled with tears as I resolved that I would return at some future time as a victorious monarch just as the first of my line had done. I also decided that it would not do for me to continue to live in the Legation, that I should at least start making preparations for my future. My earlier wish to go to Japan to study was revived, and although the Minister had no opinion on the matter, one of the Legation secretaries with whom I discussed the idea was very enthusiastic.

Not long after this, Lo Chen-yu informed me that he had arranged with one of the Legation officials that I should complete my preparations for going abroad in Tientsin since it was not convenient for me to remain at the Legation. It would be best, he explained, for me to find a house in the Japanese concession in Tientsin since the one I already owned, which was in the British concession, was not suitable. This seemed sensible enough to me, especially since I wished to see the big city of Tientsin. I therefore agreed to go at once and sent a Companion of the Southern Study to find me a house in the Japanese concession there. A few days later Lo Chen-yu told me that the Chang Garden, which was the house I finally selected, was ready and that since Feng's Army was in the process of changing its garrisons along the railroad we should at once take this opportunity to move. The Japanese Minister Yoshizawa approved and sent for the Police Chief of the Japanese Consulate General in Tientsin. He arrived in Peking accompanied by several plainclothes policemen to escort me during the trip. Once I was safely in Tientsin it was arranged that my wives would follow me.

At 7 P.M. on February 23, 1925, I took my leave of the Japanese Minister and his wife. We posed for photographs, I thanked them, and they wished me a safe journey. I then left by the back gate of the Legation with a Japanese official and some plainclothes policemen as guards and we walked together to the Chienmen Railway Station. Here I met my tutor Lo Chen-yu and his son. At every stop between Peking and Tientsin several Japanese policemen and special agents in black suits would get on the train so that, by the time we reached Tientsin, my special car was almost half occupied by them. As I got out of the train I was met by the Japanese Consul General in Tientsin, Shigeru Yoshida, and several dozen officers and men of the Japanese garrison who escorted me from the train. Three days later the press carried a statement issued by the Japanese Legation in Peking declaring that the sudden nocturnal departure of the former Ch'ing Emperor had been the result of the unstable situation there and that the provisional government of China had been notified of it the following day.

14

Tientsin

UPON MY ARRIVAL AT TIENTSIN[1] I FOUND THAT LO CHEN-yu had not told me the exact truth when he had said that my house was suitably prepared, and I therefore had to stay for one day at the Yamato Hotel. The next day Wan Jung and Wen Hsiu, as well as the others who had been in the Japanese Legation with me, arrived and we all moved into the hastily furnished Chang Garden.

The Chang Garden covered over three acres and included a large two-story house in the center. Originally used as an amusement park, it belonged to a former Manchu general who would not accept any rent for it from me, and at first, every day, personally swept the yard as a sign of loyalty. I stayed in the Chang Garden for five years, but after his death I moved to the Quiet Garden when his son assumed the face of a landlord and asked me for rent.

My reason for coming to Tientsin had been to enable me to voyage abroad, but I ended up by spending seven years there, seven years in which I wavered back and forth between different factions among my advisers. The princes,

---

[1] A highly important seaport of North China connected by rail with Peking. It was one of eleven Chinese ports opened to foreign trade in 1858. Foreign concessions were granted to many of the Western powers and Japan who garrisoned them with their own troops.

my father included, had far less power over me, and Johnston, who had returned to Wei-hai-wei, ceased to be my
tutor. He did, however, visit me in 1926 and canvassed
unsuccessfully for support for me from the war lord Wu Pei-
fu and others. Later he returned to England, was knighted,
and became a professor at the University of London.

One could divide the people who struggled to win my
favor in those seven years into various groups. There were
the "old ministers" led by Chen Pao-shen who at first hoped
for the restoration of the Articles of Favorable Treatment
and later were content with the status quo. They could be
called the "back to the palace" faction. Another group
around Lo Chen-yu put their hopes in my going abroad and
in getting help from foreign countries, principally Japan;
they could be considered as the "ally with Japan" or "going
abroad" faction, and they included retired Ch'ing officials
as well as one or two of the Manchu princes, such as Pu
Wei. A third group, of which I was the leading figure, thought
the best method was to get in touch with and "buy up" the
war lords. This "employing military men" group was rather
heterogeneous and included retired Ch'ing officials and Republican politicians.

When Cheng Hsiao-hsu, who had unsuccessfully sought
to reorganize the Household Department, came back to my
service, he did not attach himself to any clique. He seemed
both to praise and to attack the proposals which the others
put forward; then he would suggest ideas that none of them
had brought up, such as the use of foreign advisers and an
open-door policy of cooperating with any country that was
willing to help me in a restoration, but his suggestions were
opposed by all the other factions. Later, when he finally
adopted the policy of relying on Japan, he overcame all his
old rivals including Lo Chen-yu, who had from the beginning
been the leader of the pro-Japanese clique.

I was able to associate with as many war lords as I liked
during my seven years in Tientsin, and they all gave me
illusions—some more, some less. In a letter Wu Pei-fu
described himself as a servant, Chang Tso-lin kowtowed to
me, and on his own initiative Tuan Chi-jui requested an

audience with me. Those in whom I had the highest hopes were the Manchurian or Fengtien war lords, and it was with them that I associated most closely. This began when Chang Tso-lin kowtowed to me.

One day in June, 1925, after I had arrived in Tientsin, my father-in-law Jung Yuan came to tell me in great excitement that Chang Tso-lin had sent a trusted envoy to give me $100,000 and to tell me that Chang hoped he would be able to meet me in the house where he was staying. I refused to go to see him on the advice of my tutor Chen Pao-shen, but, to my surprise, Jung Yuan brought Chang's envoy again the following night. The man insisted that I would be in no danger in Chinese territory, and explained that it was not convenient for Chang Tso-lin to enter the concession and that was why he was repeating his invitation. Without telling anyone else I got into an automobile and set off.

That early summer evening was the first time I had ventured out of the Japanese concession. When I arrived at the Tsao Family Garden, where Chang Tso-lin was staying, I saw a strange guard of honor—tall soldiers dressed in gray who carried ancient swords and spears as well as modern rifles. The car passed slowly between their double ranks from the main gate to the house.

When I got out of the car I was led into a brightly lit hall, where a very short man with a moustache wearing civilian clothes came toward me. I recognized him at once as Chang Tso-lin, and hesitated since I did not know how to greet him. This was the first time I had sought out an important Republican figure and Jung Yuan had given me no instructions. But to my astonishment, Chang knelt on the floor without a moment's pause and kowtowed, saying, "How is Your Majesty?"

"How are you, Marshal?" I replied as I helped him to his feet and we walked toward the reception room together. I was in very good spirits and grateful for what he had just done to end my uneasy feeling that I had lowered my dignity by coming to see him. What made me even more pleased, of course, was to discover that this very powerful and influential man had not forgotten the past.

The room was furnished expensively in a melange of furniture that included Chinese hardwood tables and chairs,

Western-style sofas, and a modern glass screen. We sat down at a round table facing each other and Chang Tso-lin started talking as he smoked one cigarette after another. No sooner had he opened his mouth than he started to curse Feng Yu-hsiang for forcing me out of the Forbidden City in order to get at the palace treasures. He himself, he claimed, attached the greatest importance to the preservation of China's ancient culture and riches, had looked after the Ch'ing palace in Fengtien very well and was planning to get possession of a set of the famous Four Libraries of books, which had been made at the orders of the Emperor Chien Lung (1707–1799), so that he could preserve them in their entirety. He said in a reproachful tone that I should not have fled to the Japanese Legation at a time when he had plenty of troops in Peking who could have ensured my safety. He asked me about my life since my departure from Peking and said that I had only to tell him if I wanted anything.

I said that I was well aware of how thoughtful he had been on my behalf, but since Feng's men were still in Peking, I had been forced to flee to the Japanese Legation. I went on to observe that I had known how well the imperial palaces and mausoleums in Mukden had been looked after and that I appreciated his understanding and sentiments.

"If Your Majesty would like to come up to our Mukden and live in the palace there, it would be quite possible for me to arrange it."

"Marshal Chang, you are too kind. . . ."

But Marshal Chang then changed the subject to my daily life. "If you need anything from now on just write to me."

The only thing I lacked was a throne, but I could scarcely say so in so many words while I was talking to him. During our conversation we were alone in the room except for a swarm of flies, and it occurred to me that there were never flies in the middle of the night in the concession.

An aide-de-camp came in after a while and said, "The Chief of Staff wants to see you, sir," Chang Tso-lin waved his hand and said, "There's no hurry. Tell him to wait for me."

I immediately got up and said that I would be going since he must be very busy. He replied at once, "No hurry, no hurry," but at that point I caught a glimpse of a woman's face behind the screen (I learned later that this was his fifth concubine) and I felt that he must really be busy. I took my leave of him again and this time he did not try to keep me.

When I had left the concession I had been accompanied by one of the plainclothes Japanese policemen who were stationed at the Chang Garden. Apparently, Chang Tso-lin had not noticed him standing beside my car, for as he saw me off he said in a loud voice:

"If those damn Japs put a finger on you, let me know and I'll sort them out for you."

The following morning, the Japanese Consul General delivered the following warning: "If Your Majesty makes another secret trip to Chinese territory, the Japanese Government will no longer be able to guarantee your safety."

My relations with the Fengtien war lords had been growing closer, and after my meeting with Chang Tso-lin they were entirely in the open. When they came to the Chang Garden the etiquette observed was no longer that of the Forbidden City: they did not kowtow to me and I did not confer upon them the right to ride a horse or be carried in a sedan chair at court. They merely bowed or shook hands, and then we would behave as equals; and I did not affect the style of an Emperor when writing to them. The closeness of the relationship between me and the Fengtien generals would be decided by their attitude toward my restoration.

In 1928 Chang Tso-lin was murdered by the Japanese. I later heard that the reason they killed him was because he was becoming less amenable to their demands because he was under the influence of his son, the "Young Marshal" Chang Hsueh-liang, who wanted to break with Japan and make friends with the United States. Although this murder frightened me, and some of the retired Ch'ing officials regarded it as an object lesson, it did not deter me from my course because I did not regard myself in the same class as Chang Tso-lin. He, after all, was a military commander for whom a substitute could easily be found. But I was the Emperor, and the Japanese could not find another one in the whole of China. As my advisers explained: "The Japanese are strong enough to take Manchuria by force, but if they did so they would not be capable of running it; without Your Majesty on the throne they will find it very difficult to achieve anything." I was completely convinced that Japan recognized these facts, and built my policy on this assumption as well as the necessity of winning the hearts of the people of the Northeast.

15

Mausoleums and the Japanese

THE YEAR 1928 WAS ONE OF EXCITEMENT—A YEAR THAT made me both sad and happy. On the one hand, the Japanese issued a statement prohibiting Chinese troops from entering Manchuria or Mongolia and sent Japanese soldiers to Shantung Province to block the northward advance of Chiang Kai-shek's Kuomintang forces. On the other, the armies of Chang Tso-lin, Wu Pei-fu and Chang Tsung-chang, the war lords with whom I had connections, crumbled away in a series of defeats. Although my tutors and the Japanese advised me that since the Kuomintang was carrying out a major purge of Communist members the threat to me from "raging floods and wild beasts" seemed diminished, they informed me at the same time that I was in imminent danger and that my enemies were operating everywhere. But the event that gave me the biggest shock was the plundering of the Eastern Mausoleums by Sun Tien-ying.

These mausoleums in Malan Valley, which is in Tsunhua County of Hopei Province, are the imperial tombs of the Emperor Chien Lung and the Empress Dowager Tzu Hsi. In 1928 Sun Tien-ying, an ex-gambler, opium peddler and gangster-type war lord, before becoming a subordinate of Chiang Kai-shek, brought his troops into this area and began to carry out a well-planned campaign of tomb depredations. First he posted notices announcing that he was going to conduct military maneuvers, and then he cut all communications. Next he set a battalion of engineers to digging, and

Pu Yi at the time of his ascension to the Dragon Throne.

The Empress Dowager, Tzu Hsi (center), with members of her court.

The second Prince Chun, Pu Yi's father.

Mrs. Wang Chiao, the imperial wet nurse.

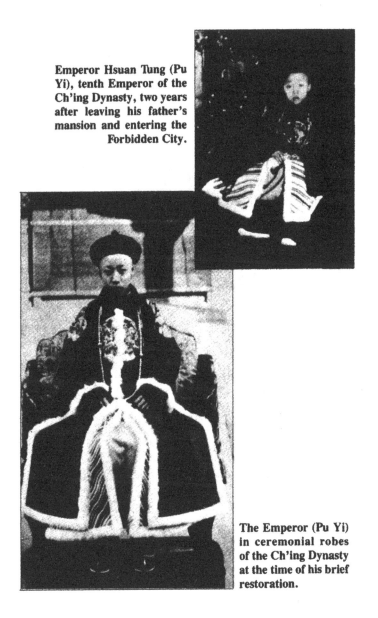

Emperor Hsuan Tung (Pu Yi), tenth Emperor of the Ch'ing Dynasty, two years after leaving his father's mansion and entering the Forbidden City.

The Emperor (Pu Yi) in ceremonial robes of the Ch'ing Dynasty at the time of his brief restoration.

Pu Yi at his wedding.

Pu Yi's British tutor, Sir Reginald Johnston, in Ch'ing robes.

Pu Yi's first wife, Wan Jung.

Birthday greetings in Tientsin.

Pu Yi with his courtiers and Japanese Army leaders in Manchukuo.

"Back to basics"; part of Pu Yi's "reeducation," at Fushun, during the brainwashing process.

Mr. Pu Yi, during the brainwashing process in Fushun, accuses the Japanese as war criminals.

A family reunion in Peking in the spring of 1961.

Pu Yi takes a look at industrial life in the "New" China.

Pu Yi leaving his house in Peking to go to the office with his new wife, Li Shu-hsien.

after three days and nights had cleared out all the treasures that had been buried with Chien Lung and Tzu Hsi.

Chien Lung and Tzu Hsi were the most extravagant Emperor and Empress of the Ch'ing Dynasty. In cultural and historical source materials I have read the following description of their mausoleums:

The tunnel to the tomb was lined with white marble and led through four beautifully carved marble gates. The "sleeping palace" or vaults in which the bodies rested were octagonal with domed ceilings on which were carved nine gleaming golden dragons. The area of the vaults themselves were about the same size as the Palace of Central Harmony in the Forbidden City. Chien Lung's inner and outer coffins were made of a special valuable hardwood. The burial pieces in these two tombs, besides the gold and silver ingots and funerary vessels, consisted of rare jewels and treasures. The funerary objects of Tzu Hsi consisted for the most part of pearls, emeralds, diamonds and other gems, and her phoenix crown was made of big pearls strung on gold wire. On her coverlet was a great peony studded with large pearls and on her arm was a bracelet in the form of a large chrysanthemum fashioned of diamonds of all sizes and six small plum blossoms paved with diamonds. This bracelet shone with a dazzling brilliance and glittering light.

In her hand was a demon-quelling wand about 3 inches long carved of emerald jade and on her feet were shoes embroidered with pearls. Besides this, there were 17 strings of pearl prayer beads in the coffin as well as several pairs of emerald jade bracelets.

Chien Lung's burial objects consisted of calligraphy, paintings, books, swords, jade pieces and also jade, coral and ivory carvings, plus gold statutes of Buddha, etc. The objects made of silk had already disintegrated beyond recognition.

The report of Sun Tien-ying's grave-robbery from the officials responsible for the protection of the Eastern Mausoleums gave me an even worse shock than the one I had received when I was expelled from the Forbidden City. The royal family and the retired Ch'ing officials were all aroused by it. Men of every faction, whether they were active in Ch'ing affairs or not, flocked to my house and expressed their hatred for the troops of Chiang Kai-shek, and Ch'ing veterans from all over the country sent funds for the restoration of the mausoleums. Spirit tablets for Chien Lung and Tzu Hsi were set up in the Chang Garden along with tablets for incense and mats for people to kneel on as if it were a funeral, and it was decided that these services should continue until the job of reconstruction was completed.

It was said that Sun Tien-ying sent some of the booty to Mme. Chiang Kai-shek and that the pearls from Tzu Hsi's phoenix crown became decorations for her shoes. My heart smoldered with a hatred I had never previously known and I made a vow before my weeping clansmen, with my face raised to heaven:

"If I do not avenge this wrong I am not a member of the Aisin-Gioro clan of the Ch'ing Dynasty."

I also swore that "as long as I am alive the Great Ch'ing shall not perish."

My longing for restoration and revenge reached a new intensity, and I resorted to divination to try to find out what the fate of the Chiang Kai-shek government and myself would be. The indications were that Chiang's power would fade by 1932 and that I should change the name of my reign from Hsuan Tung to Hsing Wu, or "Flourishing Valor" in English, but that such a change was a "heavenly secret" and the divinations concerning it should be revealed to no one. This kind of activity, which besides divination included fortune-telling and other forms of soothsaying, were accepted practices in the circle in which I moved in Tientsin and were part of its daily life. It gave me spiritual strength as well as guidance. Although it was secondary to the advice I received from my privy counselors, it was nonetheless important.

Nobody burning with ambition and longing for revenge as I was could have left everything to the will of heaven and not tried to do something himself. My experience of the past few years and the story of Chiang's rise to power combined to make me believe that if one wanted to achieve anything it was necessary to have military power, for the foreigners would support the man with an army as a matter of course. If an orthodox "Great Ch'ing Emperor" like myself had troops, then the foreigners would be bound to take me more seriously than some marshal who had started out as nothing more than a bandit chief or a gangster. I decided to send some of the most trusted members of my family to military school in Japan and regarded this as more important than going abroad myself.

I chose my brother Pu Chieh and a brother-in-law, Jun Chi, and asked the Japanese Consul General in Tientsin to recommend a private tutor to teach them Japanese. The man he selected, Takeo Toyama, turned out to be a member of the Black Dragon Society who knew many Japanese politicians. When he had taught my brother and brother-in-law Japanese for some time he went back to Japan to try to make arrangements for them to study there. He reported that although they would not immediately be able to enter the Japanese Army Cadet School, they could first go to a special academy for the sons of the Japanese nobility and receive the support of one of the most illustrious families in Japan. My two future generals left for Japan with Toyama in March, 1929, seven months after the plundering of the Eastern Mausoleums.

By 1929 most of my advisers in the Chang Garden believed that a restoration was only possible with Japanese assistance and that an arrangement with them was possible.

During my first year in Tientsin, the Japanese Consul General had invited me to visit a primary school for Japanese children. The children lined my route with paper flags in their hands and welcomed me with shouts of "ten thousand years"—a scene that made my eyes fill with tears. When the fighting between war lords was approaching Tientsin, the foreign garrisons in the various concessions organized an allied army and announced that they would deal with the Kuomintang Army if it came too close to the concessions. But only the Japanese garrison commander at Tientsin paid a special visit to the Chang Garden to say, "Please do not worry, Your Majesty. We are determined not to allow the Chinese soldiers to put one foot inside the concessions."

At New Year and my birthday the Japanese Consul General and the senior officers of the garrison always called upon me to offer their congratulations. They also invited me to attend the military parade on their Emperor's birthday. At one of these celebrations, when I arrived at the parade ground, the commander rode over on horseback to salute me, and when the review was over I and the other Chinese guests joined the Japanese in shouting "Long live the [Japanese] Emperor."

For many years colonels of the Japanese garrison used to come to tell me about current affairs, and they did this job most conscientiously, sometimes bringing along diagrams and charts which they had specially prepared. One of these was a General Yoshioka who was later Attaché to the Imperial Household and was with me for ten years in Manchukuo.

The main subjects of these talks by the Japanese staff officers were the civil wars, and they would often put forward their analysis that the "root cause of China's confusion is that she lacks a superior dragon or emperor." They would go on to discuss the superiority of the Japanese imperial system and say that the hearts of the people of China could be won only by the "Hsuan Tung Emperor." The corruption and impotence of the Chinese armed forces was a favorite topic of theirs, and, of course, they made invidious comparisons between the Chinese troops and the Imperial Japanese Army.

Once when I was taking a stroll beside the White River I saw a Japanese naval vessel moored along the shore. I do not know how the captain knew about me, but he suddenly appeared on the riverbank and respectfully invited me to visit his ship, the *Fuji*. When I went aboard the vessel, I was saluted by the officers. Since this was an impromptu occasion there were no interpreters on either side and we had to communicate in writing.[1] The captain later paid me a return visit with a number of his officers. I gave him a signed photograph when he asked for one, and he indicated that he regarded this as a very great honor.

At first I considered the Japanese as a single entity, which

---

[1] Chinese and Japanese can communicate to a certain extent by writing the Chinese characters that are used in the script of both languages.

consisted of the Japanese of the Peking Legation and the Tientsin Consulate General and garrison as well as the friends of Lo Chen-yu and my other advisers who held neither military nor civil office. The reason I had this view of them was that they all "protected" me and treated me as an emperor, all shared the same contempt for the Republic, all praised the Great Ch'ing and all expressed their willingness to help me.

But one day my father-in-law Jung Yuan informed me that some friends of his had told him that assassins in the service of Feng Yu-hsiang had been arriving in the British and French concessions. The situation became more alarming when a member of my household observed a suspicious person loitering near the main gate and trying to peer into the grounds. I hastily summoned the head of my General Affairs Office and the commander of my guard and told them to ask the Japanese police to tighten the precautions at the gate. I also gave instructions that the guards keep a careful watch on strangers outside the gate and allow no one in or out at night.

One night I was awakened by a gunshot outside the window and then another shot rang out. I jumped up from my bed and ordered the guard to muster, convinced that Feng Yu-hsiang's secret agents were in our midst at last. The whole household was roused and guards were posted everywhere. The policemen at the main gate were put on the alert and Japanese detectives stationed in the garden went out to investigate. When they captured the man who had fired the shots he turned out, to my utter astonishment, to be a Japanese.

The next day the head of my General Affairs Office told me that the man, whose name was Kishida, was a member of the Black Dragon Society. When he was taken to police headquarters the Japanese military authorities had rushed in and removed him at once. Apparently, it was pointed out to me, certain Japanese had sought to frighten me into becoming more dependent on their protection.

Besides the tutor to my brother Pu Chieh and my brother-in-law Jun Chi, I had had previous contact with members of this powerful secret Japanese espionage organization. In 1925, at my tutor Lo Chen-yu's urgings, I had met Nobuo

Tsukuda, an important figure in the society. Lo had told me that many powerful people in Japan, including some in the Army, were planning to help me achieve my restoration and had sent their representative Tsukuda to have a private talk with me. This society, the biggest of the Japanese "nongovernment" activist organizations, had originally been called the Black Ocean Association. Founded by Kotaro Hiraoka right after the Sino-French War, 1883–1885, it was the first organization of secret agents to carry out espionage activities in China. It started out with bases in Foochow, Chefoo and Shanghai and operated under such covers as consulates, schools and photographers' shops.

The name Black Dragon Society, which implied "beyond the Amur River" (the Chinese name for the Amur is the Black Dragon River) and thus the expansion of Japanese interests in the Northeast, was first used in 1901. The society played a useful role in the Russo-Japanese War of 1904–1905 and its membership was said to have reached several hundred thousand with correspondingly huge financial resources. Mitsuru Toyama was the most famous of its leaders and under his direction its members penetrated deep into every stratum of Chinese life. They operated everywhere: at the side of Ch'ing nobles and high officials, and among peddlers and servants, including the attendants in the Chang Garden. Many distinguished Japanese personalities in the late twenties and thirties were disciples of Toyama, a Buddhist with a long silver beard and a "kindly" face who loved roses and hated to leave his garden. Yet he was the man who, in an aroma of roses and while gently stroking his beard, planned the Society's appalling espionage conspiracies, "black" propaganda and murders on behalf of Japanese expansionism.

16

Living in the Temporary Palace

It seemed to me that the Chang Garden was free of all the things I disliked about the Forbidden City while preserving all the essentials. What I had most hated in the Forbidden City were the rules which did not even allow me to ride in a car or go for a walk in the streets and the infuriating people of the Household Department. However, I now had the freedom to do as I liked, and while others could remonstrate, they could not interfere.

The essential element of my life in the Forbidden City, my dignity, was preserved. Although I now wore an ordinary Chinese jacket and gown, or, more often, Western-style clothes instead of the cumbersome dragon robes, people still kowtowed and bowed to me. Built as an amusement park, the place where I now lived had no glazed tiles or carved and painted beams, but it was called a "temporary palace." I found the foreign-style two-story building with flush toilets and central heating far more comfortable than the Mind Nurture Palace. What had been the ticket office in the days when it was an amusement park was now a substitute "Guard Office of the Cloudless Heaven Gate." Although there was no longer a Southern Study, a Great Diligence Hall or a Household Department, people saw the "Office in Charge of the Affairs of the Ch'ing House During Its Stay in Tientsin" as their combined reincarnation. Nobles would come from Peking to stand in attendance before me. I was still addressed in exactly the same way as before and dates were given in terms of the reign period of my imperial title, "Hsuan Tung." All this seemed to me both natural and essential.

The only former senior official of the Household Department still with me was my father-in-law Jung Yuan. The others were either looking after my property in Peking or had retired. My former tutors Chen Pao-shen and Lo Chen-yu, and also Cheng Hsiao-hsu were the privy counselors whom I saw daily. They and other advisers came every morning and waited in a row of single-storied buildings to the west of the main building to be "summoned to audience." People who asked for an audience would wait to be called in a small lodge by the main gate, and these included military men, politicians, former Ch'ing officials, all kinds of "modern" figures, poets, writers, doctors, soothsayers and astrologers. Japanese police stationed at Tientsin, known as "white-caps," who lived in a house opposite the Chang Garden, used to note down all the comings and goings. Whenever I went out a Japanese plainclothes police-man would follow me.

The economics of the Chang Garden were naturally on a far smaller scale than those of the Forbidden City, but I still had a considerable fortune. Of the large quantities of valua-bles I had brought with me from the Forbidden City, some had been converted into money which was now earning interest in foreign banks and some had been turned into real estate to bring in rent. I still owned a lot of land in the Northeast and North China. The Ch'ing House and the Republican authorities set up a special office to deal with the renting and sale of these lands which were the "encircled" property of the Emperor. These lands had been obtained after the dynasty had moved to China from Manchuria and the term "encircled" was derived from their original seques-tration when their limits were described as being as exten-sive as a horse can run around within a given period of time. The numbers of these "encirclements" were very large. The two sides divided these properties 50/50 and our share from the sale of some of it was one of our sources of income. In addition we still had the great quantities of art treasures that Pu Chieh and I had moved out of the palace over a period of six months as I described earlier.

After I moved to Tientsin there were many places in Peking, Mukden and Tientsin to which money had to be sent every month and a number of offices were set up for this purpose: the Peking Office, the Office of Mausoleums and Temples, the Liaoning Provincial Office, the Imperial Bannerman Bureau and the Office for the Administration of Private Property. There were also officials appointed to look after the Eastern and Western Mausoleums of the Ch'ing House. According to a document I have found, the monthly expenditure for Peking and the mausoleums alone was $15,800; and the Tientsin figure must have been over $10,000. The biggest item on the budget was the money spent to influence war lords and this was in addition to my regularly budgeted expenditures. Purchases, excluding such items as cars or diamonds, probably accounted for two thirds of an average month's expenses. I spent far more money on buying things when in Tientsin than I had in Peking, and the amount increased every month.

We never tired of buying pianos, watches, clocks, radios, Western-style clothes, leather shoes and spectacles. Wan Jung had been a young lady of Tientsin, and so she knew even more ways of spending money on useless objects than I did. Whenever she bought for herself, Wen Hsiu would follow suit, and, when I bought something for Wen Hsiu, Wan Jung would want something too, as if a failure to receive something would detract from her status as Empress. This, in turn, would make Wen Hsiu complain and ask for more. This competitive buying eventually compelled me to set a quota on their monthly expenditures. Naturally, Wag Jung's allowance was somewhat higher. At first it was a thousand dollars, with Wen Hsiu's about eight hundred, but when we ran into financial difficulties the allowances were cut to $300 and $200 respectively. There was, of course, no limit to my personal spending.

As a result of this extravagance, the Chang Garden was reduced to desperate financial straits just as the Forbidden City had been, and sometimes we were unable to pay our bills, our rent, and even the salaries of the privy counselors and advisers.

While spending incalculable sums of money on quantities of useless objects, I also became far more convinced than I had ever been in the days when Johnston was with me that everything foreign was good and everything Chinese, except the Imperial System, was bad. A stick of Spearmint chewing gum or a Bayer aspirin, the cost of which was just a few cents, would be enough to make me sigh over the utter foolishness of the Chinese.

The treatment I received in the foreign concessions was quite unlike that accorded to other Chinese. In addition to the Japanese, the consuls general and senior military officers of the United States, Britain, France and Italy and the heads of foreign firms were all extremely respectful to me and addressed me as "Your Imperial Majesty." On their national days they would invite me to review their troops, visit their barracks and see their newly arrived aircraft and warships; and they would all come to congratulate me at New Year and on my birthday.

Before Johnston left me, which was not long after my arrival in Tientsin, he introduced me to the British Consul General and the Commander of the British garrison. They introduced me to their successors, who in turn introduced me to theirs, so that my social contacts with the British military commanders continued unbroken. When the Duke of Gloucester, the third son of King George V of England, passed through Tientsin, he visited me and accepted a photograph of me to take to his father. George V later wrote a letter thanking me for it, and asked the British consul to present his picture to me. I also exchanged photos with the King of Italy through the Italian Consul General.

I visited a number of barracks and attended many reviews of foreign troops. When these soldiers—whose presence in China had been conceded by my ancestress Tzu Hsi in the 1901 treaties—marched before me in their martial splendor, I was very pleased and felt that the way the foreigners were treating me proved that they still regarded me as Emperor.

There was a country club in Tientsin run by the English, a very grand establishment where Chinese were forbidden to pass through the main entrance. I was the only exception to this rule. I was allowed to enter freely and even bring along family members, and we all enjoyed the delights of being "special Chinese."

I made the most of the clothes and diamonds of the foreign

stores such as Whiteway, Laidlaw and Co. to dress myself up like foreign nobility. Whenever I went out I used to wear the very latest in Western clothes tailored from British cloth. I would have a diamond pin in my tie, diamond cuff links on my sleeve, a diamond ring on my finger, a "civilization stick" in my hand, and German Zeiss spectacles on my nose. My body would emit the combined odors of Max Factor, eau de cologne and camphor and I would be accompanied by two or three Alsatian dogs and a strangely dressed wife and consort.

This mode of living drew much criticism from my former tutors and advisers Chen Pao-shen and Hu Sze-yuan. They never opposed my excessive spending or my relations with foreigners, but when I attended the theatre or the movies, or wore Western clothes on an official visit, they would always remonstrate about this loss of imperial dignity. When repeated protests had no effect, Hu Sze-yuan submitted a memorial in which he took the blame on himself and asked my permission to retire.

He had previously asked leave to retire when he had run into me at the theatre with my wife Wan Jung who had accompanied me to see the famous Peking opera actor Mei Lan-fang. After I repeatedly begged him to stay, rewarded him with two fox-fur coat linings, and stressed my determination to accept his criticisms, his sorrow had turned to joy. He had then praised me as an "illustrious ruler" because I accepted the remonstration. I dealt with his new resignation in much the same way.

Wan Jung's twentieth birthday[1] occurred in our first year in Tientsin and my father-in-law wished to arrange for a foreign orchestra to come and play for the occasion. Some of the former Ch'ing officials heard about this, and hastened to remonstrate, protesting that "foreign music had a mournful sound' and could not possibly be played on an empress's "thousand year" day. As a result, we had no orchestra, and the old official who had protested was given $200. This must have been the time when I started to bestow rewards on ministers who criticized me.

From this time until my imprisonment in the Soviet Union

---

[1] The nineteenth, by the Western calendar.

I never went out to a theatre or a barbershop. The reason I followed Hu's advice was not because I was worried that he might go on complaining but because I thought he was right in saying that it was undignified for me to attend the theatre. One example of the "progress" I made occurred when a Swedish prince visited Tientsin and asked to meet me. I refused because I had seen a picture of him in the press with the actor Mei Lan-fang and thought that I should show my disapproval of his loss of dignity.

Hu Sze-yuan and other members of Chen Pao-shen's group differed from Cheng Hsiao-hsu, Lo Chen-yu and their associates in that they seemed to have despaired of a restoration and were opposed to trying anything desperate. They attached more importance than Cheng and the others to my imperial dignity, which was another reason I obediently did as they told me. Although I found many of their suggestions bigoted, I always accepted those which reflected their loyalty. True, I was living a strange life in a foreign settlement, but I never forgot my position and always remembered that an emperor had to abide by precedent.

When my consort Wen Hsiu suddenly asked for a divorce in 1931, the old officials, before the final settlement, asked me to issue an edict demoting her from the rank of consort to that of commoner, and I naturally complied.

The divorce from Wen Hsiu is evidence of my irregular family life. Instead of attributing the cause of divorce to emotions, it would be better to attribute it to the emptiness of our life in the Chang Garden. Even if I had had only one wife she would not have found life with me interesting since my one preoccupation was my restoration. Frankly, I did not know anything about love. In other marriages husband and wife were equal, but to me wife and consort were both the slaves and tools of their master.

Even in the Forbidden city, Wen Hsiu had written a short essay that reflected her sentiments about her sterile life.

She had been brought up from her earliest years to accept the old-fashioned three obediences and four virtues, and since she began the life of a palace consort before she reached the age of fourteen, her ideas of her duty to her sovereign husband were very deeply embedded in her. That she dared to ask for a divorce in spite of this upbringing was a sign of extraordinary courage. She overcame all kinds of obstacles to obtain it, and was badly treated afterward. It has been said that she was egged on to ask for the divorce by her family in order to obtain a considerable alimony, but in fact the difficulties her family created for her caused the greatest distress to someone of her mentality. After she had paid her lawyers and the middlemen, and after her family had taken what they wanted, she had very little left of the $50,000 alimony, and her psychological losses were even greater. A brother of hers actually published an open letter to her in a Tientsin paper in which he accused her of ingratitude to the Ch'ing House.

I do not know much about what happened to Wen Hsiu after the divorce, except that she became a primary-school teacher and died in 1950. She did not remarry.

In July, 1929, I moved from the Chang Garden to the Quiet Garden, which was also in the Japanese concession. This house previously had a different name, and the change to "Quiet Garden" was not without significance.

After the Northern Expedition the power of Chiang Kai-shek's Kuomintang extended to the north of China. The war lords with whom I was on good terms had collapsed, and the three provinces of the Northeast, in which I had placed such high hopes, had proclaimed allegiance to Chiang's Nanking Government. Everyone in the Chang Garden had relapsed into pessimism. Some of the Ch'ing veterans in my entourage had scattered and of the ministers who stayed with me only Cheng Hsiao-hsu and Lo Chen-yu still talked about restoration. The only question that the others considered was how the new "dynasty" of Chiang Kai-shek which had just conquered the country was going to treat me, the last Manchu. I too was very worried about this.

But this situation did not last long. We soon saw that under the Nanking Kuomintang Government, civil wars continued just as they had under the Peking war lord regime. The "unification" achieved by Chiang Kai-shek became more and more illusory and hopes revived in the Chang Garden when all had seemed lost. It seemed to us that the great enterprise of "unification" could be accomplished only by me, a view that was expressed not only by retired Ch'ing officials in my service but also by the Japanese staff officers who advised me on developments every week. Thus, the name I chose for my new residence—Quiet Garden—did not mean that I was looking for peace and quiet. It meant that I intended to wait, *quietly*, for my opportunity. And in the Quiet Garden I waited day after day, and month after month.

17

The Unquiet "Quiet" Garden

IN THE SUMMER OF 1931, AFTER TWO YEARS OF WAITING IN the Quiet Garden, we received some news.[1] A letter finally came from one of my advisers Tung Chi-hsu, who had gone to the Northeast, in which he said that he had uncovered the real feelings of General Honjo, the Commander of the Japanese Kwantung Army. Honjo felt that since the three Northeast provinces were not yet entirely under his control, it

---

[1] The crisis in Manchuria had been building up during the previous twelve months. The Manchurian war lord, "Young Marshal" Chang Hsueh-liang, with Chinese capital, had begun to build railroads in Southern Manchuria to compete with those of the Japanese-owned South Manchuria Railroad. Tokyo viewed this as a challenge to its dominant position in the area dating back to 1905. Also the Chinese took steps to restrict Korean immigration to Manchuria and Japan claimed it had jurisdiction over Koreans in China. A Japanese military officer was killed by Chinese soldiers and on September 18, 1931, Japanese forces seized Mukden. This was followed by almost unopposed occupation by the Japanese of all large cities in Manchuria and by the end of the year the victorious Japanese had pushed toward the Great Wall of China and occupied Jehol Province. These moves were not opposed by the Nationalist Government of Chiang Kai-shek who was busy elsewhere in China fighting the Communists. They did, however, lead to Japan's international isolation and raise the possibility of concerted action against it by the great powers through the League of Nations.

would be better for me not to come to Mukden until they were unified and stable. Since this was the opinion of the supreme arbiter of my destiny and the highest authority in Manchuria, I had no alternative but to obey and wait.

The days dragged by like years. Meanwhile I issued numbers of imperial edicts and sent my two nephews Hsien Yuan and Hsien Chi, who had just graduated from the Japanese Staff Officers' College, to the Northeast to win over some Mongol princes. I also gave beautiful jade pieces to some of the Manchurian leaders who had been among the first to submit to the Japanese occupation forces and, at the request of a Japanese officer, I wrote letters to the resistance fighter Ma Chen-shan and some Mongol princes advising them to surrender. I made a number of official appointments and prepared a plentiful reserve of edicts of appointment to official posts with blank spaces for names.

At this time I acted on a suggestion from Cheng Hsiao-hsu, who was becoming less cautious, and sent my brother's Japanese teacher to Japan to make contact with the new Army Minister and the leader of the Black Dragon Society. I wrote each of them letters in my own hand on yellow silk, copied from drafts by Cheng Hsiao-hsu. About three weeks after the dispatch of these letters, I met the Kwantung Army Staff Officer and representative, Doihara,[2] who conveyed a message to me from his superiors advising that I should now leave Tientsin and go to the Northeast.

Doihara, who built his military career out of aggression against China, first came to China in 1913 and was adjutant to a Kwantung Army major general. In 1924 he was closely associated with Chang Tso-lin, but in 1928, when the Kwantung Army decided to eliminate Chang, Doihara took part in the plot to blow up his train at Huang Ku Tun. Soon after this he was promoted to the rank of colonel and was placed in charge of a secret service organization headquartered at Mukden. From 1931 to 1937 he was involved in many secret Japanese plots against China, including riots, the setting up of local puppet authorities, and the engineering of outbreaks of fighting, as well as other subversive activities. In 1937, he

---

[2] Doihara was tried by the International Military Tribunal for the Far East and executed as a war criminal in 1948.

gave up covert work for overt activities and became a full general.

Because of the mysterious stories that were told about him, the Western press at that time described him as the "Lawrence of the East" and the Chinese papers said that he usually wore Chinese clothes and was fluent in several Chinese dialects. But when I met him he was dressed in Japanese-style Western clothes, and his spoken Chinese was not much. He used the services of the Tientsin garrison interpreter Yoshida to be sure that there would be no misunderstandings.

He was forty-eight at the time and the flesh around his eyes was flabby. He had a little moustache under his nose, and throughout our interview his face wore a bland and kindly smile, which made one feel that every word he spoke was completely reliable.

After politely inquiring about my health he turned to business. First he explained the Japanese action to me. He said it was aimed at dealing with the "Young Marshal" Chang Hsueh-liang, under whose rule "the people of Manchuria were reduced to destitution and the Japanese had no alternative but to use force." He claimed that the Kwantung Army had absolutely no territorial ambitions in Manchuria and "sincerely wants to protect the Manchurian people and enable them to set up their own independent state." He hoped that I would not miss this good opportunity and would soon return to the land from which my ancestors had arisen to undertake the leadership of the new state. Japan would sign a treaty of alliance with this country and its sovereignty and territorial integrity would be protected by Japan. As sovereign of this new state I would take charge of everything.

But there was still one big problem that worried me, and I asked Doihara what form the new state would take.

"As I have already mentioned, it will be independent and autonomous, and it will be headed by you."

"That is not what I asked. I wish to know whether it will be a republic or a monarchy? Will it, or will it not, be a monarchy?"

"This problem will be solved after you come to Mukden."

"No," I insisted. "I will only go if there is to be a restoration."

He smiled slightly and without changing the tone of his voice replied: "Of course it will be a monarchy; there's no question of that."

"Very well. If it is to be a monarchy, I will go."

"In that case I must ask Your Majesty to leave as soon as possible and to be in Manchuria by the sixteenth without fail. We can discuss the details in Mukden. Yoshida, the interpreter can arrange your journey."

After Doihara's departure, Yoshida told me that I should say nothing to the Consulate General about the meeting and that he would arrange my journey as far as Dairen. I decided that I would discuss the matter with no one but Cheng Hsiao-hsu, but since the news of my interview with Doihara was in the press the next day and its purpose was explained I had to answer advice and criticism from many quarters. Meanwhile, however, I did not reveal my own intentions.

Chen Pao-shen was horrified by this affair as were several of my other close advisers. Three days or so after Doihara's visit an emissary arrived from the Chiang Kai-shek Government in Nanking and unexpectedly offered to revive the Articles of Favorable Treatment and pay me either a yearly grant or perhaps a single lump sum provided that I lived anywhere except in Japan or the Northeast. I gave the emissary a noncommittal answer and by the time he tried to see me again I had already left Tientsin. I also received warning letters. One from a member of my own family implored me not to "acknowledge the enemy as my father" and advised me to treasure the dignity of the Chinese people. Two days before I left I was sent a basket of fruit which contained two bombs. Fortunately, the basket was intercepted and turned over to the Japanese police. The interpreter Yoshida informed me that the bombs had been produced in the arsenal of the "Young Marshal" Chang Hsueh-liang. A trusted young manservant, whom I later sent to military school in Japan, received a phone call from a waiter in the Victoria Café telling him that "suspicious people" who looked as if they had weapons concealed in their clothing had been making inquiries about me and that he was certain they were agents of the "Young Marshal."

After the bombs, the threatening letters, and the telephone call came the "Tientsin Incident." This was one of Doihara's masterpieces. The Japanese arranged for a crowd of Chinese in their pay to make trouble in the Chinese-administered part of the city. A state of emergency and martial law was then announced in the Japanese concession and communications with the Chinese city were cut. Armored cars drove up to "protect" the Quiet Garden, which was now isolated from the outside world. The only people allowed in and out were Cheng Hsiao-hsu and his son, Cheng Chui.

18

Crossing the White River

THE DAY OF MY DEPARTURE WAS SET FOR NOVEMBER 10, 1931. I used lots of ingenuity in developing what I hoped would be a safe plan and scheduled my departure for after dark so that I could slip out, unseen, through the main gate of the Quiet Garden. Originally, I had hoped to avoid the main gate and leave through the garage door which opened directly on the street. Thus I told my servant, Big Li, to see whether it could be opened, but he reported that it had not been used for so long that the posters which had been plastered over it on the street side had sealed the door fast. It was therefore decided that I was to hide in the rumble seat of a roadster. One of my aides would serve as chauffeur while another would sit beside him.

Waiting for me in his car not very far from the main gate was the Japanese interpreter, Yoshida. As soon as he saw our car it was arranged that he would follow in his.

My departure occurred on the third day after the Tientsin Incident. Martial law prevailed in the Japanese concession as well as in the neighboring Chinese-controlled areas. Although no Chinese vehicles were allowed on the streets, whenever my car was stopped at a crossroad, or at a barbed-wire obstacle or by Japanese soldiers, it was allowed to pass after Yoshida gave a signal. My driver was completely inexperienced and a very poor chauffeur. As soon as he had passed through the main gate of the Quiet Garden, he ran into a light pole so that I bumped my head on the lid of one of my suitcases, and throughout the trip I was shaken up most uncomfortably by his bad driving. Nevertheless, we managed to reach our destination, which was a Japanese restaurant.

After the automobile came to a stop at the restaurant, my aide and Yoshida opened up the rumble seat and helped me out. The three of us entered the restaurant together. Here a Japanese captain, who had been waiting for us for some time, produced a Japanese Army greatcoat and cap and hurriedly put them on me. Then the captain and I entered a Japanese military car sent by the Commanding Officer of the garrison of the Japanese concession. This car had no trouble at all passing the various roadblocks, and we went straight to a dock on the bank of the White River. Yoshida and the captain helped me from the car. I noticed right away that we were no longer in Japanese territory and became somewhat worried. Yoshida whispered to me in a low voice: "Never mind, this is the British concession."

Yoshida and the captain each took one of my arms and hurried me along a concrete wharf until we reached a small darkened motor launch, which we boarded. In the cabin, I found Cheng Hsiao-hsu and his son Cheng Chui, as planned, as well as three Japanese. The captain of the launch explained that there were also more than ten Japanese soldiers on board in charge of an officer whose sole duty was to escort me safely. The boat had been sent out by the Transport Section of the local garrison, and because of its special "transport" mission, there were piles of sandbags and steel protective shields aboard. About twenty years later, in a Japanese magazine I read some reminiscences about my escape in which the author claimed that if the launch had been detected by Chinese soldiers there was a big drum of gasoline aboard with which to blow us up if escape was impossible. According to the article my seat in the cabin was only a few feet from this incendiary bomb!

As soon as Yoshida, the interpreter, and the captain who had brought me to the launch left, we pulled away from the dock. When the lights of the boat came on, I gazed at the night scene on the river and let my mind be overwhelmed by thoughts. I had been to the White River quite a few times before, in daylight, and had visited aboard a Japanese destroyer and gunboat. On each of these occasions I gave myself up to dreams of my restoration. I had thought of the White River as the road of my escape to the ocean and to foreign help. Now I was actually sailing on it and was immensely happy. But, as it turned out, my happiness was premature. For Cheng Chui told me that we were now beyond the foreign concessions and would soon be within Chinese jurisdiction where we might encounter hostile troops.

After hearing this my heart nearly jumped into my throat. When I looked at the faces of the Japanese, I saw that they were all fixed and grim. No one spoke. Then, from the riverbank, I heard a voice: "Stop! Halt!"

Suddenly, as if my nerves had been severed, I nearly fainted and collapsed on the floor. The Japanese soldiers rushed onto the deck, and I heard orders given in low voices and the scurry of running feet.

When I looked out of the cabin window I saw soldiers behind each sandbag aiming their rifles toward the shore. The speed of the boat seemed to decrease and we were heading directly toward the riverbank. This puzzled me. I could not understand why we should be heading in the direction from which the order had come to halt. The boat's lights were turned off, and I heard a burst of gunfire from the bank. All of a sudden, the motor roared into full speed and the boat shot forward while it veered to one side as if we were about to leap over the bank itself. Meanwhile the shouting from the bank and the gunfire receded into the distance. The Japanese plan had succeeded! First they had pretended to obey the order to halt by approaching the bank slowly; but then, when the Chinese were taken in by the ruse, they had veered off from the bank and bounded away.

After a while, the lights came on again and life returned to the cabin. About midnight we reached the mouth of the river at Taku, and while we waited for the merchantman, *Awaji Maru*, to pick us up, the Japanese soldiers produced *miso* soup, pickled cabbage and sake. Cheng Hsiao-hsu became very lively and started talking about the racial and cultural ties between China and Japan. He described our escape as a "heroic episode" and offered toasts to the Japanese soldiers. Then he began to sing and compose poems, one of which ran something like this:

Two Emperors of the same Continent wish to be almighty and deserving of respect,
While seven guests, passengers on the same ship, speak of Imperial coexistence.
It is not an empty boast to say that man can triumph over his destiny,
For when there are common goals there is no need for lengthy talk.

Because we had eaten a Japanese meal together, Cheng Hsiao-hsu later was inspired to design two personal seals for me in commemoration of the event. One seal told of the times of civil wars in the remote past when a prince escaped his captors and managed to regain his throne. The other seal celebrated the eating together of a meal of rice paste and oatmeal which symbolized the revival of the Later Han Dynasty.[1] By recalling these two incidents from the historical past of China, he sought to remind me of how we had survived a crisis and shared the common experience of a new beginning.

Once we were aboard the *Awaji Maru*, Cheng Hsiao-hsu talked incessantly about his ambition to govern the country, and his words seemed not to cease until the morning of November 13th when we put in at the South Manchuria Railway dock at Yingkow in Liaoning Province. I had imagined that there would be a crowd to give me the sort of welcome I had received when I visited the Japanese primary school in Tientsin—people waving flags, cheering, and shouting "Long live the Emperor." But the nearer the boat drew to the dock the fewer signs I saw of any such welcome. There were no crowds, no flags. When I went ashore I discovered that the handful of people there to meet me were all Japanese.

---

[1] The Later Han Dynasty occurred during a period of political unrest. At one time the Han Emperor fled, ate a coarse meal and was then restored to power. Since then the partaking of this particular food has become symbolic of an Imperial restoration.

I was immediately taken to the station and, without being given a word of explanation, was transported to the warm springs resort of Tangkangtzu, where, full of suspicion, I entered the Tuitsuike Hotel. Run by the Japanese South Manchuria Railway Company, this hotel was a luxuriously furnished Western-style building in the Japanese manner and was reserved for Japanese army officers, high officials of the South Manchuria Railway, and Chinese bureaucrats. I was shown to a suite of rooms on the second floor where my former tutor and adviser Lo Chen-yu, the head of my general affairs office in Tientsin Tung Chi-hsu, and my counselor Shang Yen-ying were waiting. After greeting me, Lo Chen-yu told me that he was in the midst of discussions with the Kwantung Army regarding my restoration and the founding of the new state. He explained that it would not do for news of my arrival to leak out before the conclusion of the discussions, and that it would also be wrong if any of us but he were to be seen outside the hotel. I did not understand the significance of his advice and simply thought that this explained why nobody had come to welcome me. I believed that the talks with the Kwantung Army would present no problem and that soon the news could be announced that I, the Great Ch'ing Emperor, had returned to the throne in the palace of my ancestors, in Mukden. I did not notice the worried expression on the faces of Cheng Hsiao-hsu and his son. I happily ate an exotic Japanese supper as I gazed out of the window at the beautiful sunset, then went to bed, at peace with the world.

The next morning I discovered that my happiness had been premature. After washing, I wished to go out for a stroll to look at the scenery.

"It's not possible! They won't let anyone out," said my attendant.

"Why not?" I asked in surprise. "Who said so? Go downstairs and ask!"

Thus I found out that I was blockaded in the Tuitsuike Hotel, that strangers were forbidden to come near the building, and that the guests on the floor below could not come up to the second floor, which was reserved entirely for the use of my little group.

"This is a safety precaution, a safety precaution for Your

Majesty," one of my Japanese escorts said in Japanese-accented Chinese.

"How long are we going to stay here?" asked Cheng Hsiao-hsu.

"That depends on Colonel Itagaki."

"What has happened to Lo Chen-yu?"

"He's gone to Mukden to see Colonel Itagaki. They are personally discussing the new state, and when they have reached agreement he will come to take Your Majesty to Mukden. To carry out so great an undertaking is easier said than done. Be patient, Your Majesty. When the time is ripe you will be invited to go."

"To go where?" cut in Cheng. "To Mukden?"

"That will also be decided by Colonel Itagaki."

Furious, I left them and sent for Tung Chi-hsu to come and see me in another room. I asked him why he had sent me a telegram from Mukden saying "everything ready."

I did not know at the time that the Japanese were in a state of desperate confusion. Japan had been internationally isolated, and, within the country, there were still differences of opinion as to what form their rule over the new colony of Manchuria should take, so that the Kwantung Army could not yet allow me to appear publicly on the scene. My only reaction was that the Japanese were not being as respectful toward me as they had been in Tientsin. After a week of uneasy waiting I received a telephone call from Itagaki asking me to move to Port Arthur, where I stayed in the Yamato Hotel. Here, as before, the whole of the upper part of the building was reserved for us and I was told that I was not to go downstairs. Subsequently, however, my Privy Councilors were allowed out and permitted to travel freely about Manchuria.

When I asked Lo Chen-yu to explain this to me, he said, "It would injure Your Majesty's celestial dignity were you to show your face. If you wait until your ministers have arranged everything, then Your Majesty can ascend the throne at the appropriate time and receive homage with decorum and propriety." He also explained that the Kwantung Army was my host for the time being, and until I ascended the throne I should regard myself as its guest. Meanwhile it was only right that I should do as my hosts thought fit. Although I was increasingly impatient, I had no choice but to force myself to wait.

Actually, however, the delay frightened me while I was in Port Arthur. The reason for my concern was not as much my isolation as the admission by the Japanese that the Kwantung Army had not yet decided the form of the new state. This situation, which conflicted with what Doihara had told me in Tientsin, was far more depressing than having nobody greet me at the harbor at Yingkow. Then I had believed that "preparations were incomplete," or my arrival had "not yet been announced." But what did they mean when they said that "the form of the state had not been settled"?

Three months later, on February 19, 1932, came the news that the Administrative Committee for the Northeast had passed a resolution to set up a republic in the Northeast. This committee, chaired by Chang Ching-hui, was composed of a number of high Manchurian officials who had already submitted to the Japanese. On the same day it issued, under the direction of Itagaki, a "declaration of independence" from the rest of China. Everyone in my entourage except Cheng Hsiao-hsu and his son became panicky and indignant.

I seethed with hatred of Doihara and his associate Itagaki as I paced back and forth like a madman, breaking cigarettes in half. I threw a book of divination called *The Art of Knowing the Future* on the floor. I remembered my Quiet Garden and thought that if I could not become an emperor I would be much better off leading a comfortable life as an exile. I could sell some of my treasures and enjoy life abroad. Finally, I decided to let the Kwantung Army know that if they would not agree to my demands I would return to Tientsin. Neither Lo Chen-yu nor Cheng Hsiao-hsu opposed this course of action when I told them about it. I agreed to a suggestion of Lo's that I should send a gift to Itagaki, and I gave Lo a few of the valuables I had brought with me. Just then Itagaki telephoned to ask Lo and Cheng to come for talks. I instructed them to stand firm and make my views clear to Itagaki and then I prepared a list of twelve reasons why my immediate restoration was essential to the proposed new and independent Manchurian state:

1. The right system is essential if we are to follow the moral code of East Asia which dates back five millennia.
2. The right system is essential to the carrying out of the Kingly Way[2] and moral principles.
3. To rule the state one must have the trust and respect of the people, and for this the right system is essential.
4. China and Japan are fraternal countries, and for their joint survival and welfare they must respect the time-honored morality and ensure that both peoples have an identical spirit. For this the right system is essential.
5. China has suffered from the disasters of democracy for over two decades, and, apart from a selfish minority, the great majority of the people loathe the Republic and long for the Ch'ing Dynasty. For this reason the right system is essential.
6. The Manchu and Mongol peoples have always preserved their ancient customs, and the right system is essential if we are to win their allegiance.
7. The Republican system is very widespread while the numbers of the unemployed daily increase. This constitutes a most serious threat to the Japanese Empire, but if the imperial order is revived in China, this will do a great deal to preserve the intellectual and spiritual qualities of the peoples of our two countries. For this reason the right system is essential.
8. The Great Ch'ing has a history of over two hundred years in China and of over a century in Manchuria before that. To observe the way of life of the people, calm their minds, maintain the peace of all parts of the country, preserve the Oriental spirit, carry out the revival of the Kingly government and consolidate the imperial order in our two countries, it is essential to have the right system.

---

[2] A political philosophy of the Confucianists of ancient China. They wished the rulers to govern with "benevolence" and "righteousness," and they called this the "Kingly Way."

9. The rise of Japan dates from the Kingly rule of Emperor Meiji. His edicts to his ministers all propagate morality and give instruction in loyalty and righteousness. While science was learned from Europe and America, morality was based on Confucius and Mencius. Since the ancient spirit of the Orient was preserved and the people were saved from the contagion of disgusting European practices, they love and esteem their elders, and protect their country as readily as one's hand protects one's head. That is why I respect him. The right system is essential if we are to follow in the steps of the great Emperor Meiji.

10. The Mongol princes continue to use their old titles, and if they are abolished under a republic they will be disappointed and disaffected, and there will be no way of ruling them. For this reason the right system is essential.

11. Japan deserves our deepest admiration for the way in which she has assisted the Three Eastern Provinces [the Northeast] and taken thought for the welfare of their thirty million people. My wish is that we should not restrict ourselves to thirty million people but should take the Three Eastern Provinces as a base from which to arouse the whole nation and save the people from the disasters that have befallen them. This would lead to the common survival and prosperity of East Asia, a matter which closely involves all of the ninety million people of Japan. There should therefore be no divergence between the political systems of our two countries. To bring about the prosperity of both countries is indispensable.

12. Since I retired from office in 1911, I have lived among the people for twenty years. I have had no thought for my personal glory and have been guided only by a wish to save the people. If someone else would undertake the responsibility for the country and bring disasters to an end with the True Way, I would be happy to remain a commoner. If I am forced to assume this burden, it is my personal

opinion that without the correct title and real power to appoint officials and administer the country, I will be unable to bring twenty years of misgovernment to an end. If I am ruler only in name and am hedged in by restrictions, I will be of no help to the people and will only make their plight worse. This would not be my original intention, and would increase my guilt, and I absolutely refuse to bear the responsibility for this. If I were only concerned about my personal glory, I would be only too pleased to be given the land and the people after two decades of living in obscurity. What would I care whether I become president or monarch? It is purely for the sake of the people, of the state, of our two countries of China and Japan, and of East Asia as a whole, and not because of the slightest self-interest, that I maintain that the right system is indispensable.

Although Cheng Hsiao-hsu agreed to present my twelve demands he never did so. Instead, he agreed to the Kwantung Army proposal that the new state be a republic, and he undertook to persuade me to become its "chief executive." When Cheng Hsiao-hsu returned from his meeting with Itagaki and admitted what had happened, he tried to pacify me by citing historical precedent, by arguing that the "chief executive" would be sovereign, and by telling me that my hopes of restoration would be finished if I did not go along with the Japanese for the time being.

When this did not work, he said that since Itagaki wanted to see me that afternoon, I could talk to him then.

"Let him come," I angrily replied.

I met Seishiro Itagaki[3] on the afternoon of February 23, 1932, in the presence of an interpreter from the Kwantung Army. Itagaki was a short man with a shaven head, and the

---

[3] Itagaki was first appointed to the staff of the Kwantung Army in 1929. He was one of the chief architects of the setting up of the Manchukuo regime. In 1934 he became Chief of Staff of the Kwantung Army, and during World War II was made Commander in Chief of the Japanese 7th Army stationed at Singapore.

blue-white pallor of his clean-shaven face contrasted with the black of his eyebrows and his small moustache. He was the most neatly uniformed Japanese officer I had ever seen; his shirt cuffs were of dazzling whiteness and the creases in his trousers were razor-sharp. This elegance and his habit of gently rubbing his hands made me feel that he was scholarly and graceful.

First he thanked me for the presents I had sent him and then he went on to say that he had come on the orders of General Honjo, the Commander of the Kwantung Army, to report to me on the "problems of the formation of the new state of Manchukuo." He elaborated systematically on the "justice" of the actions of the Japanese Army and its "sincerity in helping the Manchurian people to establish a paradise of the Kingly Way." As he spoke I nodded in approval and in my heart I hoped he would hurry up and answer the question about which I was most concerned. At last he came to the point.

"The new state will be called 'Manchukuo' [Manchuland]. Its capital will be Changchun, which will be renamed Hsinking [New Capital]. This nation will be composed of five races: Manchus, Hans, Mongols, Japanese and Koreans. . . ."

Without waiting for the interpreter to finish translating, he produced from his briefcase the "Declaration of Independence of the Manchu and Mongol People" and the proposed five-colored Manchukuo flag and put them on the table in front of me. Pushing them aside with a trembling hand, and with my lungs ready to burst with rage, I asked:

"What sort of state is this? Certainly it isn't the Great Ch'ing Empire!"

"Naturally, this will not be a restoration of the Great Ch'ing Empire," answered Itagaki, unflustered. "This will be a new state. The Administrative Committee for the Northeast has passed a unanimous resolution acclaiming Your Excellency head of state. You will be the Chief Executive."

The phrase "Your Excellency" enraged me. My blood rushed to my face. Never before had I been thus addressed by the Japanese, and I was not prepared to tolerate the abolition of my imperial title, not even in exchange for the two million square *li* of territory and the thirty million people of the Northeast. I was so worked up I could scarcely sit still.

"If names are not right then speech will not be in order," I shouted, "and if speech is not in order then nothing will be accomplished! The people of Manchuria are longing not for me as an individual, but for the Great Ch'ing Emperor. If you abolish the title, their loyalty will be lost. I must ask the Kwantung Army to reconsider this."

Itagaki gently rubbed his hands and, his face wreathed in smiles, he said, "The Manchurian people have already expressed their wishes by acclaiming Your Excellency as head of the new state, and the Kwantung Army is in full agreement with them."

"But Japan has an imperial system! How can the Kwantung Army go about founding republics?"

"If Your Excellency does not like the term 'republic' then we will not use it. This will be a state built on the 'chief executive' system."

"I am very grateful for all the enthusiastic assistance your honorable country has given, but I cannot accept a 'chief executive system.' The imperial title has been handed down to me by my ancestors, and were I to abandon it, I would be lacking in loyalty and filial piety."

Itagaki seemed most understanding. "The office of chief executive will be for the transitional period. It is perfectly well known that Your Majesty is the twelfth Emperor of the Great Ch'ing Dynasty, and I am sure that after the formation of a national assembly, a constitution will be adopted restoring the monarchial system."

"There are *no* good national assemblies! Furthermore, the first Great Ch'ing Emperor was never given his title by an assembly!"

The argument continued for over three hours. Itagaki remained calm and continued to smile, while he rubbed his hands gently. Finally, he picked up his leather briefcase as a sign that he did not wish to go on any longer. The smile vanished from his face and, when he addressed me, he reverted from "Your Majesty" to "Your Excellency." "Your Excellency should think it over carefully," he said. "We will continue our discussions tomorrow." With that frosty remark he left me.

That evening, in an effort to improve the relations between us, I gave a banquet for Itagaki and the next morning he summoned my advisers to the Yamato Hotel and asked them to give me his final decision: "The demands of the Army cannot be altered at all. We will regard rejection as evidence of a hostile attitude and act accordingly. This is our final word."

These words, when relayed to me, left me stunned. My legs turned to jelly and I collapsed speechless onto a sofa.

"Since things have developed to such a stage, there is no use in regrets," was Lo Chen-yu's dejected view. "Our only course is to set a time limit of one year for this transitional period and if the imperial system is not restored by then, Your Majesty can resign. Let us see how Itagaki reacts to this condition."

Seeing no other way out, I sighed and sent Cheng Hsiao-hsu to see if Itagaki would agree.

Cheng soon returned, his face beaming, to say that Itagaki had agreed and was going to give a small banquet that evening in honor of "the future Chief Executive."

IV

MY FOURTEEN-YEAR RESTORATION

19

Chief Executive of Manchukuo

AT ITAGAKI'S BANQUET MY THOUGHTS WERE CONFLICTING and I did not know whether to be happy or sad about my future destiny. He had assigned a Japanese prostitute to each of his guests in an effort to make his party festive, and he himself was having a good time and embracing them right and left.

He drank a lot and laughed aloud, making no effort to conceal his mood of satisfaction. At first, when he still had some control over himself, he drank a toast to me in a most respectful fashion. He smiled a subtle hint of congratulations when he said, "May your future be smooth and may your interests be fulfilled." This pleased me, but later, as he drank more and more, his face became pale and the situation changed.

When one of the prostitutes, in broken Chinese, asked me, "Do you make a living as a businessman?" Itagaki roared with laughter.

After the banquet, my mood of uncertainty persisted for several days until several old Ch'ing courtiers came to visit me after having obtained permission from the Kwantung Army. They were all very happy. Although they claimed to be saddened by my demotion to the rank of Chief Executive, they gave me a long list of historical precedents to illustrate that in the past many founders of new dynasties frequently had to rely on friendly neighbors at the outset of their careers. Their words of encouragement, as well as some favorable divination obtained by one of my high officials, gradually soothed me.

On February 28, 1932, the All Manchurian Assembly of Mukden, at the direction of the Kwantung Army, passed a resolution declaring the independence of the Northeast and recommending that I become Chief Executive of the new state. I was advised by the Japanese and Cheng Hsiao-hsu that representatives from this conference would come to Port Arthur to petition me and that I should be ready. It was decided that there would be two replies; the first would be a refusal, and the second, to be delivered after the representatives had asked me a second time to assume the role, would indicate my acceptance.

On March 1, nine representatives of the conference arrived in Port Arthur. Cheng Hsiao-hsu welcomed them on my behalf and gave them my first message. Later I received them personally in audience for twenty minutes. They urged me to accept and I refused politely. On March 5, according to plan, the number of representatives was increased to twenty-nine and they came a second time to "request me" to accept. This time they accomplished their mission.

The day after I had performed this little show, my wife Wan Jung and I, accompanied by several others including Cheng Hsiao-hsu, returned to Tangkangtzu, where we spent the night. The next morning we all proceeded to Changchun, arriving at three o'clock on the afternoon of March 8. Even before the train came to a stop, I could hear army bands playing martial music and the shouting of the crowds at the station. As I walked down the platform, I was pleased to see a great number of Japanese gendarmes and soldiers as well as a horde of people dressed both in long Chinese gowns and Western-style clothes. Everyone was waving a small flag and I was deeply moved. The reception more than compensated for the lack of any welcome at the Yingkow dock. One of my aides pointed to some yellow dragon flags in the midst of the Japanese flags. "Those are former imperial bannermen," he explained. "They have been hoping to see Your Majesty for over twenty years." Upon hearing this, I couldn't hold back the tears, for I felt more than ever that I had great expectations.

As I sat in the automobile, my thoughts went back to the

Forbidden City. I recalled the time when I had been ejected from the palace by the Christian General, Feng Yu-hsiang, as well as the affair of the Eastern Mausoleums and the vows I had once taken. My heart became so inflamed by hatreds and desires that I did not notice the sights along the streets of Changchun or the sullen, intimidated faces of the people.

Before very long we drove into a courtyard and arrived at the "Chief Executive's Mansion," which had formerly been an imperial district government office. Even by Changchun standards it was not large and was in a dilapidated state. I was told that this would be my home only temporarily. On the following day, a large parlor, which was hurriedly prepared for me, served as the hall for the ceremonial assumption of my new duties.

The General Director of the South Manchurian Railway, General Honjo of the Kwantung Army, his Chief of Staff, Itagaki, and other important celebrities came to attend the ceremony. Other participants were former Ch'ing officials, several Manchu and Mongolian princes as well as a number of former war lords and local leaders such as Chang Ching-hui. Some of the lawyers who had handled my divorce were also present.

For the ceremony I wore a Western-style formal suit. Under the eyes of important Japanese personalities, all of the "founding" officials bowed to me three times and I acknowledged this obeisance with a single bow. Chang Ching-hui, representing the Manchurian people, presented me with the seal of office as Chief Executive. It was wrapped in yellow silk. Cheng Hsiao-hsu then read my "declaration as Chief Executive."

The human race must emphasize virtue. But if there is racial prejudice and one race suppresses others and glorifies itself, virtue will decline. The human race must also treasure benevolence. But if there is international conflict and one country damages another in trying to serve itself, benevolence will decline.

I am founding a new State based on virtue and benevolence. We want to do away with racial bias and conflicts among nations. The Kingly Way and Paradise on

Earth will then be realized. I hope all my countrymen will try to understand.

The foreign guests were received after the ceremony. The Director General of the South Manchurian Railway presented me with a "message of felicitation" and my old tutor Lo Chen-yu read aloud my message of reply. Then we all went out into the courtyard where the flag was raised and we had our pictures taken.

That same afternoon I took up a pen and signed my first official document as Chief Executive. It was the appointment of Cheng Hsiao-hsu, my former Privy Councilor and the man who had originally tried to help me reform the Household Department in the Forbidden City, as Prime Minister with a mandate from me to form a cabinet. General Honjo as Commander of the Kwantung Army had concurred in this appointment.

When I walked out of my office I ran into two old courtiers whose faces were sad because they knew they were not on the list of appointees as either cabinet officers or ambassadors. I told them I wished to keep them near me as personal aides. One of them, while sighing, thanked me, but the other said that he had to attend to family matters in Tientsin and requested that I let him go.

On the following day, Lo Chen-yu came to see me to tender his resignation. In the list of appointments the position he had received was only that of Counselor and he was not satisfied at all. Although I indicated my desire to keep him, he returned to Dairen where he became a dealer in imitation antiques.

The dragon flags and the army band at Changchun station, the ceremony that was performed on my assumption of duties as Chief Executive, and the messages of felicitation at the reception for foreign guests had impressed me deeply and made me very happy. Since I had already openly appeared in public there was absolutely no turning back, and besides, I thought that if I could maneuver the Japanese well, they would perhaps support my restoration as Emperor. I no longer believed that I had humbled myself by becoming Chief Executive, but actually regarded the position as a "stairway" leading to an Emperor's throne.

My main problem seemed to center on how best to utilize this stairway to climb to the throne. After thinking about this for several days, I gave Cheng Hsiao-hsu and Hu Sze-yuan[1] the result of my deliberations. "I want to tell you," I explained "that I have taken three vows. First of all I wish to change all my past habits. My tutor Chen Pao-shen, more than ten years ago, told me that I was lazy and undignified. I therefore vow from now on never to be that. Second, I am not going to avoid hardships and I vow diligently to restore my ancestral heritage. Third, I hope that heaven will bestow on me an imperial heir to succeed to the Great Ch'ing Dynasty. If my three wishes are fulfilled I can then die with my eyes closed."

About a month later, the Chief Executive's Mansion was moved to a remodeled and refurnished building. In order to show my determination I named it the "Mansion of Respect for the People" and also renamed my office building the "Mansion of Diligence for the People."

From this time on I arose early every morning and went to my office to work until night. Since I had vowed to restore my ancestral heritage, I readily accepted the directions of the Kwantung Army so that I could rely on it in the future, and I worked diligently to utilize my position and power as a "sovereign." But my hard work from morning to night did not continue for very long. I had no business to administer and I soon discovered that the power and authority of the Chief Executive were only shadows without substance.

---

[1] A close associate of Pu Yi's tutor Chen Pao-shen.

20

Imperial Dreams

IN THE ORGANIZATIONAL STATUTE OF MANCHUKUO WERE 13 clauses dealing with the authority of the Chief Executive. Article 1 stated that "the Chief Executive controls Manchukuo." Articles 2, 3 and 4 stipulated that I should direct the "legislative power," administer the "executive power," perform the "judicial power" and that I should have the right to issue "emergency decrees" which would have the effect of laws, to set up the "personnel system and appoint officials" and to be "Commander of the Army, Navy and Air forces." I was also placed in control of "general and special problems, the commutation of punishment, the restoration of civil rights," and so on. In fact, however, I didn't even have the power to decide whether or not I could pass out of the door to go for a walk.

One day I decided to take a stroll to Tatung Park with my wife Wan Jung and two of my younger sisters. Soon after we entered the park, automobiles full of Japanese gendarmes and Chief Executive Mansion Police drove up and asked me to return. Later, the Japanese Advisor to the Chief Executive Mansion told me that in order to preserve my prestige and dignity, as well as for my safety, I could not go out in private, and from that time on, except for special arrangements made by the Kwantung Army, I never left the Executive Mansion.

After I had worked diligently for a few days I began to have doubts about my prestige and dignity. Although, on the surface, I seemed to be busy from morning to night seeing the new ministers and counselors of cabinet rank, they never talked business with me. Whenever I asked them about "official business" their replies were either to the effect that the problems already had been handled by the Deputy Minister or "we shall have to ask the Deputy Minister about that." The Deputy Minister was always Japanese and he did not come to see me.

Hu Sze-yuan was the first to complain of this situation officially. He agreed with Cheng Hsiao-hsu that all authority in each ministry should belong to the Minister and that important affairs should be decided by the Chief and then handed down through the ministry for administration. The Deputy Minister, he maintained, should not be allowed to have the final say. Cheng replied that since we were using the cabinet system, all political affairs should be decided by the Council of State and each week the Prime Minister could take all important documents and cases passed on by the Council to the Chief Executive for approval. He claimed that this was the procedure followed in Japan. He agreed however, that the Deputy Ministers should not be all powerful and said that he planned to discuss this matter with the Commander of the Kwantung Army.

Just how Cheng negotiated the matter I was not told, but Hu Sze-yuan subsequently described to me an actual meeting of the State Council so that I could understand the relationship between the Minister and Deputy Minister. At this particular meeting there was a discussion of the salaries of the Ministers and Deputy Ministers. As usual, all the resolutions to be acted upon had been prepared and printed and distributed by the General Administrative Bureau of the Kwantung Army. In the past, the ministers, usually without any discussion, had indicated their approval. But in this case the ministers themselves gave serious thought to the proposal and opinions were expressed, indicating their dissatisfaction. The crucial point was that in the draft resolution it was stipulated that the Japanese officials' salary scale would be 40 percent higher than the Manchukuo officials. The Minister of Finance argued that "since this is a very complex racial state all the races should be treated equally. Why should the Japanese receive special treatment," he asked, "and why should they receive higher salaries?" This led to an extensive discussion and various opinions were expressed by the Manchukuo officials. The Director of the General Affairs Bureau then called in the Section Chief for Personnel who had drafted the resolution.

The Chief of Personnel said: "If one wishes to talk about equality one must find out if ability is or is not equal. Since the Japanese have greater ability, naturally their salaries should be higher. Besides, the Japanese standard of living is higher. They were born to eat white rice; they cannot live on sorghum like the people of Manchukuo."

Upon hearing this, all the Ministers indicated their dissatisfaction and the meeting adjourned. The following day, when it was reconvened, the Japanese Bureau Director explained that he had analyzed the matter, and, with the approval of the Kwantung Army, all the ministerial salaries would be raised to the same level as the Deputy Ministers. But, since the Japanese were away from their homes and had come abroad to establish a Kingly Way Paradise for the Manchurian people, the Manchurians should gratefully give them a special living allowance. This decision was final and there could be no further discussion.

When the Ministers heard this, they realized it would do them no good to continue the argument, especially since their own salaries had been increased. But after this affair, the truth of the cabinet system and the Council of State was evident to everyone. All resolutions at the Council of State were already decisions passed on by the Deputy Minister's Conference which was held regularly each Tuesday. But real power was in the hands of the Director of the General Affairs Administration Bureau of the Kwantung Army. Cheng and I were Prime Minister and Chief Executive in name only; the Cabinet officers were Ministers in name only; and the Council of State was a Council in name only.

All this was no secret to anyone, and I should have been awakened from my dream. But the courtiers around me kept reminding me that I was the most important man in Manchukuo. This made it hard for me to forget the rationalizations, formed in Tientsin in the Chang Garden, that "Japan, without me as Emperor, would not be capable of running Manchuria and would achieve nothing."

21

The Treaty

WHEN WE WERE FIRST IN PORT ARTHUR, CHENG HSIAO-hsu had negotiated with Honjo the conditions under which I would take office as Chief Executive and the provisions for his own status as Prime Minister. This understanding was not reported to me until the eve of Honjo's departure from Manchukuo. On August 18, 1932, Cheng came to my office with a heap of documents. "This," he explained, "is an agreement that your humble servant has made with General Honjo. I request Your Majesty to approve." As soon as I saw what it was I was furious.

"Who asked you to negotiate this agreement?" I asked.

"These are all conditions that Itagaki stipulated in Port Arthur," he replied with considerable formality. "Itagaki informed Your Majesty of them a long time ago."

"Nonsense! I never heard him talk about them. And even if he had, you should have told me before you signed."

"I did this on Itagaki's instructions. He was afraid that since your other advisers did not really understand the true situation, it would only add to your troubles if they found out."

"Just who is in charge here—you or me?"

"Your obedient servant would not dare to presume prerogatives. This agreement is actually just a temporary convenience. We can still negotiate other treaties stipulating a time limit, after which we may resume all privileges and powers."

What Cheng said was in fact true. All the privileges demanded by Japan in the agreement were already in their hands. The major items of the agreement stipulated that Manchukuo's national defense and security would be entrusted entirely to Japan, that Japan controlled Manchukuo's railroads, harbors, water routes, air routes, and could carry out future constructions and additions; that supplies needed by the Japanese Army would be supplied by Manchukuo, that Japan had the authority to develop Manchukuo's mines and natural resources and that Japanese nationals could be employed as Manchukuo government officials. Also Japanese had the right to immigrate to Manchukuo. Finally it was stipulated that the agreement would become a basis for a formal treaty between the two countries.

Since all the provisions were an accomplished fact, I signed the agreement and Cheng Hsiao-hsu took it away with him. A short time later Hu Sze-yuan entered. I told him about the agreement and Hu was furious. "Cheng Hsiao-hsu is really a disgrace," he said. "Chen Pao-shen always claimed that Cheng is accustomed to be generous with others' belongings and now he has dared to take it on himself to do this."

"Well, now the wood had already been made into a boat," I said despondently, "there is nothing we can do. At any event, let's wait for the latest news from Tokyo and see. After all, there is really nothing else I can do."

Several days previously we had learned that Honjo, as Commander in Chief of the Kwantung Army, was going to be replaced and that Japan was going to recognize Manchukuo officially. Hu Sze-yuan attached special importance to this development and felt that when Japan changed the commander of the Kwantung Army there might be a change in attitude and that we should take this opportunity to send people to Japan to support our point of view. He argued that we would have to give Japan some advantages such as mines, railroads, natural resources and even national defense, but the power of appointment and dismissal should be retained by me.

I adopted his proposal and sent the lawyer who had handled my divorce case and a Taiwanese recommended by Hu Sze-yuan to lobby for us in Tokyo. After a couple of days Hu reported good news from Tokyo. According to our negotiators, the elder statesmen and some people in the Army Ministry were quite sympathetic toward me and were not satisfied with the attitude taken by Honjo. I therefore decided that as soon as a new commander of the Kwantung Army arrived in Manchukuo I would personally take up my demands. Hu Sze-yuan urged me to insist on the removal of Cheng Hsiao-hsu as Prime Minister because of his disgraceful generosity to the Japanese.

Nobuyoshi Muto, the new commander of the Kwantung Army, arrived in Changchun in September and on the 15th he and Cheng Hsiao-hsu signed the Japan-Manchukuo Protocol, the official public treaty derived from the secret agreement.

After we had drunk champagne following the ceremony, I was impatient to have a personal discussion with Muto. I was confident about the outcome because I had the secret reports from my emissaries in Japan which indicated that Muto was sympathetic to my problems and was willing to consider restoring my imperial title. Muto had come to Manchukuo with an illustrious army carrer behind him. During World War I he had led the Japanese forces that had occupied Siberia. He was a full general with three concurrent official positions—Commander of the Kwantung Army, Chief Executive of the Kwantung Bureau, and Ambassador to Manchukuo. Soon after his arrival, he was promoted to the rank of Marshal. He was in fact the true emperor of Manchukuo. The Japanese press referred to him as the "guardian deity of Manchuria," and in my eyes this white-haired old man of sixty-five seemed to have the powers of a god. When he bowed to me for the first time, with the greatest politeness, I immediately had the feeling that I was especially favored by the heavens. After I finished my talk, he replied very politely: "Regarding Your Excellency's opinions, I will refer them to Japan for a thorough analysis." When he left he took with him a memorandum drawn up by Hu Sze-yuan.

But I never received any word about the analysis. According to the routine that was established, I had three meetings each month with the Commander of the Kwantung Army, and after ten days, at the second meeting, I asked him about the result of his studies.

"Studies," he replied. "Studies . . . studies . . . research . . . research?"

Each time he met me he was always very polite, bowed deeply, smiled and addressed me as "Your Excellency." But he never mentioned the memorandum. If I touched on the subject he would shift the conversation to something else. After two or three of these incidents, I no longer had the courage to ask him about my demands. Whenever I met him, up to the time of his death in July, 1933, I could only discuss Buddhism, Confucianism and "friendly relationships," never anything substantive.

22

Emperor for the Third Time

In May, 1932, the Commission of Enquiry of the League of Nations arrived in the Northeast. Cheng Hsiao-hsu and his son had placed high hopes in this Commission. When it published its report in October of that year they were sure that their dream of international control of Manchukuo (as distinguished from Japanese control) would materialize in a short time with the result that I would then be able to play off one power against the other to my own advantage, instead of remaining at the mercy of the Japanese. Later, when the Chengs were discarded by the Japanese, it was said that their enthusiasm for international control of Manchukuo was the cause of their dismissal.

On May 3 I met with the Commission of Enquiry for about a quarter of an hour in Changchun. They asked me only two questions: how did I come to the Northeast and how had Manchukuo been established?

Before I replied to their questions, a thought flashed through my mind. I remembered how in the past my tutor Johnston had told me that the gates of London would always be open to me, and I wondered, in view of the trickery of Doihara and the threats of Itagaki, whether I dared beg Lord Lytton (the head of the Commission) to rescue me and take me with him to London. Would he agree or not? But as soon as this idea swept into my mind, I recalled that, seated next to me, were the Chief of Staff of the Kwantung Army and Itagaki. I looked at Itagaki's bluish white face and felt

173

compelled to repeat exactly what he had "reminded" me to tell the Commission: "The masses of the people of Manchuria begged me to come. My stay here is absolutely voluntary and free. . . ."

The members of the Commission all smiled and nodded at my reply. They did not ask for more. Later, we had our pictures taken, drank champagne and toasted one another's health. After their departure a smile floated across the blue-white face of Itagaki and he praised me: "Your Excellency, the Chief Executive's manner was really excellent. How strong and clear your voice sounded!"

Later, Cheng Hsiao-hsu came in shaking his bald head. "All those Westerners," he explained, "met with your slave. We talked only about equal opportunity for all in Manchukuo and the interest of the great powers in the 'open door' policy. It was just as I had expected."

After the departure of the Commission, the Chengs predicted that the League of Nations might adopt a resolution proposing international control of Manchuria. When the Commission's report was announced it gave the Chengs even greater confidence, for it stated that China should accept international control of Manchukuo. It described Japan's wish for "stable government" as not "unreasonable" and added that "it is only in an atmosphere of external confidence and internal peace . . . that the capital which is necessary for the rapid economic development of Manchuria will be forthcoming." It looked as though the Chengs had been right in expecting that the Commission would advocate international management with international guarantees for all the foreign powers.

In the first few days after seeing the Commission's report, Cheng Hsiao-hsu told me with great glee that things were "very hopeful" and that several Chinese scholars had also expressed a favorable view of the report. But the Chengs became dispirited when they learned the Japanese reaction. Although the Commission had repeatedly stressed that it respected Japan's "rights and interests in the Northeast" and even described the seizure of Mukden on the night of September 18 as an act of self-defense by Japan, a Japanese Foreign Ministry spokesman indicated Japan was not in the least interested in a plan for international control and administration. It soon became clear that the League of Nations would do nothing to enforce its recommendations on Japan.

It therefore became more important than ever that I not offend the Japanese if I wished to ascend the throne again. Now I must rely on the Japanese, *or else* . . . !

At one of the routine meetings a few days before my first anniversary as Chief Executive, General Muto unexpectedly raised the question of the restoration of my imperial title. He explained that Japan was analyzing the problem of the Manchukuo state system, and as soon as the time was opportune, it would be resolved.

Soon afterward, on March 27, 1933, Japan, in order to exercise more freedom of action, withdrew from the League of Nations. Meanwhile Japanese armies conducted an encircling movement against Peking and Tientsin, and the Nanking Government, busily engaged in a civil war against the Communists, signed the Tangku Agreement with Japan by which the area south of the Great Wall and east of Hopei Province was designated as a demilitarized zone from which all Chinese troops were withdrawn. This agreement enabled the Japanese to extend their influence and control over North China itself.

Cheng Hsiao-hsu explained that the Japanese military occupation óf North China, and even South China, was only a matter of time, and it was therefore more urgent than ever that the form of the Manchukuo state system be settled. He said that the final decision on this issue would not be decided by the Kwantung Army in Changchun, but in Tokyo itself. Since he repeated the claim that many of the elder Japanese statesmen had already advocated my assumption of the throne, I felt that I should send a new emissary to Tokyo to learn what was going on there.

The man I chose for this job was a Japanese police officer named Tetsusaburo Kudo who had accompanied me from Tientsin to the Northeast. He had always been an active supporter of mine and when I was in Port Arthur he had not behaved like the other Japanese and had even indicated his dissatisfaction with the Kwantung Army. Once when I had noticed that the color of the tea in my cup seemed odd and was afraid that someone might be trying to poison me, I asked for it to be analyzed. Before the tea could be removed, Kudo drank it down. He was the only Japanese who addressed me as Your Imperial Majesty and his loyalty was no less than the most devoted Ch'ing official. I had therefore bestowed on him the Chinese name of Chung ("Loyal") and treated him as a member of my family.

When he returned from his short mission to Japan he told me that he had met with the Minister of the Army as well as Black Dragon Society leaders and had learned that all the military authorities were in favor of the imperial system. I now believed that my restoration was soon to come.

In October, 1933, three months after Muto's death, Kudo's report was verified. The new commander of the Kwantung Army, Hishikari, informed me that the Japanese government was now prepared to recognize me as the "Emperor of the Manchukuo Imperial State."

As soon as I received this news I was so happy that all the flowers in my heart burst into full blossom. My first thought was that I must have a set of imperial dragon robes to wear.

These robes were brought to Manchuria from Peking where they had been in the keeping of one of the High Consorts, but the Kwantung Army informed me that since Japan was recognizing me as "Emperor of Manchukuo" and not as the Great Ch'ing Emperor, I could not wear the dragon robes of the Ch'ing Dynasty at my coronation. I was told to wear the dress uniform of a Grand Marshal of the Land, Sea and Air Forces of Manchukuo.

"How can this be?" I asked Cheng Hsiao-hsu. "I am the descendant of the ruling Aisin-Gioro clan. How can I ignore my ancestral regulations? All the Manchu nobility from Peking will come to see me crowned. What will I look like if I wear a Western-style uniform when I ascend the throne?"

"What Your Majesty says is true," Cheng Hsiao-hsu said as he nodded his head and looked at the dragon robes laid out on a table. "Your Majesty is quite right, but what will the Kwantung Army say?"

"Go and negotiate for me."

After Cheng Hsiao-hsu had gone, I gazed in admiration at the dragon robes that had been preserved for me for twenty-two years by the High Consort Jung Hui. My heart was filled with emotion. These robes had once been worn by the

Emperor Kuang Hsu. They were a real Emperor's dragon robes, the ones I had been dreaming of for twenty-two years. I *would* wear them to reascend my throne and this would mark the restoration of the Ch'ing Dynasty. . . .

When Cheng Hsiao-hsu returned, he reported that the Kwantung Army insisted that I wear the marshal's uniform for the enthronement ceremony. "Did you negotiate for me?" I asked.

"How would your servant and slave official dare not to?" he answered. "But this decision has been personally delivered to me by Itagaki."

"But it cannot be," I said as I jumped up. "Before I ascend the throne I must perform the ceremony of praying to heaven. Do you mean to say that they want me to kowtow to heaven in a marshal's uniform?"

"Your servant and slave official will talk to Itagaki again."

This time the Kwantung Army agreed to let me wear my dragon robes when I paid tribute to heaven. On the early morning of March 1, 1934, at the Apricot Flower Village in the suburbs of Changchun, on an earthern "Altar of Heaven" that had been piled up for the occasion, I wore the dragon robes and performed the ancient ritual of announcing my ascension to heaven. Later, on my return to the city, I changed into a marshal's uniform and went through the actual ceremony of my ascension to the throne.

The ceremony was held in the Mansion of Diligence for the People. The floor of its principal drawing room was covered with a crimson carpet and the northern wall was hung with silk draperies in front of which was placed a specially made high-backed chair on which was carved the "imperial emblem" of orchids. I stood in front of it, flanked by high officials of the Household Department, my Chief Military Aide, Japanese attachés to the Household and other palace officials. The civil and military officials headed by Premier Cheng Hsiao-hsu stood before me and bowed low three times. I replied with a half bow. Then Hishikari, the new commander of the Kwantung Army and, concurrently, the Japanese Ambassador, presented his credentials and felicitations. After the ceremony, the princes and nobles of the Aisin-Gioro clan who had come from Peking in almost full strength, as well as some former members of the old

Household Department of the Forbidden City, performed the traditional Ch'ing ceremony of kneeling three times and kowtowing nine times before me as I sat on the throne.

Many retired Ch'ing officials living inside the Great Wall sent congratulatory memorials and even the boss of the Shanghai underworld sent a memorial proclaiming himself a loyal subject.

On June 6, Prince Chichibu, the brother of the Emperor of Japan, came to congratulate me on behalf of Hirohito. He awarded me the Japanese Cordon of the Chrysanthemum and on my wife Wan Jung he bestowed the Order of the Crown.

In July, my father, a younger brother and a sister came to Changchun to see me. Their visit illustrates how deeply intoxicated with myself I had become. When they arrived at Changchun, I sent a group of palace officials and also a company of the Palace Guard to welcome them at the station. Wan Jung and I waited outside the palace gate. She was dressed in Manchu court dress and I wore my marshal's uniform with three sets of medals—one from the Japanese, one from the state of Manchukuo, and a third consisting of Great Ch'ing decorations. Since I did not dare wear this third set in front of the Kwantung Army, I was glad of this particular chance to show them off.

When my father's automobile arrived at the palace, I stood at attention, saluted in a military manner and Wan Jung knelt in Manchu fashion. Then I accompanied him into the drawing room and, before taking off my uniform, I also knelt to him in Manchu fashion and paid my respects.

That night I held a big family banquet at which Western-style cuisine and etiquette were observed. According to my arrangements, as soon as I entered the banquet hall, a military band began to play.

As the banquet proceeded to the stage of drinking champagne, Pu Chieh, as I had arranged, stood up, raised his glass and shouted: "Ten thousand years to His Majesty the Emperor, ten thousand years, ten thousand years." My family all joined in the toast. As soon as I heard the shouting, my head reeled as if I had already reached a point of intoxication.

The following day, a senior palace official told me that the

Headquarters of the Kwantung Army had protested in the name of the Japanese Ambassador that in sending an armed guard to the station to welcome my father I had violated the agreement between the Northeastern authorities and Japan which Manchukuo had undertaken to observe. Under this agreement a strip of land on either side of the railway was to be the territory of the South Manchuria Railway Company and no armed men were to be allowed into it except those of the Japanese army. The Kwantung Army Headquarters wanted an assurance that no such incident would occur again.

This incident should have been enough to awaken me from my dream world, but at least on this occasion, the Japanese showed me the courtesy of not protesting openly, and after I had sent someone to apologize and to assure them it wouldn't happen again, they said nothing more.

I reached the pinnacle of authority and the nadir of my misconceptions after the first of my two state visits to Japan, in April, 1935. The Kwantung Army had made all the arrangements for this trip which was undertaken to demonstrate my gratitude to the Japanese Emperor for sending his brother, Prince Chichibu, to congratulate me on my ascension to the throne as well as to show my personal interest in promoting friendly relations between Japan and Manchukuo.

The Japanese government had organized a reception committee of fourteen consisting of high-ranking peers headed by Baron Hayashi, a Privy Councillor. A battleship, the *Hie Maru*, was sent over to take me to Japan and other warships provided an escort. When I set sail from Dairen I inspected three destroyers and, on arrival at Yokohama, there was a formation of over 100 airplanes to welcome me.

During the voyage I was seasick and wrote the following poem:

> The sea is as flat as a mirror,
> I travel 10,000 miles.
> Thus two nations join hands,
> To strengthen the East.

On the fourth day of the voyage I witnessed a maneuver of over seventy warships and I penned some more verses in an effort to forget my seasickness. Even before landing in Japan I was so flattered by the honors given me that I no longer knew who I was. I was not only impressed by the power demonstrated by the Japanese but also looked at it as a demonstration of respect for me. All my misgivings of the past I now attributed to my own misunderstandings.

On my arrival in Tokyo, the Emperor Hirohito personally came to the station to welcome me, and also gave me a big banquet. After I had paid him a visit of respect, he returned my visit. I also received many felicitations from important Japanese elder statesmen. I inspected troops with Hirohito and even participated in a ceremony at the Meiji Shrine. I also went to pay my special respects to Hirohito's mother, the Japanese Empress Dowager. The Japanese press reported that as I strolled with her in the garden I used my hand to help her up a small slope as I had once helped my father up the steps of the palace in Changchun, but the truth is that I had never helped my father up a single step. On the last day of my visit, Prince Chichibu represented his older brother at the railroad station to bid me good-bye.

The treatment I received from the Japanese Imperial Household really went to my head, and the air seemed to have a different aroma to it now that I had paid an imperial state visit. Since I and the Emperor of Japan were equals, I reasoned, my status in Manchukuo was exactly like his in Japan. I therefore believed that the Japanese would treat me the same way they treated their own Emperor.

Intoxicated by these illusions, as soon as I returned to Changchun I asked the latest commander of the Kwantung Army, General Minami, to come to see me so that I could give him my impressions of the trip. On the following day, April 29, I participated in the celebration of Hirohito's birthday, and on April 30 I sent for all the officials in the capital, Chinese and Japanese, to come to hear me talk about my visit. I had not discussed what I was going to say with the Japanese in advance and did not prepare a draft of my remarks for them to examine beforehand. In my talk I described in detail how the Japanese Emperor had entertained me, elaborated on the respect his subjects had shown me, and concluded by asserting that disloyalty to the Emperor of Manchukuo was the same as disloyalty to the Emperor of Japan.

Less than a month after my return to Changchun, the Commander of the Kwantung Army, during one of our routine meetings, told me that "Premier Cheng Hsiao-hsu wished to retire." He advised me to grant the request and replace him with a new Prime Minister. I had already learned that Japan was dissatisfied with Cheng, and since I was also looking for an excuse to get rid of him, I immediately agreed and proposed that my Minister of Civil Affairs and Governor of Fengtien Province, Tsang Shih-yi, be appointed Cheng's successor. I thought that General Minami, who had heard my views on Japan-Manchukuo friendship twice in recent days, would be bound to comply with my request. But to my surprise I ran straight into a brick wall.

"No," he replied, shaking his head. "The Kwantung Army has already considered the question and chosen a suitable man. Your Majesty need not worry about a thing. It would be better to let Chang Ching-hui be the Prime Minister."[1]

Not long before this, Cheng Hsiao-hsu had expressed his annoyance with the Japanese by saying that Manchukuo was no longer a child and that it should be let alone to take a walk. This remark had irritated his Japanese masters and they therefore kicked him aside. Cheng was not even allowed to draw his money out of the bank and was forbidden to move out of Changchun. Under constant surveillance, he could only practice calligraphy and compose poems at his home. He died suddenly three years later, a disappointed man. His son, Cheng Chui, met a sudden death a few years before his father, and it was rumored that both had been murdered by the Japanese. Even if this rumor were untrue, their tragic ends should have been enough to smash my illusions about the restoration of my ancestral heritage. Yet it took one more year after Cheng's death, until it began to dawn on me what my position really was.

---

[1] Chang Ching-hui at this time was serving as Minister of Defense in the Manchukuo Cabinet. Prior to Pu Yi's arrival in Manchukuo he had at one time been second in command of the Fengtien (war lord) Army of Marshal Chang Tso-lin.

23

Illusions Vanish

FROM THE TIME OF ITS WITHDRAWAL FROM THE LEAGUE OF Nations in early 1933, Japan proceeded to prepare for war and the total invasion of China. Even before the July 7 incident in 1937,[1] Japan continued to use armed force and engineered many coups in North China. Meanwhile, the Nanking Government of the Kuomintang surrendered step by step and repeatedly indicated to Japan that it did not contemplate any anti-Japanese action, insisting that there was no reason for it to be against Japan. As a result, Japan's influence was greatly strengthened within the Great Wall.

In view of all this and the fact that the Kwantung Army had ignored my advice in choosing a replacement for Cheng Hsiao-hsu, I should have understood the unreality of my position. But I was still utterly intoxicated and had not awakened from my dream. The first real taste of disillusion came over the Ling Sheng affair.

Ling Sheng was the son of a former Ch'ing military governor in Mongolia and had been an adviser at Chang Tso-lin's headquarters. He had been one of the members of the delegation that had come to Port Arthur to urge me to become Chief Executive and had thus been listed as one of

---

[1] On the night of July 7, 1937, fighting broke out between Chinese and Japanese troops at the Marco Polo bridge south of Peking. In August Japan attacked Shanghai and the full-scale war between the two countries began.

the "founders of the nation." When he was suddenly arrested by the Kwantung Army in the spring of 1936 he was governor of a province of Manchuria.

According to Colonel Yasunori Yoshioka, the Kwantung Army's "Attache to the Imperial Household," Ling Sheng was arrested because he had been engaged in anti-Manchukuo and anti-Japanese activities. From other sources, however, I had been told that he was arrested because at a recent governors' conference he had expressed complaints which irritated the Japanese. Apparently he had argued that the Kwantung Army had not fulfilled the promises Itagaki had made at Port Arthur concerning the recognition of Manchukuo as an independent country. Ling Sheng had claimed that as governor of Hsingan Province he had no real power or authority.

I found the news of his arrest especially disquieting because only six months previously my fourth sister had become engaged to his son. Just as I was debating whether I should discuss the matter with the Kwantung Army, the Commander came to see me.

"A few days ago we broke a case and the one who committed the crime was known to Your Majesty," he explained. "It was the Governor of Hsingan Province, Ling Sheng. He had established an alliance with foreign countries to plot a revolt against Japan. A military tribunal has found him guilty of crimes against Japan and Manchukuo and he has been condemned to death."

"Condemned to death," I repeated in surprise.

"Yes, death. This will be a warning. By executing one, we warn another hundred."

After he left, Colonel Yoshioka advised me to break off the engagement between my sister and Ling Sheng's son, and I immediately complied.

Ling Sheng's sentence was carried out by decapitation and several of his relatives were similarly executed at the same time. This was the first case of execution by the Japanese of a high Manchukuo official. Since Ling Sheng had sought a marriage relationship with my family, I had supposed he respected me and was loyal. Yet the Kwantung Army had judged him solely by his attitude toward Japan. The incident made me realize that the Japanese would apply the same standards to me, and when I thought of the Commanding General's statement about killing one to warn a hundred, his remarks seemed most ominous.

The incident also made me think of a man whose fate had been the direct opposite of Ling Sheng's—Chang Ching-hui, the new Prime Minister. Clearly the Japanese intended me to see the contrast between the two. How Chang Ching-hui had ingratiated himself with the Japanese is evident in a remark he once made at a Council of State meeting. "Japan and Manchukuo," he stated, "are like two dragonflies tied to a single string." On another occasion he said: "Manchukuo has thousands of square miles of land but the Manchurians are illiterate and ignorant. If the Japanese come to open virgin land and teach them modern techniques, both sides will benefit."

When the Japanese stepped up their grain requisitions and bought up grain at a low fixed price, Chang Ching-hui pointed out that "soldiers of the Japanese Imperial Army are giving their lives, and for us, the Manchurian people, to pay with grain is quite fair." The Commander of the Kwantung Army was always praising Chang Ching-hui as a good minister and as a man who was adept at giving effect to Japanese-Manchukuo friendship.

After the Ling Sheng affair, I was even more deeply disturbed by a meeting I had with Prince Te.

Prince Te was a Mongol prince whom the Japanese had placed in charge of the "Inner Mongolian Autonomous Military Government." When I had lived in Tientsin he had sent me money, and given well-bred Mongol ponies to Pu Chieh, and had shown his loyalty in many other ways. When he came to see me in Changchun he complained that the Japanese were too powerful and ambitious. After hearing his complaints, I couldn't help but comfort him a little. I didn't anticipate that on the following day, Colonel Yoshioka would come to see me with a grim expression on his face.

"What did Your Majesty discuss with Prince Te yesterday?" he asked.

Realizing that something was wrong, I said that we had only been talking about unimportant things.

"The talk you had yesterday," Yoshioka said, "indicated some dissatisfaction with the Japanese, did it not?"

My heart began to pound. I knew that the only thing I could do was deny it. "That is a false statement manufactured by Prince Te," I exclaimed.

Even though Yoshioka did not continue the inquiry, I was on edge and worried. How had the Japanese learned of my talk with Prince Te? There were two possibilities. Either the Japanese had installed some kind of listening device or Prince Te had acted as an informer. I spent a long time searching for a listening device, but since I found none I inclined to the view that Prince Te had deliberately tried to betray me. I thus learned from this incident, better than from the Ling Sheng affair, not to talk frankly with any outsider, and I became very cautious toward all visitors. As a matter of fact, there were very few and in 1937 the Kwantung Army insisted that Yoshioka, the Attache to the Imperial Household, should be present whenever I saw a visitor.

Many of the policies and laws to which I gave my assent in these days were connected with Japan's war preparations and the strengthening of her rule over the Northeast. They included the First Five Year Plan for Developing Production, the Property Control Law, the Reorganization of the Government to strengthen Japanese rule, and the adoption of Japanese as a "national language." But none of these had an impact on me equal to that of my brother Pu Chieh's marriage.

After Pu Chieh had graduated from the school for children of the Japanese nobility in Tokyo, he had been transferred to the Japanese Army Cadet School. He returned to Changchun in the winter of 1935 and was appointed a second lieutenant in the Imperial Guard. From this time on, the Kwantung Army people who knew him were always bringing up the subject of his marriage. When I first heard about it, I only laughed it off and didn't give it a thought. I didn't anticipate that Yoshioka would come to see me to say that the Kwantung Army hoped that Pu Chieh would marry a Japanese girl in order to promote friendly relations between the two countries.

This suggestion made me uncomfortable and I discussed the problem with my second sister. We decided to get Pu Chieh a wife from Peking in order to forestall this Japanese plot, for it was now clear that the Japanese wished to obtain, via Pu Chieh, a child of Japanese descent who could succeed me on the throne, and I warned Pu Chieh that if there were a Japanese wife in the family the husband would be under the supervision of the Japanese. Pu Chieh respectfully promised not to marry a Japanese, but when Yoshioka put pressure on him by telling him that General Honjo, himself, was acting as matchmaker on his behalf in Tokyo, he obeyed the Kwantung Army. On April 3, 1937, he married Hiro Saga, daughter of Marquis Saga of Japan. Less than a month after their marriage, under instructions from the Kwantung Army, the Council of State passed a succession law by which Pu Chieh and his son would be the successors to the throne if I had no male offspring.

After Pu Chieh and his wife's return from Tokyo I decided that I could no longer speak frankly in front of him or eat the food that his wife sent me. If Pu Chieh and I were dining together and there were food on the table prepared by his wife, I would wait until he had tasted the food first. Later, when Pu Chieh was about to become a father, I became so worried for my own safety and even for his, that I consulted divination. I was sure the Kwantung Army was capable of killing us both in order to obtain an emperor of Japanese descent. However, when his wife gave birth to a daughter, I was very much relieved.

I even became worried about what would happen if I myself were to father a son. Would he be safe or not? For the Kwantung Army had asked me to sign a document saying that if there should be a crown prince he would be sent to Japan at the age of five and brought up under their control.

On July 7, 1937, when the fighting broke out that led to the Japanese occupation of Peking, some retired Ch'ing officials in Peking began to hope for a revival of the Great Ch'ing, but I now knew this was impossible. My only concerns were how to preserve my own safety in the face of the Japanese and how to deal with Yoshioka, the Attaché to the Imperial Household and the incarnation inside my own palace of the Kwantung Army.

24

Yasunori Yoshioka—My Adviser

IF ONE WERE TO COMPARE THE KWANTUNG ARMY TO A source of high-tension electric current and myself to an electric motor, then Yasunori Yoshioka was a wire of high conductivity.

A short man with a small moustache and high cheekbones, he never left me from the time he first came to the palace in 1935 to the Japanese surrender in 1945 when he was captured by the Soviet Army at the same time I was. During those years he rose from the rank of an army lieutenant colonel to lieutenant general. He had a dual status: one was a senior staff officer of the Kwantung Army and the other was "Attaché to the Manchukuo Imperial Household." This was a Japanese term, similar to the title of "Companion of the Inner Court" in Chinese, but it does not make much difference how one translates it, for the words do not describe his real function. He was in fact the piece of wire through which the Kwantung Army transmitted its intentions to me. The tours of inspection I made, the visitors I received, the protocol I observed, my admonitions to my subjects, the toasts I proposed, and even my nods and smiles were all under Yoshioka's direction. He decided whom I should and should not see, the meetings I should attend, the speeches I delivered—everything.

When Japan launched its full-scale invasion of China in July, 1937, it wanted Manchukuo to contribute grain, men and supplies. I ordered Chang Ching-hui to make public an exhortation, actually written by Yoshioka at a meeting of the provincial governors, in which I urged the people to "carry out their duties diligently to support the holy war." When the Japanese entered the Pacific War they wanted Manchukuo troops to replace some of the Japanese units engaged in the Chinese War. I read out another of Yoshioka's speeches, this time at a banquet given for the commanders of the various military zones, in which I expressed my determination to "live or die with Japan, and, united in heart and virtue, smash the power of Britain and America."

Whenever Japan occupied a major Chinese city inside the Great Wall, Yoshioka would ask me to stand up with him and bow in the direction of the battlefield as a mark of mourning for the Japanese soldiers killed in the fighting. After he had me do this a number of times I needed no prompting.

When the "National Foundation Shrine" was built I used to go there every month to pray for the victory of the Japanese troops, and this too was done after receiving an impulse along Yoshioka's electric wire.

The Kwantung Army did not interfere much in my personal and domestic affairs before the outbreak of full-scale fighting between Japan and China in 1937, but the situation changed after that. Before the invasion, some of my family members would come up from south of the Great Wall every year to celebrate my birthday. But after July 7, the Kwantung Army allowed only a few of them to come to Changchun at specified times. They also stipulated that with the exception of my closest relations the others could bow to me but could not address me. All mail sent to me from outside Manchukuo was read by Yoshioka's staff and he decided whether or not I was to see it. The Kwantung Army was of course perfectly well aware that I was not anti-Manchukuo or anti-Japanese, but they were still worried that I might establish a relationship with people inside the Great Wall for the restoration of the Ch'ing Dynasty and this was not in accordance with their plans.

Yoshioka had shown considerable ability in getting his post in the palace. Some accounts say that he was a friend of mine before I went to the Northeast, but actually he had only lectured to me a few times on current affairs when we were in Tientsin. He managed to use his friendship with Pu Chieh, whom he had known when he was an instructor at the Army Cadet School in Japan, to convince the Kwantung Army that he was a personal friend of mine. Although this was not true, it was on the strength of his claims that he got his twin appointments as Attaché to the Manchukuo Imperial Household and as a senior staff officer of the Kwantung Army.

Yoshioka loved to paint pictures in ink. Once he painted a bamboo scene and asked Cheng Hsiao-hsu to write a poem on it and then asked me put on some writing in my own hand. Later he took this ink picture to Japan and presented it to the Japanese Empress Dowager. The Japanese press published the picture and praised Yoshioka as being a soldier with a colorful pen. Subsequently he often carried little presents back and forth between me and the Dowager. These gifts often included pastries, but because of my suspicious nature, I always insisted that someone else taste first those sent from Japan.

Yoshioka's Chinese was not too good, but in our conversations we encountered little difficulty since he also knew English. When Yoshioka spoke he would always intersperse his words with "uhs" and "ahs" while twitching his eyebrows, a habit that got worse with time and which I found increasingly irritating. As this habit grew more pronounced our relationship changed.

After my visit to Japan in 1935 the Japanese Empress Dowager gave me some poems and what Yoshioka said then was music in my ears: "Her Majesty the Empress Dowager is the equivalent of Your Majesty's mother, and since I am almost a relation of yours, I feel very honored at this!"

But by 1936 he said to me, "Japan is the equivalent of Your Majesty's father, uh. The Kwantung Army represents Japan, uh? Thus the commander of the Kwantung Army is the equivalent of Your Majesty's father, ha!"

As the Japanese troops at the front ran into more and more difficulties, my standing went down in Yoshioka's eyes. He even went so far as to say, "The Kwantung Army is your father, uh, and I am the representative of the Kwantung Army, ha!"

Yoshioka made more frequent daily visits to the palace as

time went on. Sometimes he would stay for less than ten minutes and then leave, only to return five minutes later. He would give ridiculous reasons for these frequent comings and goings, such as "I forgot what I wished to say at our last interview," or "I forgot to ask you what will be my assignment tomorrow," and so on. I naturally became worried that he was using these lightning visits as a way of spying on me, and I thought that the only way I could avoid suspicion was to agree to see him as soon as I heard he had come and never keep him waiting. I would even see him in the middle of a meal and put down my rice bowl to talk with him. In my relations with Yoshioka, I had reached a position similar to that of the great Duke of Chou[1] who would "stop his meal three times, and hold his hair up three times in the midst of washing it, in order to attend to state affairs."

---

[1] A public official much admired by Confucius.

25

Majesty Without Power

SINCE I WAS NOT ALLOWED TO PARTICIPATE IN POLITICS, OR
to go out as I pleased, or to send for my "high officials" for
talks, I had nothing to do when the Kwantung Army was not
transmitting current to me. I thus developed the habit of
going to bed late, sometimes at 3 A.M., and getting up late. I
ate two meals a day: my breakfast at noon or at one P.M.,
and dinner between nine and eleven at night. I would take a
nap between 4 and 6 P.M. Apart from my eating and sleeping,
my daily life could be summarized as follows: floggings,
curses, divinations, medicine and fear.

These elements were mutually interrelated. As the signs
of the Japanese collapse became more apparent, I grew more
and more frightened that the Japanese would kill me before
their final defeat in order to destroy evidence of their conduct. Convinced that I faced death at their hands, I became
more affable toward them and flattered them. At the same
time, within my own house, my temper became worse and
worse. I cursed people out and had them flogged over the
slightest irritation and I became more and more superstitious. I ate only vegetarian foods, and spent the whole day
reciting Buddhist incantations, consulting oracles, and praying to Buddha and the gods for protection. In this neurotic
and unstable state, my health, which was already poor,
deteriorated.

My tendency toward cruelty and suspicion had originally
taken root in the Forbidden City, and had been strengthened

in Tienstin where I had made the following set of "household rules" for the servants:

1. Irresponsible conversations are prohibited in order to prevent bribery and corruption.
2. Covering up for each other is prohibited.
3. Embezzlement and profiteering is forbidden.
4. Misdemeanors by colleagues must be reported at once.
5. Senior staff must beat their juniors immediately after the discovery of wrongdoing.
6. Punishment is to be increased one grade for slackness in enforcement of rules.

After we came to the Northeast I made my staff swear an oath: "If I break these rules I am willing to receive the heavenly punishment of being struck down by a thunderbolt."

My severity and cruelty reached the point where I would have my staff beaten incessantly and I would sometimes have them tortured. This job was not limited to one or two but was entrusted to any of the members of my household who might be present. They had to flog very heavily. Otherwise, I would suspect that they were siding with my victims and then they themselves would be subject to the rod.

My victims included almost everyone in the household except my wife, my brother, my sisters, my brothers-in-law and my sister-in-law. In those days a number of my nephews were studying in the palace. They would often talk to me and serve me as I was bringing them up to be my trusted relatives. But this did not save them from scoldings and beatings. What they most feared was the phrase "ask him to go downstairs," since this meant they were to be taken below for a flogging.

I suffered from hemorrhoids while in Changchun. When a young nephew saw the suppositories I had purchased for treatment, he innocently remarked, "They surely look like bullets." This infringed on one of my taboos. Did he mean that I would meet my death from bullets? At my order, another nephew belabored him with the rod.

The sorriest victims of my rule were the pages. They came

from a charity orphange in Changchun and there were about a dozen of them. Most of their parents had been killed by the Japanese, and, out of fear that they would grow up longing for revenge, the Japanese had asked the Manchukuo Government to set up a charity orphanage for them. When they had first learned that they were to be sent to the palace, they thought their lives would be much better than in the orphanage. In fact, however, there was no improvement. They ate the lowest grade of sorghum, were dressed in shabby clothing, had to work fifteen to sixteen hours a day, and sometimes had to sit up all night on duty as well. They were always being beaten; for falling asleep on the job, for not sweeping the floors clean enough, or for talking too loud. When my personal servants were in a bad mood they would always take it out on the pages and would sometimes put them in solitary confinement. Their life was so wretched that at the age of seventeen or eighteen they were as small as ten-year-olds.

My precautions against being swindled by the kitchen staff were similar to those one would take for protection against robbers and thieves. When the cooks went out to do their shopping, I sent agents secretly to spy on them and would question my younger sisters about the price of meat and chicken. If the dishes were not well prepared, or if I found some dirt in them, I would have the cooks fined. Of course, they were also rewarded if I was pleased. Although powerless and without authority outside my own household, I was the absolute ruler in my own palace.

At the close of the Manchukuo period, my temper became worse than ever, and I behaved even more viciously than before.

In early 1944 one of the elders of my family who came to greet me on my birthday fell innocent victim to my wrath. An evening skating party had been arranged in the palace and some professional skaters had been hired to perform for us. While we were watching the performance, this elderly prince, who came from south of the Great Wall, politely greeted some Japanese officers in my presence. This apparently harmless act was in fact a severe breach of palace etiquette, since it was forbidden to pay respects to anyone else while in the presence of the Son of Heaven. The matter was reported to me, but I was in a good mood at the time and since he was of an older generation, I let the matter drop. Later at dinner, the old prince became curious and asked what my nephew, when he had reported the incident to me, had whispered in my ear during the performance. This second act of "gross disrespect" was too much for me. I became very angry and shouted at him. "I give you respect, but you don't deserve it. Is there any limit to your incivility?" The old prince became white with terror and immediately knelt on the floor and kowtowed to me. But the more I thought of the incident, the angrier I became and I left my seat to shout at him that he was not only disloyal to me but also to our imperial ancestors. All the guests fell silent. In my vanity I thought that he was worse than the Japanese who, at least, were never rude to me in public.

While in Changchun I read a number of books about spirits and ghosts and became addicted to them. When I read that all living things had their own Buddha-nature, I became concerned that the meat I ate was really the reincarnation of my own relatives. Therefore, in addition to my twice daily study of Buddhist scriptures, I would read a prayer before every meal for the better reincarnation of the soul of the animal whose meat I was about to eat. When I first started this routine, I prayed silently in front of others, but later I made everyone else leave the room until I had finished praying and only then allowed them back in again. I remember that once when I was eating my meal in the palace air-raid shelter, I kowtowed to an egg three times before eating it. By this time, with the exception of eggs, I had become a complete vegetarian.

I did not allow my staff to kill flies, insisting that they drive them outside instead. I knew that flies could carry disease and so I never ate food that a fly had touched. If one brushed my lips, I would wash the spot with cotton soaked in surgical alcohol from a kit I always carried about with me. If I discovered any trace of a fly in my food I would fine the cook; but despite all this I did not allow anyone to kill a single fly. Once, when I saw a cat pouncing upon a mouse, I mobilized my entire family to chase the cat away in order to save the mouse's life.

The more Buddhist books and sutras I read, the more

superstitious I became, and these fears were intensified by my dreams of visiting Hell. I once read that if one recited scriptures for a long time, the Buddha would appear and would want something to eat. So I prepared a room, and had food put on an altar. After reading some prayers, I proclaimed to everyone that "Buddha has come" and crawled into the room on my knees. Of course, the room was empty; nevertheless, because I believed, I kowtowed to empty space with fear and trembling.

Under my influence, the whole household started intoning Buddhist sutras, while the air echoed with the sounds of wooden drums and brass gongs. The palace sounded like a temple.

I continued with my old practice of consulting oracles and I would not stop until I got a good omen. Later, when I became afraid that the Kwantung Army was going to murder me, I used to resort to divination every time Yoshioka came to see me. Avoiding calamity and enticing good fortune became the central theme behind every action. I kept asking myself what location, what garment, or what food was propitious and what was unlucky. There were no set rules about good and bad omens. For instance, if I was walking along a path and saw a brick in front of me, I would immediately make an arbitrary ruling in my mind: "If I pass it on the left it is lucky, and if I pass it on the right it is unlucky." Each time I crossed a threshold I had first to decide whether to step over it with my right or left foot, depending on which was my lucky foot. And when I ate, I had to decide whether to eat something white before I ate something green, and so on.

Wan Jung became as engrossed in these rituals as I and she too made her own rules. If she encountered something unlucky, she would blink her eyes or spit. This became such a habit with her that she would often blink or spit unnecessarily as if she were suffering from some sort of mental illness. All my nephews, young men of about twenty, turned into ascetics under my guidance. Some of them would practice yoga every day, some would not go home in the evening although they were newly married, some would hang pictures of white skeletons over their beds, and some intoned spells and prayers all day as if they were constantly seeing ghosts.

I used to "meditate" in a yoga posture every day with the palms of my hands and my feet facing upward as I squatted on the floor. All sounds were forbidden while I was thus engaged, even that of heavy breathing. I kept a large crane in the courtyard which ignored this rule of silence, screeching out whenever it happened to feel in high spirits. I made my servants responsible for its silence and fined them fifty cents whenever it made a noise. After they had lost a lot of money because of this, they found a way of dealing with the bird. Whenever the crane started to stretch its neck, preparatory to making a screech, they would hit it and it would then keep quiet.

Since I feared death, I was terrified of illness. I became a medicine addict. I maintained a special dispensary for Chinese medicines as well as one for Western medicines, and I spent thousands of dollars importing drugs from abroad that I never used. Several of my nephews had to spend time, when they were not studying, looking after both my Western and Chinese dispensaries and they, and my personal doctor, gave me injections for my health every day.

When I lived in the Forbidden City I had often suffered from imaginary illnesses, but now I was really ill.

One day, as I went into the courtyard to play tennis, I saw written on the wall in chalk: *Haven't you had enough humiliation from the Japanese?* I forgot about tennis and immediately ordered someone to erase the writing. Then I returned to my bedroom with a pounding heart and felt so weak that I didn't see how I could carry on much longer. I was terrified that the Japanese would find out about the writing and hold a full-scale investigation of my "inner court." Heaven only knew what this would lead to! I was also terrified by the realization that there were anti-Manchukuo and anti-Japanese elements in my own household. If someone dared to write such a phrase under the eyes of so many people, would he stop short of killing me?

I was so confused and terrified every day that I had no interest whatever in family life. I had married a total of four wives, or, to use the terms employed then, I had one empress, one consort, and two minor consorts. But in fact, none of them were real wives. Although each received different treatment from me, they were in fact all my victims.

The experiences of Wan Jung, who had been neglected by me for so long, would be incomprehensible to a modern Chinese girl. If her fate was not determined at her birth, her end was the inevitable result of her marriage to me. I often thought that if she had divorced me in Tientsin as Wen Hsiu had done, she might have escaped her fate. But she was quite different from Wen Hsiu. To Wen Hsiu a normal man-woman family relationship was more important than status and medieval pomp. Wan Jung, however, attached great significance to her position as Empress and she was therefore willing to be a wife in name only.

Ever since she had driven Wen Hsiu away, I had great resentment against her. I seldom talked to her or paid attention to what she did or thought. She never talked to me directly about her own sentiments, her despairs, or her desires. I only knew that eventually she became an opium addict, which was something I could not tolerate. When Wan Jung and I parted after the Japanese surrender on August 15, 1945, her opium addiction was very serious and her health was impaired. She died the following year in the city of Kirin in Central Manchuria.

In 1937, in order to punish Wan Jung and to acquire an additional "piece of furniture" about the palace, I chose another second wife called Tan Yu-ling. She had been recommended by a relation in Peking and became a minor consort. She was of the old Tatala Manchu clan and was sixteen years old when I married her. She too was a wife in name only, and I kept her in the palace as I might have kept a bird in a gilded cage until she died in 1942. The cause of her death is still a mystery to me. She was suffering from an attack of typhoid which, according to the Chinese doctor who was caring for her, should not have been fatal. But she died suddenly the day after a Japanese doctor took over the case and Yoshioka had assumed responsibility for her health.

What seemed most odd to me was that the Japanese doctor was at first diligent in his care of her, but after he had a long private talk with Yoshioka, he fell silent, was no longer as attentive as he had been and stopped his injections and blood transfusions. Yoshioka made the Japanese gendarmes telephone the nurses in the sickroom all night for information, and the following morning Tan Yu-ling was dead.

No sooner had I been informed of her death than Yoshioka came to express the condolences of the Kwantung Army commander and produced a floral wreath. The amazing speed with which this wreath was delivered made me suspicious, but Yoshioka's action a little later made me even more so. Soon after Tan Yu-ling's death, he brought me a sheaf of photographs of Japanese girls and urged me to choose a new wife from among them.

I refused to consider such a proposal while Tan Yu-ling's corpse was still warm. However, he insisted that he wanted to arrange a match for me to console me in my grief. I argued that it should not be done in haste since it was a matter of great importance, and furthermore, there was the language barrier.

"You will be able to understand each other, uh," he said. "They all know how to speak Manchukuoan, ha!"

I hurriedly explained that it was not a problem of race, and that I had to have someone who was suited to me in her habits and interests. I made up my mind that I would not have a Japanese wife, for I did not want a woman close to me who would serve as their eyes and ears. Yet I dared not refuse in so many words.

Yoshioka continued to bother me about it day after day. Finally he realized that I was adamant—or perhaps the Kwantung Army changed its mind—and showed me some pictures of Chinese students in a Japanese school in Port Arthur. Although my second sister reminded me that these girls would be so educated as to be virtually Japanese, I felt that I could not put the Kwantung Army off any longer. I decided to select the youngest and least educated, feeling that she might be the easiest to handle.

I told Yoshioka of my choice and the marriage was arranged. This sixteen-year-old schoolgirl became my fourth victim as a minor consort. Within two years of her arrival, Manchukuo collapsed and she was sent back to her own home.

26

Collapse

IN 1942, THE JAPANESE ARMY IN NORTH AND CENTRAL China launched a large-scale mopping-up campaign. They applied their "three-all" policy of burning all, killing all and looting all, thus making a no-man's-land of certain areas. Yoshioka once told me of the different tactics used by the Japanese Army against the Communist armies of North China, such as "iron encirclements" and the "use of a fine comb." He said that "the fighting history of the Imperial Japanese Army has been immeasurably enriched" by these experiences. After listening to his account, I asked a few questions, thinking to please him. "Since the Communist armies are so tiny, why does His Majesty the Emperor of Japan use all these new tactics?" I asked.

I didn't anticipate that my question would lead to sarcasm. "If Your Imperial Majesty had any experience in real warfare you would not ask this kind of thing."

"May I ask why?"

"The Communist army is not the same as the Kuomintang. There is no distinction between soldiers and the people, uh, no distinction at all, uh. It's like, uh, red beans mixed up with red sand. It's like fish eyes mixed with pearls." He then went on to say that when the Japanese Army was fighting the Eighth Route Army or the New Fourth Army it often found itself completely surrounded. The enemy armies were becoming bigger and bigger and their members were not deserting after a year of service, which was unprecedented in the history of China. "Terrifying, quite terrifying." He sighed and shook his head. The sight of an officer of the Imperial Japanese Army describing the enemy in these terms made me so uneasy I did not know what to say. I finally screwed up my courage to remark, "They really are dreadful the way they burn and kill and the way they communize property and wives."

"Only an idiot could believe that," he interrupted rudely. A few moments later he stared at me with a mocking expression and said, "That was not an official comment. Your Majesty must now listen to the report of the Chief of Staff of the Kwantung Army."

Later, I gradually came to realize that Yoshioka's unofficial comments were comparatively closer to the facts than the official briefings of the Kwantung Army's Chief of Staff.

As I listened to the radio news broadcasts, however, I gradually came to understand Yoshioka's anxieties more clearly. There were increasing reports of Japanese military defeats on all fronts and these were confirmed by reports of "smashed jade" and "heroic sacrifices" in the Manchukuo press. Even in my isolation, I could see that there was a shortage of supplies and materiel. Doorknobs, spittoons and other articles of brass and iron began to disappear from the palace, and the officials of the inner court came to me for assistance because of the shortage of food for their families.

What made the deepest impression on me was the fear that the Japanese Army began to reveal. Tomoyuki Yamashita, who had been so proud and arrogant when he had been transferred to the Northeast after capturing Singapore, was a changed man when he came to take his leave of me on being reassigned to Southeast Asia in 1945. Covering his nose with his hand, he started weeping. "This is our final parting," he said. "I shall never come back again."

I saw even more tears at a farewell ceremony for "human bullets"—soldiers selected from the Japanese Army for stopping aircraft and tanks with their own bodies. Yoshioka always spoke of such *kamikaze* conduct with the greatest respect, but it horrified me. This particular ceremony had been arranged by the Kwantung Army so that I could encourage the men who had been chosen and wish them success. It was a cloudy day and there was a dust storm blowing. The courtyard of the palace was made even more depressing by the sandbags that were piled up as an air-raid precaution. The dozen or so "bullets" were drawn up in a line in front of me, and I read out the speech of good wishes that Yoshioka had written for me. Only then did I notice the ashen gray of their faces and the tears flowing down their cheeks, and I heard some of them sobbing.

The ceremony came to a tawdry end in the swirling dust, and as I hurried back to my rooms to wash, my mind was in turmoil. Yoshioka followed close behind me, so that I knew he must have something to say and waited for him to catch up. He cleared his throat, hummed and hawed, and finally said, "Your Majesty spoke well and moved them deeply, which is why they were shedding such manly Japanese tears."

You really are frightened, I thought. You're frightened that I've seen through your "human bullets." Well, if you're frightened, I'm even more scared.

The German surrender of May, 1945, made Japan's position more desperate than ever, and it was now only a matter of time before the Soviet Army entered the war in the East. Even I realized that Japan's situation was hopeless.

The collapse finally came. On the morning of August 9, 1945, the last commander of the Kwantung Army, Otozo Yamata, and his Chief of Staff came to the palace to report to me that the Soviet Union had declared war on Japan.

Yamata was a short, thin, elderly man who was normally grave in manner and slow in speech. But on this day he was completely different; he gave me a rushed account of how well prepared the Japanese troops were and told me that they were confident of victory. Before he could finish speaking an air-raid siren sounded and we all went to the shelter. We soon heard bombs exploding nearby and he did not refer again to his confidence in victory before we parted after the all-clear.

From that time onward I slept in my clothes, kept a pistol in my pocket, and ordered martial law in the palace.

Yamata and his Chief of Staff came again the next day to tell me that the Japanese Army was going to withdraw and hold southern Manchuria so that the capital would have to be moved to Tunghua. Realizing that it would be impossible to move my large household and all my property so soon, I asked for and won a delay of two days.

I now underwent new mental torments. These resulted from a further change in Yoshioka's attitude as well as from my own morbid suspicions. After Yamata had gone, Yoshioka had pointed out: "If Your Majesty does not go, you will be the first to be murdered by the Soviet troops." He uttered these words in a sinister tone, but what made me even more frightened was the obvious implication that the Japanese suspected I did not wish to go and was planning to betray them.

I therefore re-enacted a scene I had used over ten years earlier to demonstrate my "loyalty and sincerity" in front of Yoshioka. I sent for the Prime Minister, Chang Ching-hui, and Rokuzo Takebe, the Director of the General Affairs Office of the State Council, and said: "We must support the holy war of our Parental Country with all our strength, and must resist the Soviet Army to the end, to the very end."

I then turned to see Yoshioka's expression, only to find that the Attaché to the Imperial Household, who normally stayed with me like a shadow, had vanished. Full of terrible forebodings, I paced up and down the room. At one point I looked out of the window and saw some Japanese soldiers advancing toward the building with their rifles at the ready. My heart almost jumped into my mouth and I thought my hour had come. Realizing I had nowhere to hide, I went to the top of the stairs to meet them. But when they saw me the soldiers went away.

I decided they must have come to test whether I would run away or not. The more I thought of this the more frightened I became, and I picked up the telephone to ring Yoshioka. But I could not get through to him. It looked as though the Japanese had gone without me, and this terrified me too.

Later I managed to reach Yoshioka. His voice was very weak and he said that he was ill. I expressed my concern, said a few kind words, and heard him reply, "Thank you, Your Majesty." He then rang off. Later I realized that I had not eaten all day and was very hungry. I asked my personal servant, Big Li, who had been with me since my Tientsin days, to bring me something. He reported that all the cooks had fled, so I had to make do with some crackers.

A little after nine in the evening of August 11th, Yoshioka showed up. My brother, sisters, brothers-in-law and nephews were already at the railway station, and of my entire family, only I and two of my wives were left in the palace. Yoshioka addressed me and the servants who were still with me in a peremptory tone:

"Whether we walk or go in automobiles, the sacred objects to be carried by Toranosuke Hashimoto will go in front. If anyone passes the sacred vessels they must make a ninety-degree bow."

I stood respectfully and watched Hashimoto, the President of the Bureau of Worship,[1] carry the bundle containing the sacred Shinto objects to the first car. I got into the second and, as we left the palace, I looked around and saw flames rising above the National Foundation Shrine.

The train took three days and two nights to reach Talitzu-kou. The original plan had been to go via Mukden, but the train was rerouted along the Kirin-Meihokuo line to avoid air raids. Throughout the journey we ate only two proper meals. We saw Japanese military vehicles all along the route, and the men in them looked like a cross between soldiers and refugees. The train stopped at Meihokuo for Yamata, the Commander of the Kwantung Army, to come aboard. He reported to me that the Japanese Army was winning and had destroyed numbers of Soviet tanks and aircraft. But his story was disproved by what I saw at the Kirin station. Crowds of Japanese women and children, screaming and shouting, were pushing toward the train as they wept and begged the gendarmes to let them pass.

On August 13, I arrived at Talitzukou, a coal-mine town

---

[1] After Pu Yi's second state visit to Japan, in May, 1940, Shinto-ism and the formal worship of the Japanese Heaven Shining Bright Deity was introduced into Manchukuo via Imperial Rescript. A National Foundation Shrine was built besides the palace at Changchun and other shrines were erected all over the Northeast. A Bureau of Worship was established, and on the first and fifteenth of each month, Pu Yi would lead the Kwantung Army Commander and others to the shrine to make offerings.

set amid mountains whose beauty I was too terrified to appreciate. Two days later the Japanese surrender was proclaimed.

Yoshioka said, "His Imperial Majesty has proclaimed our surrender, and the American government have given guarantees about his position and safety." I immediately sank to my knees and kowtowed to heaven, intoning, "I thank heaven for protecting His Imperial Majesty." Yoshioka also knelt down and kowtowed.

Yoshioka then explained that the Kwantung Army had been in touch with Tokyo, and it had been decided to send me to Japan. "But," he added, "His Imperial Majesty cannot assume unconditional responsibility for Your Majesty's safety. This will be in the hands of the Allies."

This remark made me feel as if a death sentence were beckoning to me. When the Japanese decided that I was to go to Tokyo they arranged for the secret return to Changchun of the Premier, Chang Ching-hui, and Rokuzo Takebe, the Japanese Director of the General Affairs Office of the Manchurian State Council, to make arrangements for the future. When Chang got back to Changchun he made radio contact with Chiang Kai-shek in Chungking and announced the establishment of a Committee for the Preservation of Public Order that was preparing to receive Kuomintang troops. He and his group hoped that they would be able to make a quick change into representatives of the Republic of China before the Soviet troops arrived, but the Soviet advance was much quicker than they had expected. The day after the Soviet Army reached Changchun, Chang Ching-hui's hopes were shattered when he and his fellow ministers were put into an aircraft and flown off to captivity in the USSR.

On August 16, Yoshioka told me that I was to go to Japan the following day. I nodded rapidly in agreement and pretended to be very pleased. He explained that I would have to decide whom to take with me. As we would be flying in a small aircraft I only chose my brother Pu Chieh, two brothers-in-law, three nephews, a doctor and my personal servant Big Li. One of my minor consorts asked me, amid sobs, what was going to happen to her. "The plane is too small," I explained. "So you will have to go by train."

"Will the train get me to the coast and to a boat to Japan?"

"Of course it will," I answered without a moment's thought. "In three days at the most you and the Empress will see me again."

"What will happen if the train doesn't come for me? I haven't got a single relation here."

"We'll meet again in a couple of days. You'll be all right."

We landed at Mukden where we were to change to a large aircraft at eleven in the morning, and sat in the airport waiting for the second airplane.

Before we had been waiting long, the airfield reverberated to the sound of aircraft engines as Soviet planes landed. Soviet troops holding submachine guns poured out of the planes and immediately disarmed all the Japanese soldiers on the airfield, which was soon covered with Soviet troops.

The next day I was put on a Soviet aircraft and flown to the USSR.

V

MY CAPTIVITY

27

Five Years in the Soviet Union

WHEN THE PLANE ARRIVED AT CHITA IN SIBERIA IT WAS almost evening. With me in this first group of Manchukuo war prisoners were Pu Chieh, two of my brothers-in-law, three nephews, a physician and a servant. We immediately entered a Soviet Army sedan that was waiting for us and left the airfield.

Through the windows it seemed as if we were traveling across a prairie; later there were endless forests, but after we had climbed over several low hills, the road narrowed and became so winding and bumpy that our speed was reduced. All of a sudden, we stopped.

Outside, I heard a sentence in Chinese: "If you wish to urinate, you may step down."

In the darkness, I became frightened. The voice made me think that some Chinese had showed up to take us back to China, and I knew that if this were true I would, without doubt, be killed. Although it was clear that we had just come from China to the Soviet Union in a Russian plane and that it was most unlikely that we would immediately be handed back to the Chinese, I was nevertheless upset. But as it turned out, the person speaking Chinese was a Soviet officer of Chinese descent.

After relieving ourselves, we again entered the car and continued our trip for another two hours. Then we drove down a narrow drive that wound between some hills until we drew up in front of a beautiful well-lighted building.

"But this is a hotel," someone said in a loud confident voice and, all of a sudden, we were happy.

Upon entering, a man in civilian clothes, about forty years old, and followed by a group of Soviet Army officers, came up to meet us. "By order of the Soviet Government, from this time onward, you will all be detained here," he said with some dignity.

This man, who was a Soviet Army major general, turned out to be the Commandant of the Chita Military District. Later he told us that he hoped we would be comfortable while waiting for the disposal of our case. He then pointed to a carafe of water on the table. "This place," he explained, "is noted for its mineral springs. The waters are very good to drink and excellent for your health."

Our life as detainees in this sanitarium began most comfortably. We had three square Russian meals a day as well as afternoon tea, Russian style. There were attendants to look after us and doctors and nurses who constantly checked up on our health and took care of us when we were ill. We had radios, books and all kinds of games to play as well as people to keep us company when we took walks. I felt very satisfied with this kind of life.

Not long after our arrival, I developed the illusion that since the Soviet Union, Great Britain and the United States were allies, I might be able to move eventually to England or the United States and live the life of an exile. At this time, I still had sufficient jewelry and objects of art in my possession to permit me to live out the second half of my life. I knew, however, that in order to achieve this goal, I would first have to make sure that I could remain in Russia, and it was with this in mind that during my five years in the Soviet Union I wrote the authorities three times seeking permission to remain forever.

The first of these three petitions was written in Chita, and the other two were written two months after I had been moved to Khabarovsk. The other Manchukuo detainees, however, took a completely different attitude regarding the future. A few days after our arrival in Chita, a group of former high officials also arrived. The following day Chang Ching-hui, Tsang Shih-yi and Hsi Hsia came to see me. "We have heard," one of them said, "that you would like to stay in Russia. But we all have our families in Manchuria and we must look after them. Furthermore there is lots of unfinished official business to be done. We therefore request that you ask the Soviets to let us return to the Northeast. Do you think this will work?"

I really had no idea what "official business" remained to be done and thus had no interest in their request. "How can I manage that?" I asked. "Even my own departure is undecided and will ultimately depend on the Soviet Union."

These men, upon learning that I would not intercede, began to beg. "I hope you will talk for us . . . we are sure you can do it," one said.

"This is all our doing and I was selected to talk to you, Master Pu," another explained.

"This concerns all of us; if, sir, we don't beg you, honorable Master, whom shall we beg?" pleaded a third.

Since they could no longer call me "Emperor" or "Majesty," they now called me by any term that came to their minds. I was so irked by the whole incident that I couldn't help but discuss it with Colonel Volokov who was responsible for looking after us. His only response was to say that "I shall submit this message for you."

At this time I didn't fully understand that these people knew that the Kuomingtang (Chiang Kai-shek) could use them and therefore they felt that if they returned to China it would not only be safe but also that they would be able to earn a living.

One day, one of the Manchukuo prisoners who had been assigned to cleaning duty, while we were in Khabarovsk, fell to the floor in an epileptic fit and began to babble. An ex-high Manchukuo official, who believed in séances, felt that this man who was writhing on the floor was speaking the words of the gods who had taken possession of his body. He immediately knelt down beside him, kowtowed and said: "We sincerely and respectfully request the great god to give us a sign that we can know when we may leave the Soviet Union and return to our homes."

Our Russian interpreters often told us the news and we were also allowed to read a Chinese newspaper published by the Soviet Army in Port Arthur called *Trud*. It was from these two sources that we were able to follow the developments in China and the fighting between the Communists and the Nationalists. I, however, was not much interested because I realized that no matter which side won it would be the same for me. Both sides would wish to have my life; my only hope was never to return to China.

The ex-high Manchukuo officials, however, were very much concerned about developments and placed their hopes in the victory of Chiang Kai-shek because they felt that with United States aid, Chiang could defeat the Communists. Therefore, when we first heard the news of the victories of the People's Liberation Army, no one chose to believe it. And later on, when the facts were proven, the officials became panicky. When the new China was declared established one of them, who seemed to feel that he was more experienced in this sort of thing, proposed that we send our greetings to the government, and this proposal received a favorable reaction among us.

During my five years' detention in Soviet Russia I was never able to dispense with my prerogatives. When later we were transferred to the receiving center in Khabarovsk and there were no attendants, I still had people to wait on me. The members of my family made my bed, tidied up my room, brought me my meals and washed my clothing. Even though they did not dare to address me as Emperor in public, they still called me "the Upper One," and every day, when they came to my room in the morning, they would first pay their respects to me.

One day, right after our arrival at a suburb of Khabarovsk, I wished to take a walk. At the foot of the stairs there was a former high official sitting in a chair who did not even nod his head or look at me. I became so angry that from this time on I preferred to stay upstairs and spend the greater part of the day reading Buddhist scriptures. But in general, the majority of the ex-officials still maintained their respect for me. For example, during these five years, on the occasion of the Chinese New Year celebrations, when we ate meat dumplings, the first bowl was always presented to me.

I did not wish to work and also I did not wish to let my family members work for other people. I remember once at dinnertime, my younger brother and my sister's husband wished to help set the table. I stopped them. How could my family serve other people? Between 1947 and 1948 when most of my family were sent for a while to another receiving center in Khabarovsk, I felt very much inconvenienced.

Although the Soviet authorities treated me with consideration and allowed me to eat by myself, I still had the problem of who would bring me my rice bowl. Fortunately, my brother-in-law volunteered. He not only brought me my food but he was also willing to wash my clothing. Meanwhile, the receiving center set aside for us a small plot of land in the courtyard where we could plant vegetables.

My family and I raised green peppers, tomatoes, eggplant, beans, and other vegetables, and when I saw how these green plants grew daily I was most impressed. Every day I would take a can to water the plants and enjoyed doing this very much because I had never done anything like it before. But my main interest in my garden was derived from the fact that I loved to eat tomatoes and green peppers! And I couldn't help but think how much more convenient it was to buy them at the grocery.

The authorities of the receiving center issued us Chinese books on *The Problems of Leninism* and *The History of the Soviet Communist Party,* and asked my brother and brother-in-law to lecture to everyone on them. But the audience was even more confused than the lecturer. In my own mind, I couldn't help but think: If they won't let me stay in Soviet Russia what earthly good would it do, even if I learned these two books by heart? Besides, my green peppers and tomatoes are much more important!

I sat at a special seat beside the lecture rostrum. While listening to "teacher" who went stuttering on about Menshivikism and nationalist dogma, the evils of which I didn't understand and in which I was totally disinterested, my thoughts kept wandering back to the question of whether I should eventually be able to settle in Moscow or London as an exile. How many years would my jewels and art objects enable me to live comfortably? Then I began to worry about my eggplants. Since the Russians did not eat eggplants what would I be able to do with my harvest?

But still I had to pretend to listen diligently even though some of the others preferred to doze. After dinner, which was a free period, the situation was completely different. All was activity and noise. On one side of the corridor there were always a few tables of Mah-Jongg and the clicking of the tiles and the hum of voices at play. On the other side, near the window, others would often hold up their hands in prayer as they intoned "Amitabha Buddha! Goddess of Mercy!" From upstairs came the strange sounds of Japanese singing "soo, oooh, wooh." Others meanwhile stood in groups telling fortunes and asked when they could go back home and what had happened to their families. In various bedrooms there were séances and sand readings.

At first the Soviet Army guards were disturbed by this cacophony of noises and cast strange looks about the rooms. But later on, even they became accustomed to it. At this time I would usually stay in my own room either trying to predict the future by tossing coins or reciting *The Diamond Sutra*.

My thoughts went through no basic changes. I knew that by Soviet law I had committed the crime of treason, but as far as I was concerned, I only thought that what had happened had been due to prearranged destiny. I recalled the old sayings; "Might is right" and "Victors become kings and dukes, but the vanquished become bandits." At this point I had never heard of "brainwashing" or "reforming one's thoughts." I thus adopted the old method of avoiding punishment. Since the Soviet Union was the deciding factor in my life, it therefore was best to be nice to the Russians and seek to gain their favor. I thus contributed my jewels and treasure to Russia on the grounds that I wished to support its postwar economic reconstruction.

I did not give away all my valuables, however, but held back some of the best and asked my nephew to hide these in the double bottom of my black leather suitcase. But it was too small for him to hide all of the things and he therefore had to conceal the rest in whatever I thought would be safe. We hid some of the jewelry in bars of washing soap. But there was still some left over, and this we had to throw away.

One day a Soviet Army officer accompanied by an interpreter came into the parlor holding something shiny in his hand. "Whose things are these?" he asked. "Who put this into a discarded radiator section in the courtyard?"

The detainees immediately surrounded the officer and saw that he was holding some jewelry in his hand. "There are the marks of a silverware shop in Peking on it," one of them said. "It is very strange. Who could have put it there?"

I immediately recognized the pieces as some of the items I had told my nephew to throw away, and the situation looked especially bad for me since at this time all the other Pekingese detainees had been put in another receiving center. But nevertheless, I kept on shaking my head and repeating: "Strange. Most strange. I wonder who did it. I wonder who could have put it there."

Unexpectedly, the interpreter who held in his hands an old wooden comb, walked up to me and said: "This comb was found among the jewelry. I remember that it belongs to you!"

"No, no," I answered, quickly. "Even that comb; it doesn't belong to me."

The two Russians stood around for a while, but finally decided to leave. Actually, I not only threw out some of the jewelry but I also had many of my pearls burned in a stove before I left the Soviet Union. Also, I asked my servant Big Li to put others into the chimney on the rooftop.

At the same time, however, I was most cooperative in supplying material to the Russians when they sought my help in investigating the crimes committed by the Japanese "bandits" in the Northeast. And later, when I was called as a witness before the Far East International Military Tribunal in Tokyo, I accused the Japanese of being war criminals in an utterly direct and unreserved way. However, whenever I spoke about this period of history I never discussed my own guilt.

In August, 1946, I appeared as a witness before the Tribunal for a total of eight days. It was said that this was the longest period of time that a witness appeared before this Tribunal and my testimony made headlines in the newspapers throughout the world.

The demand for my appearance as a witness was derived from the desire to illuminate the real background of Japanese relations with China. It was intended to explain how Japan had tried to utilize me, the last Emperor of the Ch'ing Dynasty, as a puppet in order to gain control of the four northeastern provinces. Today I have considerable regrets about my testimony. My difficulty was that I was in constant fear of eventual punishment in China for what I might say.

Even though I did mention some of the facts regarding Japanese behavior, I also covered up a lot of things owing to my fear and to my sense of pride. I therefore did not expose everything concerning the conversations between the Japanese imperialists and myself which had commenced long before the September 18 Incident. After all, what had happened after the incident was clearly the result of prior long-term connections between ourselves and the Japanese. But in order to safeguard my own position I only spoke of how I was compelled to behave as I did and how I suffered at the hands of the Japanese.

On several occasions during the trial, I became excited, and once spoke most impulsively about being forced to worship the ancestral Shinto gods of Japan in Manchukuo. A Japanese attorney rebutted me with the remark that the way I had attacked the Japanese Emperor's ancestors seemed quite incompatible with my own Oriental traditions of virtue. "I never compelled them to treat my own ancestors as if they were theirs," I shouted back.

My reply caused laughter in the courtroom. But even so I still felt angry and thus when I came to the death of my wife Tan Yu-ling, I turned my suspicions into established facts. "Even she was murdered by the Japanese," I said.

The defense counsels tried many methods in order to mitigate the crimes of the accused war criminals. They sought to reduce the value of my testimony and they even tried to deny my qualifications as a witness. Of course they failed. But even if they had been able to refute everything I said, they would have been unable to change the fate of the accused. However, they were able to get me to talk less about the real situation by exploiting my fears of punishment.

I still remember that after I had enumerated the criminal actions of the Japanese, an American lawyer shouted at me: "You have put all the crimes on the Japanese. But you are a criminal too. You will ultimately receive the judgment of the Chinese Government!"

This remark had, of course, touched on the point that I feared most, and it was because of these fears that I had purposely sought to explain away my own conduct by arguing that I had been "kidnapped by the Japanese" and denying that I had entered into intrigues or negotiations with them. And even though the Tribunal produced a letter of mine written to the Japanese, I denounced it as a forgery.

28

Back to Manchuria—A Prisoner

THE RUSSIAN TRAIN THAT WAS USED TO TRANSPORT US arrived at the Sino-Soviet frontier on the evening of July 31, 1950. The captain in charge explained that he would have to wait until morning to complete our transfer to the Chinese government officials and exhorted me to sleep well and with a composed mind. Ever since boarding the train I had been separated from my family and placed in a compartment with the Russian officers. Although they had joked with me and given me beer and candy, I still felt that they were sending me to my death. I was sure that as soon as I set foot on Chinese soil my life would be finished.

I kept my eyes open and could not sleep. Later, I sat up to repeat some Buddhist prayers and heard footsteps approaching the train from the station. They sounded like a company of soldiers, but when I looked out, I could see no one. After a while, the sound went away and all that was left was a distant electric light glinting with an ill-omened beam. I sighed, turned over in my berth and stared absent-mindedly at the empty wineglass on the table near the window.

The captain had said to me, while he had been drinking, "By daybreak you will see your homeland. It is an important event in one's life to return to one's motherland and you can rest well. The Communist Party is the most civilized in the world and the people of China are, of all peoples, the most broad-minded." I stared maliciously at him. He was in the opposite berth and had begun to snore.

Your words, your wine and your candies, they are all lies, I thought to myself. My life is like the dewdrops on the windowpane. Once the sun comes up, everything will evaporate. *You* surely sleep very soundly!

In my mind, I had no motherland, only ancestors. To me the Communist Party could only be associated with "raging floods and wild beasts" and it was absurd to speak about civilization in the same breath. Admittedly the Soviet Russians had not given me inhuman treatment. However, Soviet Russia was one of the Allies and could not do what it wished, but as far as China was concerned, the situation was different. The Communist party of China had defeated Chiang Kai-shek and could do whatever it liked without restrictions or fear. Once I fell into the hands of these people, there would be no way for me to stay alive.

The following morning, when the captain asked me to follow him to the Chinese representatives, I wondered whether I would have the courage, once I reached the moment of truth, to shout "Long life to the ancestors of the Great Ch'ing." It was in such a state of mind that I was led into a compartment in which there were seated two Chinese, one in civilian clothes and the other in a khaki uniform without insignia or rank but with a label on which was written *Chinese People's Liberation Army*. The two stood up and said a few words to the Soviet captain and then the one in civilian clothes turned around and said to me, "I am here by order of the Prime Minister, Chou En-lai, to receive you. Now you have returned to your homeland."

I bowed my head waiting for him to handcuff me, but he only stared at me emotionlessly. They know I cannot escape, I thought.

Later, I followed the Soviet captain out of the compartment to the station platform, where there were two rows of soldiers drawn up; on one side Russians, on the other, Chinese. We walked between them toward a train on the opposite side of the platform. In the short moment it took to cross the platform I thought of the 8,000,000 soldiers of Chiang Kai-shek who had been eliminated by these people and felt, as a result, that in their eyes I was perhaps no more important than a tiny insect.

As soon as I boarded the train, I saw my family and the

other Manchukuo detainees. They all sat straight, but they were neither handcuffed nor bound with rope. I was led to a seat near the end of the car where one of the soldiers placed my leather suitcase on the baggage rack overhead. After I sat down, I tried to see what the troops outside were doing, but discovered that the windows had been pasted over with newspapers. When I looked at the ends of the car I noticed a guard at each end with a rifle and fixed bayonet.

The atmosphere was so ominous that my heart nearly came to a stop, and when I looked at the prisoners near me I saw on their faces the color of death. After a while, a man who was not carrying a rifle, and who seemed to be an officer, walked to the center of the car.

"Well, you have rejoined the homeland," he said. "You people can rest assured that the Central People's Government have made proper arrangements for all of you. There are medical attendants on the train and whoever feels ill may visit them for treatment."

What did this mean? "The homeland!" "Proper arrangements; rest assured that if you feel sick you may see the medical attendants." Oh, I understood. It was to calm our minds in order to avoid an incident while en route!

Later, several soldiers brought in a basket of rice bowls and chopsticks and distributed a set to each of us. "Take good care of these and don't break them because they cannot be replaced en route," they explained.

I immediately concluded that the road to the execution site would be a long one. Otherwise, why should they be so solicitous?

For breakfast, there were preserved vegetables, eggs and congee. Our appetites were aroused by this Chinese food, our first in a long while, and, in a very short time, the whole pail of congee was consumed. The soldiers then let us have another pail which they themselves had been eating. This puzzled me, since I knew that there were no cooking facilities on the train and that they would have to wait for the next stop until they could get more to eat for themselves.

After breakfast, quite a few of the prisoners in the car began to talk about this incident. They concluded that since the soldiers had let us have their breakfast they were well trained and disciplined and would not maltreat us during the journey.

But I did not share their opinion. I thought just the opposite. I felt that the Communist Party people hated me the most. It was impossible for me to believe that they would not do something to me before the coming night was over.

Although many of the other prisoners began to nap after breakfast, I was unable to put myself at ease. I desperately wanted to find out from those who held me prisoner whether I would meet death or not. A very young soldier sat opposite me and, after looking him over, I chose the emblem on his chest as a device with which to start a conversation.

"The Chinese People's Liberation Army," I said, pointing to the emblem. "You are a soldier of the Liberation Army. You know," I continued, "that the word 'liberation' is really excellent. I am one who believes in Buddhism and even we, in our Buddhist classics, have that same word, 'liberation.' Buddha was devoted to benevolence to the extent that he sought to 'liberate' all living creatures."

The young soldier did not utter a sound, and when I reached the point in my discussion where I explained that I had never killed a living thing, that I had never even swatted a fly, the expression on his face became so blank and his eyes so wide with confusion that I found I could not continue.

Thus, my despair became even greater, and even the clicking noise of the car wheels on the tracks made me feel that death was coming closer and closer. I left my seat and aimlessly walked down the corridor until I reached the other end of the car and then began to walk back again. In the middle, I thought I heard my nephew, Little Hsiu, say the words "democracy" and "monarchy" to someone in a low voice.

Suddenly I began to shout. "How can you talk about monarchy at such a time as this," I screamed. "If there is anyone in this car who still believes in monarchy I will be happy to fight a duel with him!"

Everyone was both astonished and stupefied, but my hysterics continued. "Why should you people stare at me? I am the one who will be shot; you others don't need to worry."

A soldier came up and dragged me back to my seat. "You should take a good rest," he said.

But apparently I had become completely bewildered, for I held on to the soldier and whispered, "That was my nephew. His thoughts are very bad; he opposes democracy just like someone else aboard this train, a former Manchukuo army officer who, while we were in Soviet Russia, said all sorts of things against democracy."

The soldier forced me down into the seat and although I closed my eyes, my lips continued to move in ranting phrases. But finally, perhaps because I had not slept in several nights, I fell into a deep sleep.

When I awoke it was already morning of the following day and the train had reduced its speed. After it came to a stop, I thought I heard someone in a low voice say "Changchun." I jumped up like a coiled spring that has suddenly been released and tried to peer through the window, but, of course, I could see nothing. All I heard were people outside, singing. This, I thought, is my place of execution. Here I was once Emperor. Now everyone is preparing to give me a public trial.

When I was in Soviet Russia, I had read in the newspaper *Trud* about the campaign against landlords, and the procedure for public trials raced through my mind. First, the militia would escort me to the public trial grounds. Just at this point in my thoughts it so happened that two soldiers entered the car together and almost overwhelmed me with fright, but as it turned out, they had come with a bucket of congee for breakfast and soon the train started to move again.

A short while after we reached Mukden a stranger came into the car with a note in his hands. "Since this has been such a hot journey," he explained, "the older people will follow me to take a rest." He then read off a list of names from the paper he still held in his hand. One of my nephews and I were both on the list, and although I was forty-four years old and could thus fit into the category of older people, it was clearly improper to include on such a list the name of my nephew, Little Hsiu, who was about thirty. I decided, therefore, that it was a trick. I was the Emperor, the rest were former high officials, and my nephew had been included because he had been denounced by me. We would soon be shot as a group, in Mukden, where my ancestors had founded the Ch'ing Dynasty.

Those of us whose names had been called were put into a big sedan and the soldiers, who followed in another car, all held rifles with bayonets at the ready.

"Everything is finished! I am taking you to see our ancestors," I said to my nephew. His face became deathly white, even though the man who had read the list laughed and asked, "What are you afraid of? Didn't I tell you this is to take you for a rest?"

I paid no attention to him. I merely kept muttering, under my breath, "A trick, a trick, a trick."

Upon our arrival at a large building, a soldier came up to the car and guided us through the gate. "Go upstairs," he said.

I was sure I would die and decided that I might as well get it over with quickly. Thus, with my coat under my arm, I walked faster and faster up the stairs so that the soldier who was leading us was forced to increase his pace in order to keep up with me. Once upstairs, we stopped at a door and the soldier told me to enter. The room was large and in its center was a long table with chairs on both sides and on it were cigarettes, fruit, and pastry. I threw down my coat, picked up a big apple, and took a bite. "This is my last supper," I said to myself. "I might as well finish it in a hurry."

Before I had half finished the apple, other people in both civilian clothes and military uniforms began to enter the room and it was soon crowded. Not far from me, a middle-aged man in uniform began to talk. But since I was trying hard to swallow what was left of the apple, I couldn't hear a thing he said. With difficulty I finally finished the apple, and I then stood up.

"You don't need to talk," I said. "Let's go."

Several of the people started laughing. The one who had been speaking also laughed. "You are too tense," he said. "You don't need to be afraid. Later when you arrive at Fushun, take a good rest and start studying diligently and faithfully."

I was utterly astonished at his words. Was this true? Were they not going to execute me? What was it all about?

Just at this moment the man who had brought us from the train approached me. In his hand he still held the list of names and explained to the man who had been talking to me that all of us who needed a rest were present and accounted for except for one who was ill.

Upon hearing this, I completely disregarded all formality and grabbed the list from his hands. Even though my conduct made everyone laugh, I didn't care, for I was still sure that the list contained the names of those who were sentenced to death.

At this point, however, another prisoner arrived. He had been among those who had been sent back to China before us and he told us what had happened to his group and their families. When we learned that they were all still alive and that their families were either in school or at work, our faces lit up. Tears came to my eyes and I began to weep.

Although this relief from tension did not last long, only for about an hour, the time it took to travel from Mukden to Fushun, it still allowed me to relax for a bit. Otherwise, I should have gone insane, because from the time I had boarded the train in Russia five days previously, I had thought only of death.

When we returned, we found the atmosphere on the train completely changed. Everyone was smoking cigarettes and chatting gaily. Some thought that we would be sent to the most exclusive and lavish club in Fushun where we would be held for a few days of study, after which the Communists would send us home. Others told of how, after our arrival, they would send telegrams to their families saying that they were well and asking their relations to get ready to welcome them. Others spoke of taking a bath once we got to the club. Illusions of all kinds and colors prevailed.

When the others spoke of their former fears, it turned out that they had all felt as I had. We could not help laughing about it. But as soon as we left the train at Fushun, we noticed that we were surrounded by sentries in uniform and we could no longer laugh and smile.

We were escorted to some trucks and from this time on I

again became sick with fear. I lost all sense of time and only knew that when the truck stopped I would find myself surrounded by walls. They would not only be high, but there would also be barbed wire on top and sentry towers at the corners.

After I got down from the truck, we walked some distance until we came to a row of one-story buildings. There were iron bars at all the windows. I began to understand—it was a prison. My fears had been correct.

The soldiers led us inside through a long, narrow passageway until we came into a large room. Here we were searched and later we were taken outside in groups. Several others and I followed a soldier down a passageway into a small room. Before I had a chance to see exactly what sort of room it was, I heard a noise behind me. It was the bolting of an iron door.

There was a long wooden *kang* in the cell and also a long table with two benches. The few who had come in with me were all former army officers of the Manchukuo government. I did not know them well and did not wish to talk with them.

A few hours later, the cell door was pulled open and a guard entered. He asked me to follow him to another cell. Here, to my intense joy, I found my three nephews, my brother Pu Chieh, and my father-in-law, Jung Yuan. They had just received new blankets, new mattresses, washbasins, and other necessities, and had taken one of each for me.

"This is a military prison," my father-in-law explained, as he touched the iron bars. "Everyone here is in uniform. I do not think we are in immediate danger. Otherwise, why should they have issued us toothbrushes and towels? Also, when we arrived, a receptionist gave us each a receipt for the personal possessions they took from us. This is not the treatment accorded ordinary prisoners. Furthermore, the food is not so bad."

By the following day I began to believe that what my father-in-law had said was true. Not only were the meals about the same as the day before, but we were also given a thorough physical examination, and were issued new white underwear and black jackets and, surprisingly enough, cigarettes. This was clearly not the treatment for prisoners awaiting death. A few days later, a somewhat stout man of about forty came to our cell and asked our names and what kind of books we had read in the Soviet Union and whether or not we had studied hard while there. Upon hearing our replies, he nodded his head. "Well," he said, "I'll issue you some books and newspapers right away and you people can learn some new ideas."

A few hours later books, newspapers, chessboards and playing cards were brought in. At the same time loudspeakers, in the passageway outside the cell, were connected. Broadcasts were transmitted twice a day; one was news and the other consisted of operatic and theatrical music.

Besides listening to these, we were allowed to walk in the courtyard for a half hour each afternoon. Meanwhile, my nephew, Little Hsiu, had found out that the man who had told us to study hard was the Director of the War Prisoner Thought Control Center in which we were held and the man who had actually brought the books, who was named Li, was the Deputy Director. At the time we had addressed him as "Mister" since we didn't know what we were supposed to call him. We also addressed all the guards as "Mister" too.

Li had brought us three books: *The New Democracy, The History of China's Last 100 Years* and *The Revolutionary History of the New People's Democracy*. He had told us that since he did not have enough books to go around, we should rotate them, or, better still, one of us should read aloud to the others. He explained that there were many new terms in these books.

Although there was much that was strange and novel in the books, actually the most novel thing of all was that they made us, as prisoners, study. One of my nephews was the first to become interested in the books. He read much faster than the rest of us and would often ask us to explain things to him. If we could not answer him, he would go to the Center Director and ask. My father-in-law castigated him for this.

"Don't think for a minute that this is a school," he explained. "It is a prison."

"But didn't the Director tell us we should start to learn?" my nephew asked.

"To learn . . . yes. To learn that this is a prison," my

226

father-in-law answered. "Yesterday," he continued, "when we went outside for exercise, I heard someone say that this was formerly a prison under the Manchukuo regime. It formerly was and it still *is*, even with books and magazines."

One day, not long after this, when we came back from our stroll in the courtyard, Pu Chieh hurriedly began to scan the newspapers. With some excitement, he said that he had overheard a discussion outside about an article in the paper that had explained the reason why the government was asking us all to study. We immediately circled around him in order to help him find it. Although I have forgotten the title, I do recall that it made the point that the new China was in need of all kinds of talent.

All of us, except my father-in-law, read the article and Pu Chieh explained that this was exactly what he had overheard; namely, that the reason the government let us study and had treated us so leniently was because the country was experiencing a shortage of talent and that it wished to be able to make use of all of us.

When I recall this incident today, his opinion seems laughable. Yet, at the time, it was actually the way the majority of us felt. In our cell, despite my father-in-law's doubts, the others seemed to go along with this line of reasoning and from this day on a great change was evident, inasmuch as all of us became devoted students. Prior to this time, with the exception of my one nephew, the rest of us had shown an interest in the propaganda pamphlets and daily study period purely as a means of demonstrating to the guards in the passageway outside the cell door what model prisoners we were.

We did not have a member of the Communist Party cadre from the prison's central office with us. Our study was thus limited to memorizing the terminology and learning its meaning. My father-in-law, of course, wasn't interested and when the rest of us studied, he would close his eyes and repeat Buddhist incantations. But this blind optimism on our part did not last very long. Like a flower that blooms for just a few hours, it soon faded away, for shortly afterward the prison announced a readjustment of cell arrangements and separated me from my family.

29

Isolated

ALTHOUGH, IN MY BRAINWASHING, THIS WAS ONE OF THE most important steps, I did not understand it at the time. I thought that the Communist Party still regarded me as the arch-enemy and was preoccupied with my past, not with how I should be reformed vis-a-vis the future. I believed that it had separated me from my family in order to facilitate my eventual prosecution.

Ever since my detention in Soviet Russia, I had consistently tried to explain away my conduct as something I had been compelled to do under pressure. Thus, I had claimed that the plot between Doihara and me had been a case of kidnapping and I had covered up my relations with the Japanese.

I had also warned the adult members of my family to cover up for me while in Soviet Russia, and now that I had returned to China it was more necessary than ever to keep the true story of my relations with the Japanese a secret. I would have to be very careful to avoid a slipup—especially with my nephew Little Hsiu. On the first day of our arrival at Fushun, I discovered that he harbored some sort of resentment against me because of the incident on the train. Soon after we were locked in our cell, I felt something crawling on my neck and I asked him to see what it was.

If this had happened in the past, he would have come over to me promptly. But on this occasion, he pretended not to hear me and did not make a move. Later, when he finally did come and discovered that it was a caterpillar and brushed it off onto the floor, he muttered under his breath, "What is the use of liberating a living creature, if, after liberation, it may be destroyed by someone else?"

I felt very much upset by his remark which was so clearly meant for me. A few days later, when Little Jui was tidying up my blanket and mattress, I asked him to pick up the blanket and shake it out. This was somewhat distasteful to the others in the cell because it was filled with dust. Pu Chieh frowned and another of my nephews put his hands on his nose and said to Little Jui, "Be kind to us. This will choke us to death."

Little Hsiu, at this point, immediately stopped what he was doing, took the blanket from Jui, and tossed it on the *kang*. "This cell is not only for you," he said. "We have to live here too. Why don't you think about us? This will not do."

"What do you mean by 'we' and 'you?' " I said, frowning. "Don't you have any manners left?"

He did not answer me, but turned his head away and sat at the table without saying a word. After a while, I noticed an angry expression on his lips as he scribbled on a piece of paper. I wanted to see what he was writing and did not anticipate that as soon as I reached for it he would tear it to pieces. But I felt sure I had seen a line which read, "Wait and see who will come out on top."

Since the incident on the train, I had tried my best to show goodwill toward him and I had talked to him in a most amicable way. Later on, I had had an opportunity to talk to him alone, specifically about the train incident. I told him that it had not been done with malicious intent; that I had loved him all the time, that I had been hysterical and had not slept for five days. Since that time, whenever I had a chance, I had explained to all of my nephews about the importance of a close family relationship according to Chinese traditions. Confronted by an emergency, we should cooperate fully. Whenever Little Hsiu was not around, I would say to the others, "Watch out for Little Hsiu. Be careful not to let him do anything wrong. Try to please him."

Thus, by the time the newspaper article had aroused hope in our minds, Little Hsiu's attitude had become completely normal and when the guard ordered me to another cell, it was Little Hsiu who, along with another nephew, Little Ku, picked up my bedding and suitcase and carried them for me to my new cell. They left immediately after they had put my things down.

I felt so desperately alone before my new cellmates that I did not know whether to sit down or stand up. There were eight prisoners besides myself in the cell and when they saw me enter, they remained silent and their attitude was very formal. Later, one of them took my bedding and placed it in the corner. At the time, I didn't realize that this was a gesture of respect since the spot they had chosen was the best in the cell, warm in winter and cool in summer. I could only think that the separation from my family was fraught with danger.

I sat down silently for a while and then stood up and paced back and forth. Finally I walked to the door and knocked several times.

"What is it?" a rather stout guard asked as he opened it.

"May I talk to the Center Chief about something?"

"What do you want to talk to him about?"

"I wish to tell him that I have never been separated from my family and I feel most distressed and uncomfortable."

The guard nodded his head and asked me to wait. Upon his return he told me that the Center Chief would allow me to go back to my original cell. This made me extremely happy. I folded my bedding myself, and one of the guards helped me pick up my leather satchel. In the passageway, I ran into the Chief. "There is a higher standard of food for those of you who are a little older," he explained. "We felt that if you continued to live with your family and I gave you better food it might have had a bad effect on them."

I refused to believe that this was the real motive and thus, without waiting for him to explain further, I immediately said, "Never mind; I guarantee that they won't be upset."

I nearly said, "How could you have supposed they would be like that?"

The Chief grinned and asked me if I had ever thought that the time might come when I should have to learn to take care of myself. "Yes, yes," I replied, immediately. "But I have to practice it slowly, bit by bit."

"All right." The Chief nodded. "But you should begin practicing right away."

By the time I had returned to the cell with my family it seemed as if the half-day separation had been for a whole year. When I explained to them how the Chief had told me to "practice bit by bit," they interpreted his remark as indicative that the government did not intend to maltreat me.

Ten days later, a guard again ordered me to pack up my things and I decided that I would take the opportunity, while Little Jui was packing for me, to pass on a few words to my family. But, fearing the guard might hear, I decided it would be best to write a note. Also, since there were two men in the cell who were former Manchukuo officials and not family members, it seemed safer to write. The note was purposely vague: "We have lived very well together. After I leave I hope you will continue to help one another. I am very much concerned for each and every one of you."

I gave the note to Pu Chieh and told him to pass it around to the others. I felt that after they had seen it they would be able to understand its meaning—to have one heart and to remain united.

My nephew again took my bedding and carried my suitcase to the cell I had been put in the previous time, and the occupants again placed the bedding in the same place as before. Unable to sleep well, I paced back and forth for a while and later knocked at the door until the same short stout guard opened it. His name was Liu.

"Mr. Liu, I have something . . ." I said.

"You want to see the Director?" he asked before I had finished my sentence.

"I wish to talk with you first. I . . . No, it isn't that I wish to move back to my old cell. I want to ask if I can meet with my family once a day. So long as I can see them, I'll feel much better."

"Every day during the exercise period in the courtyard, won't it be possible for you to see them?"

"But I wish to talk to them privately. Do you think the Director will permit this?"

"According to regulations, people are not supposed to talk to one another who do not live in the same cell. But I'll ask for you."

I got permission and, from that day on, when I took my stroll in the courtyard each day I could meet with my family and talk with them for a while. My nephews would then tell me what was going on in their cell and whom they had talked with. Little Ku still maintained his carefree attitude, Little Hsiu did not show any sign of bitterness and Little Jui still continued to wash my clothing and darn my socks. Thus, one problem that had bothered me was solved.

But meanwhile new problems had arisen. For the past forty years, I had always reached for the clothing that had been readied for me and eaten the food that had been placed in front of me. Now these habits were a great hardship. Things like a rice ladle, a carving knife, a pair of scissors, a needle and thread were utterly foreign to me. I had to do everything myself and I was trapped in a very distressing situation. In the morning, by the time everyone else had finished washing their faces, I would just be ready to dress; and by the time I was ready to wash, everyone else had finished. When I brushed my teeth, I would realize that I had forgotten the tooth powder, and by the time I had finished dressing everyone else had already eaten breakfast. I was always late and always behind schedule and yet was always rushing about the cell like mad.

But what bothered me the most was that I knew my cellmates, all of whom were former military officers of the Manchukuo imperial regime, were laughing at me behind my back. In former times, these people had not been qualified to raise their heads in front of me, and when I had first arrived in the cell, even though they did not call me the "Upper One" as my family members did in private, they had not dared to use the familiar "you." They had either called me "Mister" or some other title in order to show their respect for me. But now I knew they were joking silently about my predicament and this made me ill at ease.

There was also something else that made me feel even more uncomfortable. Since the first day of our arrival at Fushun, each cell had established a "duty" system by which the cleaning and honey bucket chores were rotated. Before I had been separated from my family, I was not required to do this, but now, what would I do if I had the "duty"? Should I empty the honey bucket for everyone? It seemed to me that this would be an insult to my ancestors and to my nephew's ancestors and their heirs. Fortunately, the Center solved the problem for me. Two days after I had been moved to my new cell, a man who was an active member of the Communist Party cadre in the Center came to the door. "Pu Yi," he said, "will not get cleaning duty." To me, these words made me feel as if I had stepped from a corner of death.

One day, while we were taking our daily walk by twos and threes, when the Center Chief appeared, as he did every day to say a few words, I noticed that he looked at me closely as if he were sizing me up. Finally, he called out my name, "Pu Yi."

"Yes," I answered as I walked over to him.

"Your clothing was issued at the same time as the others. Why is it that your suit is not in the same condition?"

He spoke quietly and in an amicable tone. I looked at my clothing and that of the others. Everyone else was neatly dressed; their suits were pressed and clean; and yet mine was rumpled; a pocket was torn, a button missing and there was an ink spot on the lower part of my jacket. My pants legs seemed of different lengths and my shoes were improperly tied.

"I'll tidy up right away," I replied in a low tone.

"You should watch more carefully how the others manage their daily lives," the Chief said. "If you learn from others, then you'll progress."

Even though the Director's tone was not unkindly, I felt embarrassed and angry. This was the first time I had ever been reprimanded in public as incompetent and it was the first time that I had ever been exhibited before the eyes of so many people as a useless thing.

Desperately embarrassed, I turned around in order to avoid having to look at my fellow prisoners, and I went to the foot of the courtyard wall and stared at its gray stones. I was seized with a terrible depression and I felt that in all my life I had never been able to get away from gray walls; all my life I had been a prisoner. But heretofore I still had some kind of dignity and position. Even in my little circle in Changchun, I had still maintained some special privileges. Now, within this particular set of walls, all was gone. I was treated as everyone else and had been humiliated before everyone else as incompetent. Thus the gratefulness that I had developed for those who had allowed me to be exempted from cleaning duty was washed away from my heart forever. It was in this mood that I spent more than two months in Fushun. By the end of October, the Center was moved to Harbin.

On the train, en route to Harbin, only a few of the younger people still had some interest in conversation. The others had little to say and if they did talk it was always in a very low tone. I was silent most of the time. Quite a few other prisoners, I noticed, could not sleep at night and could not eat properly in the daytime.

I was not as apprehensive as I had been when I had first returned to China, but I was still more tense than anyone else. This was the time that the American armies were approaching the Yalu River, during the Korean War, and it was not long after the Chinese People's Volunteer Army had left China to enter the Korean campaign. I noticed that Pu Chieh could not sleep either and I stealthily asked him how he felt about the war situation. "To leave the country to participate in war is like making an offering of incense before ghosts," he replied in a dull tone. "The end is soon in sight."

What he meant was that China would soon be defeated and Manchuria would be occupied by the American Army. Pu Chieh feared that when the Communists realized that the situation was hopeless and the country would soon be lost, they would kill us to prevent our falling into American hands. Later I found that this was how all the other detainees felt.

When we arrived in Harbin, I felt even more hopeless after seeing the new Thought Control Center which was a prison, originally built by the Japanese to house those who had opposed their regime. It was two stories high and in the center was a watchtower; circling it were two fan-shaped buildings. The gates were all made of iron bars one inch in diameter. The cells were partitioned by cement walls; each could accommodate seven to eight persons, but in my cell there were only five. Owing to the Japanese design there were no *kangs* and we had to sleep on the floor. I stayed in this prison almost two years.

One night, in the city nearby, there was an air-raid alert and the wailing noise of the sirens stayed in my mind a long while before it was erased. At this time, I believed that the Chinese would be defeated and, as a result, I would die. I still remember very clearly that when we learned about the first victory achieved by the Chinese People's Volunteer Army on the Korean front none of us chose to believe it. By the end of that year, when we learned that the Chinese and Koreans had driven the American Army to the 38th parallel we were very suspicious. After the New Year, when a member of the Center's Communist Party cadre got up on the watchtower and announced the news that the Chinese and Korean armies had retaken Seoul, I still held to my belief in a United States victory. In February, when the press announced new regulations for punishing antirevolutionaries, the Center feared that we would become unduly alarmed if we should read them and withheld the newspapers from us. We, of course, who did not know the real reason, supposed it was because of a defeat in Korea and were thus strengthened in our conviction that the earlier reports of a Chinese victory had been false. I came to believe that I was approaching a period of great danger. At night, I was afraid to hear the sound of the cell doors and, in the daytime, the sound of automobiles. Whenever I heard them, I suspected that soldiers were coming to take us to a public trial.

My cellmates' situation was no better than mine. Like me, their appetites became smaller and smaller and their voices lower and lower. I remember that at this period whenever there were sounds on the stairway, all of us tried to peer through the iron bars of the cell door to take a look. If a stranger appeared, all the occupants of the cell became stony silent. It seemed as if each and every one of us were facing his last day of judgment.

Just at the point when all of us were plunged into the deepest despair, the Chief of Public Security came to the prison to give us a talk. From his speech, which lasted over an hour, we got some hope. He told us that the People's Government did not wish to send us to death; it only wished us to pass through a reorientation and re-education process in order to be reformed. He said that the Communist Party and the People's Government believed that the majority of us could be remolded into new men, and that the ideal of Communism was to reform the whole world, society and the human race.

"You people," he explained, "have only thought of death and you people seem to believe that all the arrangements we have made for you are preparatory to your execution. But you should realize that if the People's Government wished to eliminate all of you, we would not have let you study.

"All of you seem to have developed many illusions regarding the Korean War. Some of you have thought that the People's Volunteer Army would most certainly lose and that the Americans would come to Manchuria. Therefore, you have been afraid that the Communist Party would kill you first. Some of you have had blind faith in the military power of the United States, but I can tell you categorically that the Chinese and Korean people will triumph.

"The reform policies of the Chinese Communist Party will be vindicated on the battlefield. Victory is assured. The Communist Party never engages in empty talk!

"Perhaps you people say to yourselves; All right, then, if you don't wish to kill us, why don't you let us out? But if we were to let you out without remolding your personalities, not only would you again commit crimes, but the people of China with whom you must live would never forgive you. Therefore, you must study hard and achieve complete reform."

At the time, none of us paid any attention to the Chief's remarks about being remolded through study and learning. As I saw it, it seemed absurd to suppose that by reading a few books one's thoughts could be changed. And as for the possibility that the American soldiers could be defeated, this was preposterous. My cellmates, who were military men, all agreed that even if the United States did not use the atomic bomb, its superiority in conventional weapons was sufficient for it to be without equal in the world.

But not long afterward, we were again allowed to read newspapers and we came to the conclusion that the information from the Korean War theatre was not entirely untrue. The ex-officers pointed out that although the number of casualties on both sides could easily be falsified, gains and losses of territory could not be altered indefinitely and that the news that the U.S. Commander in Chief had indicated his willingness to negotiate could not be a fabrication. Furthermore, they thought the reports that the Americans were talking about a cease-fire were significant. As a result, the ex-officers began to have doubts about a U.S. victory and, needless to say, I was thrown into complete confusion. In one way, however, I began to feel more comfortable. For if the Communist Party were not to collapse, then it would not execute me before its dissolution.

Meanwhile, our study and brainwashing routine was changed. Previously our studies had seemed to be on a *laissez-faire* basis and the Center did not interfere with us. Now, however, Communist Party cadre members who were in charge of the Center personally took a hand and guided us. We were given topics to study such as "What is a feudal society?" and we were required to discuss them and to take notes. Later, one of the cadre said, "As I have mentioned before, in order to remold one's thoughts it is necessary to understand what one's original thoughts were. Each man's thoughts are inseparable from his past history and from the position he held when he started out in life. Therefore, you must begin with your own history in order to conduct an analysis. To achieve thought reform, each one of you must, without any hesitation, and with complete objectivity, reflect on your own history and write an autobiography."

Is this what they call reform? I thought to myself in silence. It is no more than a pretense at using "thought reform" in order to secure a confession. Perhaps the Communist Party feels that now the war situation is more or less stabilized it will have time to try us publicly instead of lining us up against a wall and shooting us.

My former attendant, Big Li, had been the actual witness of my departure from Tientsin for the Northeast. Before I had left, he had prepared all my baggage and clothing and when I had hidden in the rumble seat of the car, it had been he who had closed it over me. If this were to leak out, no one would believe my kidnapping story at the hands of Doihara. It was thus imperative that I see Big Li, but this could be handled only during our exercise period in the courtyard when I had the privilege of meeting with my family group.

At this time the routine was somewhat different than before. With the exception of my father-in-law, who had died, and my former physician, who had arthritis, the remaining members of our group all participated in service work, such as carrying water or rice, helping in the kitchen, and doing other menial tasks. It was therefore not easy for me to meet them all at once since they had to be at different chores. However, there were some benefits from this arrangement, since it meant that their movements were comparatively free and they could relay messages. I thus utilized this situation to ask Little Jui to tell Big Li to come and see me quietly.

Big Li approached me in a very obedient manner, as if he were waiting for my instructions. I lowered my voice. "Do you still remember when we moved from Tientsin?" I asked him.

"You mean when we actually left for Manchuria, or slipped out of the gate, or when I packed up your things?" he asked.

"If the Center should ever ask you about how I left Tientsin, you should say you don't know a thing. It was *after* I left that you packed my things; do you understand?"

"After you left."

"Yes, after I left. You took orders from another man that you should pack my things and send them to Port Arthur."

Big Li nodded and left quietly. The next day, Little Jui told me that Big Li had asked him to give me this message: The previous night he had told one of the clerks of the prison that when I was in the Northeast I had been kind to my servants and I had never scolded people or beaten them. Also, he said that when I was in Port Arthur, I locked my door for a whole day and refused to see the Japanese.

When I heard this, I felt that Big Li was fabricating a little too much. Why should he mention Port Arthur? I told Little Jui to tell him not to talk any more and that if anyone should ask about the situation in Port Arthur he should say that he knew nothing.

I was most satisfied with Big Li's loyalty and felt secure.

Meanwhile, I reminded my nephews again that I had commenced to write my autobiography. I wrote down my genealogy, how Tzu Hsi had designated me Emperor, how I had spent my youth in the Forbidden City, how I had to seek refuge in the Japanese Legation, how I had spent my life in Tientsin. Then I wrote about my "kidnapping" and the unfortunate years in Changchun.

This draft of my autobiography, after much editing, was finally put in its final form and presented to the authorities. From the way I had written it, I was sure that everyone would see that I was a repentant man. But after I had delivered it, I felt that my writing was not a sufficient demonstration of my repentance. I ought to think of another way to prove to the government my "sincerity" and "progress." What should I do?

At this time the prisoners felt that they only needed to demonstrate repentance in order to dupe the authorities. But even from this standpoint, I did not think I could compare favorably with the others. There were three phases of work in which the prisoners could demonstrate their repentance: study, "duty" functions and daily life. In my cell, the best performance in the study phase was shown by our Section Chief, Wang, a former major general in the legal division of the Manchukuo army. He had studied politics and law in Peking. His cultural standards were comparatively high and he could comprehend new terms and new ideology faster than the rest of us. The other three ex-officers in my section were like me. They could not understand terms like "subjective point of view" and "objective point of view." But still their progress was faster than mine.

During discussion sessions they all could repeat set talks. What was most difficult for me was that after we had completed talks on, for example, "a feudal society," each of us had to write a summary of what he had learned. During the discussion period I managed to talk simply about what I knew of the subject, but writing down my own understanding was not so simple. In addition, the process added to my fears. For example, a feudal emperor was the biggest landlord and this fact seemed to contain a judgment against me personally. If I had been the biggest landlord, then not only could I be punished from the standpoint of being a traitor to my country, but it also meant that I could be executed from the standpoint of land reform and there would be no way out for me.

I also had difficulty with my "duty" functions. After I had arrived in Harbin, I had volunteered to participate in these, but this act of volunteering was really the only evidence of my progress; my actual work was without any such indication. This was the first time in my life that I rendered service to others. But the first time that I served meals in the cell, I nearly spilled a bowl of vegetable soup on someone's head. Thereafter, whenever it was my turn to serve, there was always someone else who volunteered to help me. They did this not so much out of kindness, but because they did not wish to run the risk of having food spilled down their backs.

My living habits were not comparable to the others. My dress was still untidy and I still had to depend on my nephew Little Jui to wash and mend for me. Since the time the Center Chief had pointed out my untidiness in public, I had a feeling of shame. I tried to look after myself and to wash my own clothing, but I always made myself wet. When I found I could not control the soap and the scrub board, I felt resentful. And when I waited in the courtyard for Little Jui to do the job for me and saw how other people looked at the clothing and socks in my hand while I waited for my nephew to wash them, I felt ashamed.

Thus, after I finished my autobiography, I decided to try once more. I felt that I must at least try to do my own washing even though it was so difficult for me. Otherwise, the Center would never believe in my reform.

After I had worked myself into a "great happy sweat" washing a white shirt, I noticed that once it was dry it had become a colored shirt—like a watercolor painting. I was shocked. Later, Little Jui came over and took the "ink painting" from the line and tucked it under his arm. "This should not be handled by the Upper One; it should be done by me," he said in a low voice.

His remark was pleasing to my ears and I felt that he was right. It was not good for me to do the washing. Even if I tried, I could never do it well. But if I did not do this kind of thing, how could I demonstrate my reform to the Center? I must find something I could do extremely well.

240

I still had some jewelry and treasures left; more, in fact, than anyone else. Even the items not concealed in the bottom of my suitcase were worth quite a bit of money. Among them was a set of seals used by Emperor Chien Lung (1707–1799), after his son had taken over the throne. They were invaluable and consisted of three separate seals carved on precious stones which were linked together by three carved chains made of precious stone. The workmanship of the carving was beautifully done. I decided to use the seals to show my "self-enlightenment" and "self-awareness."

It so happened that on this day some government officials came to conduct an inspection, and through the iron bars of my cell, I saw the man who had told me, when I was in Mukden, not to be too tense.

By the manner in which the Center Chief accompanied him, I decided that he must be of a higher rank. Even though he did not wear an army uniform, I felt that if I should present my contribution to him, it might have a beneficial result. I waited until he passed in front of my cell. Then I bowed and said to him, "I request your permission, Mr. Chief; I have something that I wish to contribute to the People's Government."

I tried to hand over the seals of Emperor Chien Lung, but he did not take them. "You are Pu Yi, I presume," he said. "Well, you should take up the matter with the Center here." He then asked me a few personal questions and left.

I thought that if he had actually bothered to examine my gift he would have appreciated its value and would not have been so casual. However, I had no alternative but to discuss it with the Center Chief and so I wrote a letter and asked one of the guards to pass it along with the seals.

For days I had no news. I couldn't help but become suspicious. Could it be that the guard had taken the treasure himself? However, a few days later, the Center Chief came up to me in the courtyard and spoke about them. "Your letter and seals of precious stones reached me," he said. "Also," he continued, "the contributions you made while in Soviet Russia have been turned over to us here. But regardless of this, I think you should know that from our standpoint, men are more valuable than treasures and a man who has been reformed and remolded is even more so."

The real meaning of his words was not understood by me for many years. At the time, I only thought that since he had mentioned the need for reform, it meant that I was in no immediate personal danger. I never dreamed that real danger had come.

One day the earpiece of my eyeglasses broke and I asked the guard to take them to Big Li to be repaired. Big Li could fix anything and whenever I had had trouble with my glasses in the past he had taken care of them for me. I never expected that his attitude would change.

It was characteristic of the Control Center that voices downstairs could usually be heard upstairs. Not very long after the guard had taken my glasses, I could hear from below the rumbling of Big Li's bass voice and even though I could not make out his words, I could tell that he was not happy. After a while, the guard brought back my glasses and, in an apologetic way, asked, "Could you think of some way to fix them yourself? He said he has no way of repairing them for you."

I felt angry and disgusted and told the guard, "If I could have repaired them myself, I wouldn't have asked him. Last time they broke he repaired them for me. I hope you will ask him again."

This time Big Li did not refuse, but I noticed the job was done carelessly; he had only used string and the original hinge was missing. Upon deliberation, I realized that Big Li had changed and that the change had not occurred suddenly.

A short time previously, because I had not seen Big Li for several days, I had sent Little Jui to fetch him during our exercise period. On Jui's return he said, "Big Li is busy and has no time."

This incident had occurred shortly before New Year, 1952. Another was to occur at the New Year celebration party itself, for which the Center had asked us to prepare some theatrical programs for our own amusement. The theatre was the empty space in front of the sentry post and the program was a play written and performed by my nephews, Little Ku and Little Hsiu, and also Big Li. My other nephew,

Little Jui, did not take part. They used a question and answer form to make jokes about the happenings among the prisoners and also imitated their gestures. I knew it had mainly been written by Little Ku and at first I thought it quite humorous; but later, I stopped laughing.

They had begun to make sarcastic remarks about people who were suspicious and who believed in ghosts, spirits, prayers and divinations of the future. Later, they talked about a man who had begun to understand lots of things in prison, even though he "still wants to be a servant to others" and "wants to serve other people obediently." As a result, he was aiding another to maintain an attitude of master and to resist reform.

Upon hearing this, I immediately understood that the one who was being castigated and the one they had in mind was me. Also, I understood why Little Jui had refused to participate in the program and became worried for fear that he might not be able to carry on in the face of this.

Actually, however, even Little Jui began to show changes. Big Li, Little Hsiu and Little Ku had been continuously absent from the courtyard, and now even Little Jui reduced his presence there. My dirty clothing had accumulated and, after the New Year party, Little Jui stopped coming to pick it up.

Then another incident occurred. It was my duty day and I was waiting to receive the food outside the cell door. Little Jui was distributing it. After he had given everything to me, he handed me a note folded into a small square. I immediately put it into my palm and then passed out the food as if nothing had happened. When the meal was finished, I pretended that I wished to go to the men's room, where I secretly opened the note and read it. "We have all committed crimes," it said. "We should confess everything to the government. In the past I have hidden things for you. Confess what you have in the bottom of your suitcase. If you can take this initiative, the government will be lenient with you."

At first I was so angry I felt as if a flame had burst in my chest. But in a while my anger subsided and I was overcome by a chill of loneliness. Everyone was leaving me. It was some sort of omen. I tossed the note into the toilet to be flushed away, but I could not erase the sentiment that the note had brought to me. I deliberated about the past and the present of these four young men and I felt that the change in them was unbelievable.

Big Li's father had served in the Summer Palace, and had waited upon the Empress Dowager Tzu Hsi. Because of this, when the palace had dispersed the eunuchs, Big Li had been allowed to become a servant at the age of fourteen. Later, he had accompanied me to Tientsin and was in my service, along with some other boy servants. Later on, he had formally become my personal attendant. When I left Tientsin, I had taken Big Li with me. In Soviet Russia, he had nearly fought with a Japanese who had refused to step aside for me. He had always been respectful and willing to listen. When he had taken my instructions to destroy the jewelry and treasures he had done it thoroughly. I could not figure out why he had changed.

Little Ku was the son of Pu Wei. When his father, as Prince Kung, had died, I had given him the title and had tried to build him up as one of the hopeful elements for the future restoration, and he had felt that this was his lifelong wish. When we had been in Soviet Russia, he had written a poem to show his loyalty. He had been educated by me to become a devout Buddhist and had become attracted to a branch of Zen Buddhism. Upon our arrival in Harbin, he still had shown his loyalty to me. I hadn't expected a man like him to have written a sarcastic program containing innuendoes against me. Apparently his loyalty was not in existence any more.

What was completely unforeseen was the change in Little Jui. I could explain the changes in others like Big Li, who did not belong to the royal family, or Little Hsiu who was still upset because I had denounced him on the train, or Little Ku who had become infatuated with Zen Buddhism. But what was the reason for the change in Little Jui? Little Jui was the descendant of Prince Tuan of the Ch'ing House. His family had declined in importance after his grandfather and uncle had become involved in the Boxer Rebellion. But Little Jui, at nineteen, had been sent for by me to come to Changchun, and I had allowed him to study along with the other members of the royal family, under the same tutors.

Among the young students of the Inner Court he was considered one of the most trustworthy and sincere. I realized that he did not have as high an I.Q. as the others, but he was not tricky and it had been better for me to have someone steady like him about.

During our five years in the Soviet Union his loyalty had been complete and, thus, when I was about to return to China and feeling that my life would be in danger, I had discussed with my brothers-in-law and my brother the problem of "selecting an heir to the throne," for I had decided to choose Little Jui. After he had learned of this decision, needless to say, his devotion was really beyond words. But now this young man had told me I was "guilty."

The unimaginable change in my nephews, and above all in Little Jui, raced through my mind. I sought to discover the reason for it in the events that had occurred since our return to China, but I found that I could find no valid reason even if I were to admit to myself the supreme power of the Communist Party.

And so I leaned for a moment against the wall and tried to find some small comfort out of what had happened. I found that my only consolation was that my brothers-in-law and my brother had not shown any signs of change, but even this could not erase my worry over whether Little Jui would actually denounce me before the prison authorities.

If he were to tell of what I had in the double bottom of my satchel, my future seemed most uncertain. This treasure consisted of 468 items of gold, diamonds, pearls, etc. I looked upon them as my livelihood for the second half of my life. Without them, even if I were set free, I would have nothing to live on. It never occurred to me that I could support myself and, furthermore, since I had hidden the jewelry for such a long time, if I were to surrender it at this late date, it would only prove how long I had been cheating. In view of this, I finally decided that all I could do was let the problem ride and do nothing.

But about a week later, when it was Little Jui's turn to bring our food to us, I noticed that although his manner was dignified, he didn't look at me. Instead, he stared at my leather suitcase. Two hours later, after we had begun our studies in the cell, he suddenly came back again and stood in front of the cell door, and then, just as suddenly, left again.

I saw clearly that his eyes had stared at the suitcase and I concluded he was about to go and see the Center Chief. I could no longer remain calm. I knew that instead of waiting to be exposed, the time had come for me to assume an active role.

30

Intensified Brainwashing

"I, PU YI, HAVE NO CONSCIENCE. DESPITE THE FACT THAT
the government has given me humane treatment I have
nevertheless concealed things and violated prison regulations. I have committed a crime against the State. These
jewels were never mine; they belonged to the people. Until
now I never understood this."

I stood in the reception room of the Center Chief with my
head bowed. On a desk near the window were the 468 pieces
of jewelry shining with a brilliance that would make anyone
wish to possess them.

The Chief stared at me attentively as I spoke. Then he
nodded his head. "Please sit down," he said. "You must
have gone through a great deal of mental anguish regarding
this affair."

I replied that I had been very uneasy and then went on to
elaborate my difficulties, but in all that I said at that time,
only the last sentence was important. "I didn't dare to be
frank with you because I was afraid that even if I should
confess, I still might not receive lenient treatment."

"Why was that?" the Chief asked as the trace of a smile
darted across the corners of his mouth. "Was it because you
were an emperor?"

I hesitated for a while and then admitted he was right.

"I don't blame you for entertaining this kind of thought,"
the Chief continued with the smile still on his lips. "You
have a special history and naturally you have many special

thoughts. However, I wish to tell you once more, the Communist Party and the People's Government are always true to their word. It doesn't matter what kind of status you once had; after you have confessed and if you can reform yourself more completely, you may even receive a reduced sentence. If you should be able to achieve an act of genuine merit you might even receive a reward. It's always up to the individual. The fact that you did not surrender these jewels prior to this time, means that you have committed a violation of prison regulations. But now, since you have confessed voluntarily and recognized your mistake, this indicates that you show regret for your previous conduct. I definitely will not give you hard treatment."

After he had finished speaking he ordered the guard outside the door to summon someone from the Custodial Section whom he asked to inventory the jewelry and to provide me with a receipt. "Even if the government is unwilling to confiscate them," I said, "I myself would like to contribute them to the State."

"No, it's better for us to keep them for you," the Chief explained. And then, just before walking out of the room, he turned to face me and said, "As I have told you previously, insofar as we are concerned, a man who has been reformed is more valuable to us than jewels."

When I returned to my cell with the receipt for the jewelry, my cellmates gave me an unprecedented welcome and congratulated me on my progress.

"Oh, Pu, we never thought of you showing such bravery, we do so admire you," they said. They had all stopped calling me Mr. Pu for some time, and I now found this familiar form of address most comforting.

This sort of praise from them was unprecedented, for since I had started to wash my clothing and do my mending myself, my appearance had become so sloppy that the respect my cellmates had shown me had been greatly reduced. Some had given me the nickname of "secondhand shop." Also, whenever I had made a mistake in class, I would at once become the object of unreserved laughter. Now they embraced me, and I immediately felt proud.

Later, during the rest period in the courtyard, I overheard our former Ambassador to Japan talking about the case in a way that touched my heart. "Pu is really not so dumb," I heard him say. "He has gained the initiative by confessing his ownership of the jewelry. What he did was correct. Besides, I don't think he could have concealed them much longer. The information the government holds in its hands today is simply unimaginable. You can understand what I mean if you consider all the cases reported in the press. Tens of thousands of people have supplied information to the government."

Hearing his talk made me think about the lies in the draft of my reminiscences and feel that I could not fool the government officials. But if I were to speak out, perhaps I could pass through this ordeal peacefully, just as had been the case with the jewelry. Of course, this was a political problem rather than an economic one and the Center Chief had said nothing about it. But, nevertheless, it made me wonder if I would receive the same kind of treatment.

According to the exposures of anti-Communist activity reported in the press, those who admitted their guilt by confession were being treated leniently. News regarding the settlement of these cases was becoming more and more frequent. I had talked many times with my cell section chief, Wang, a former judge of the Manchukuo regime, about these cases, and his analysis of them always had the effect of making me see the relationship between my particular case and the ones receiving such publicity.

Not long after this, the Center asked us to supply material on the criminal actions of the Japanese in the Northeast for use in connection with its proceedings against them. When the Communist cadre in the Center announced this to us someone asked whether, besides the behavior of the Japanese, we should write about something else.

The cadre member replied, "Of course, you can, but the main thing we want to know about is the criminal action of the Japanese bandits."

Upon hearing this exchange, I couldn't help but become worried again. What did this mean, writing about "something else"? "Something else" clearly meant the Chinese, and the war criminals among the Chinese meant me. Would my own family write about me?

When my fellow prisoners wrote about criminal action

regarding the Japanese in Manchukuo they were very accurate. In my own section, on the first day, more than ten copybooks of material were produced, and Wang, after collecting all the material submitted, said, "Our result is very good. Tomorrow I'm sure we'll produce even more."

On the second day we wrote all day long. I, however, had produced much less than on the previous day. But as Wang collected it, he still seemed satisfied, at least with what the others had produced.

"You people can well imagine," he said, "how much more material the people in the Northeast themselves will write. Thus, you can estimate the enormous amount of material in government hands. Those of you who have had judicial experience will know how it works. Once you have evidence you need not worry about those who do not talk. In the old days, the judicial organ of government felt that it was very difficult to gather evidence, but now, in the People's Government, the common people all gladly supply material. The situation is completely different."

My heart nearly jumped through my throat on hearing this. It was not the first time I had heard how the government was in possession of lots of material. That very morning we had discussed an item in the newspaper about the arrest of a counter-revolutionary in Hunan who had assassinated a Red Army general way back in 1935, and who had hidden in the mountains for many years. How had they found his hiding place? Perhaps the Communist Party had been collecting evidence on this man for years and had it available in its files, pending investigation.

On the third day of our writing about the Japanese in the Northeast, I heard footsteps at the foot of the stairs. Turning around, I saw a middle-aged stranger who was followed by the Center Chief. Based on previous experience, I judged that he was someone from high up in the Public Security Organization who had come for an inspection of the prison.

The inspector examined each and every cell and also listened to the names of the prisoners as read off by the Chief. His face remained expressionless and, although he did not wear an army uniform, he looked like a military man.

"What are you doing?" he asked as he stopped outside my cell. His eyes bored into me.

I stood up and reported that I was writing about the criminal actions of the Japanese. He seemed interested in my reply. "What kind of criminal actions of the Japanese bandits do you know of?" he asked.

I told him about a report I had once received on the execution of workers at a construction site of a secret base. Perhaps it was due to my supersensitivity, or perhaps it was really the case, I do not know, but I sensed that the trace of a smile that had originally shown on his face seemed to disappear. His eyes became stern.

"At the time I originally heard the story I was much agitated. I had never expected the Japanese to be so cruel," I added, most uncomfortably.

"Why didn't you protest to the Japanese?" he asked, as he looked straight into my eyes.

I felt that he was very angry and immediately I bowed my head. ". . . I . . . didn't dare," I replied.

"You didn't dare? Were you afraid? Was that it?" He did not wait for my reply. "Fear . . . fear, to think that fear could change a man to this extent."

"No," I answered. "It was not fear. . . . It happened as a result of my own crimes and mistakes. I can only admit my crimes to the people. Even if ten thousand deaths were meted out to me, I could not wash away my guilt."

"You don't need to be like that," he said quietly. "Don't try to take everything on your own shoulders. You can only be responsible for what is yours. You should deal with facts. What is yours you cannot erase, but what is not yours, you should not assume."

But I still continued to talk on about my guilt and how I had made up my mind to reform. Meanwhile, I noticed that he was conducting an inspection of my cell. He even asked one of my cellmates to hand over his mouthwash cup for inspection. After I finally finished speaking, he shook his head and said, "We must depend on facts. So long as one can really admit guilt and show by facts the degree of his guilt he will receive very lenient treatment. You must use facts to explain and illustrate your progress and not empty talk. Do your best."

He then glanced casually at the things I had written and went to the neighboring cell. From this time on, the inspector's pair of stern eyes stayed with me, as well as his words: "You must base your story on facts, not empty talk."

He had made me feel that I myself was confronted with an irresistible and driving and thrusting force, the kind of force that was able to get to the bottom of everything. It was because of this same force that a man who had murdered a Red Army Chief in 1935 could not escape his fate, even though he had hidden for years deep in a mountain. I now felt that because of this thrusting force, nothing could escape revelation.

A few days later, I took up my pen and put down in detail, far greater detail than heretofore, all the facts about my activities in Tientsin and the relationship between me and my courtiers on the one hand, and the Japanese on the other, as well as my meeting with Doihara.

Two days later, our Section Chief told me that the Center authorities had read what I had written and felt I had shown important progress which should be commended.

At the end of 1952 we moved to another building with larger rooms where there were new wooden boards for beds, as well as tables, wooden benches and bright windows. I began to feel that what the Center Chief had said about my reformation was true, especially since I had received no punishment, but rather a commendation for what I had written about my collaboration with the Japanese.

In the spring of 1953, the Center entered into a working agreement with a pencil factory in Harbin. The prisoners pasted up the paper boxes that contained the pencils and, from this time on, every day, we would work at making paper boxes four hours a day and would study four hours.

The authorities explained that this arrangement would be useful in breaking the monotony of our lives and, furthermore, since we had never before worked as laborers, it would be good for us.

These words were to have a particular meaning for me. Needless to say, in the past I had never even sharpened a pencil, to say nothing of having pasted a pencil box. I had never paid any attention to the boxes pencils came in and I did not know how much trouble it took to make them. But after a while, all my curiosity over the process was lost.

Pencil boxes and paste became synonymous and I was reduced to a state of confusion. By the time others had finished several boxes, I had not yet completed one of them. I had no concept of manual work.

"What have you done to this one?" Hsien, who had been Chief of Military Hospitals in Manchukuo, asked me one day as he picked up one of my boxes. "How come it cannot be opened? What do you call it?"

Hsien was the son of Prince Su. He and several of his brothers and sisters had been educated in Japan and he had studied medicine there. Lady Yamagishi was his younger sister. One of his brothers had been mayor of Harbin and his whole family was pro-Japanese. When we had met for the first time in Soviet Russia, he had knelt before me, saying, "Your slave now has the opportunity to see his master."

Now he was in my section and enjoyed picking bones with me. He was a very irritable man, easily aroused against others, and, yet, if he got into an argument, he could never win it. Since my work was incomparably poorer than others and since I never had the courage to argue, I had become the escape hatch for his own emotions.

Hsien's meddling in my affairs aroused the attention of the other workers in our section and they came over to observe my problems and began to laugh. I grabbed the box from Hsien and threw it on the discard pile. "Why do you set yourself up arbitrarily as the official reporter on waste?" I asked him.

"Who has reported waste?" he answered as he stared at me and opened his eyes wide.

"Even though my pasting is a little inferior, it doesn't mean that the boxes can't be used," I muttered. Then I picked up the pencil box from the waste pile and put it back on the pile of finished boxes.

"And even though you put it over there," he answered, as he pointed at the box, "it's still a waste item."

I became so angry that I began to tremble uncontrollably. "You can only cope with me. You are someone who always jumps on a weak person. I'm about the only man you can handle."

This remark touched him on his raw spot and he blushed. "Who have I bullied? Who am I afraid of?" he shouted.

"You still think you are the Emperor; do you want people to worship you?"

Fortunately, none of the workers paid any attention to him and he stopped shouting when the Section Chief came up, but this did not end the quarrel because Hsien was not a person to give up easily. The following day when we went to work, he selected a seat next to me. From the moment we commenced, he began to look at my work with a critical eye. I turned my back on him and, even though my day's work could not compare with the others, at least it showed some progress.

The Center used the money it obtained from our labor to buy candies and sweets for us. This was the first time in my life that I enjoyed something as the result of my own physical labor and I felt that the candy I received was really better than any I had ever tasted. But, unfortunately, as soon as it was issued to us, Hsien started talking, "Today Pu Yi's results have not been so bad."

"Not bad, nothing was wasted," I answered him.

"You would do better to be more humble," he said, chuckling.

"Am I not humble when I say I did not have any waste?" I was really angry at heart and the candy no longer seemed sweet. What I disliked the most was that Hsien had a compulsion to be critical when others were happy. "If I produce any more waste items, you can be critical of me again," I added.

I hoped that when I said this he would stop and I would not have to talk to him again. I did not expect that he would pick up one of my finished boxes, hold it up in the air, and say to everyone, "Please look at this!"

As I raised my head to look at it, I nearly swallowed my candy. I had pasted the label on upside down. I became so mad, I felt like taking a box and throwing it at Hsien's face. "Do whatever you wish to do," I growled after a while.

"Uh, now look at all the big talk! Still showing the smelly pomp of an Emperor," he droned on. Then he raised his voice. "When I criticized you it was for your own good. Why don't you admit it?" As he heard the footsteps of the guards outside the door, he raised his voice even louder.

"Do you still entertain the illusion of becoming an emperor again?" he asked.

"You are talking utter nonsense," I said. "I am dumber than you; I cannot compare with you in either talking or working. By nature I am not as able as you. Now, will that do?"

Everyone had left their benches and come over to try and stop our quarrel. Our workroom held eighteen people. There were, besides me, three former Manchukuo civilian high officials and fourteen military officers. Our Section Chief, Wei, was a former military man and Chang Ching-hui, the former Premier of Manchukuo, was one of the three civilians, but he had become senile and did not study or work and seldom talked.

That evening, with the exception of Chang Ching-hui, the others participated in a discussion regarding the now famous "paper box incident." One man criticized Hsien saying, "He should not have raised his voice." Another criticized me saying, "If I had not pasted the box right, I should have admitted it at once and not taken an unfriendly attitude." A Mongol named Kuo felt that the attitude of Hsien was wrong from beginning to end and that I was entirely justified in getting angry. Another, who was friendly with Hsien, opposed Kuo and another believed that the whole incident should be discussed at our Saturday review and self-criticism session with the prison authorities.

As the talk went on, neither side would give in. But all of a sudden, everyone became quiet. I turned my head and saw that Chief Li, a cadre member in charge of our study section, had come into the room. After he heard the story, he picked up the paper box on which I had pasted the label upside down, and said, "This is a very small item; it's not worth quarreling about. Since the label was pasted upside down, paste another label right side up on top of it."

The suggestion quieted everyone, but the incident was not yet finished. A few days later, Little Jui, who was responsible for distributing paper box material to us, told us that several of the working groups wanted to start a labor competition and asked whether we wished to participate. All of us indicated our approval. Little Jui also told us that the group to which Little Ku belonged had initiated a "speedy pasting process," the efficiency of which was 100 percent higher and thus our group felt that if we were to join the competition we could no longer use our old method and that we would have to devise a newer and more efficient one. Someone advocated a "water flow" or mass production system by which each man would specialize on one phase of the work; one would paste the bottom of the box, another put on the paper, another the label, etc., etc. We all agreed to try it out and I was pleased because I felt that, in this division of labor, the work would be simpler and less confusing. I didn't foresee that new problems for me would develop.

Under this new "water flow" system, everything piled up on me and the "water" could not flow through my hands. Hsien noticed it at once. "If one of the workers on the production line is not up to scratch, then what do we do?" he asked.

On this occasion, I did not pick a quarrel with him. I looked at the pile of half-completed boxes in front of me and, when I heard one of my colleagues say that my production was not up to standard and that the waste rate was high, I knew that this time neither the Mongol Kuo nor our Section Chief would oppose Hsien.

Thus, I decided to withdraw from the "water flow" process and undertook to labor alone. This was the second time since my return to China that I endured the horror of loneliness. The first time had been when I was separated from my family members. I felt as if I had been stripped naked in front of everyone and this emotion was made doubly acute when I saw on Hsien's face, which was like the rough skin of an orange, his satisfaction over my misery. I wanted to find someone sympathetic to talk with, but in my unit everyone was working and not interested in talking.

Soon after this, I caught the flu and the night I came down with it I had a nightmare in which I saw Hsien's orange-skin-like face approaching me. "You are a good-for-nothing man, you are only fit to be a beggar," he said.

Then I dreamed I was standing on a bridge. The scene was exactly like the ones the eunuchs used to describe to me of the Peking beggars standing on the bridges of the city. Suddenly someone put a hand on my head and woke me up.

In a blurred way, I was aware that a person in white was standing over me and feeling my forehead with his hands. "You have a high fever; your flu is getting worse. Let me examine you," a voice said.

I was dizzy and my head felt as if my blood vessels were jumping. As I pulled myself together, I began to understand what had happened. The prison guard had heard me talking and shouting in my sleep and had tried to wake me, but couldn't, so he had reported my condition to the Center Chief who, in turn, had asked the military doctor to come and see me.

The doctor took my temperature and a nurse gave me an injection. I fell asleep again immediately and didn't even know when they left. I was sick for nearly a half month. During this period, I spent most of my time in bed. I neither studied nor worked.

I did more thinking during this half month than I had during the past few years. My mind raced back and forth between the paper box incident and the face of the Dowager Empress Tzu Hsi, which had frightened me as a child and made me cry. Heretofore, whenever I recalled that blurred image, I had only felt that the Empress Dowager had been someone to be feared. But now I felt that she was to be hated. Why should she have chosen me Emperor? I was an innocent and pure child at the time. My natural disposition and endowments were no different from those of my brother, Pu Chieh. But since I was to become an emperor, I had been raised in a vacuumlike atmosphere and no one had taught me the basic things of life. Thus, today, my practical knowledge and ability could not be compared with Pu Chieh's; in fact, they could not be compared with a child. Because of this, I now received insults, jeers, sarcasm and bullying from men like Hsien. I really didn't know how I could go on living.

In the past, whenever I had heard jeering or suggestive innuendoes, or whenever my lack of ability was pointed out by others, my heart had been filled with hatred. But now I began to feel that I should not hate them, for I was no longer in a position to avoid being laughed at and scolded.

In place of this hatred, a new kind of hostility developed in me against the Forbidden City. Shortly before my recovery, the Center Chief sent for me and we discussed my health and the quarrel with Hsien, as well as the education I had received as a child.

I said to him, "At the time the quarrel occurred, I was really very much agitated, but now I'm no longer angry and can only blame myself for being so difficult. Also, I blame the people in the Peking Palace."

"Very good; you have recognized your weakness! This is progress. Inability is not something to worry about, so long as you are willing and able to recognize it and turn it into ability. It is even more important that you have found out the reason for it. Can you think why the princes and high officials educated you as they did?"

"They were only thinking about themselves," I answered. "They disregarded me. They were selfish."

"I'm afraid it wasn't at all like that," the Center Chief replied, not unkindly. "Can you honestly say that your father and your tutor Chen Pao-shen purposely tried to harm you?"

I couldn't reply.

"You may take time to think about this problem. If you can understand it, then your illness will have had great value for your future life."

After I returned to my cell from the Center Chief's office, I could not dismiss the problem from my mind and, by the time I attended our regularly scheduled self-criticism review session, the first I had gone to since my illness, I had been over it several times. During this meeting, someone criticized Hsien, saying that he was unfriendly and had purposely sought to attack me. A majority seemed to be against him and there was one person who even laid the responsibility for my illness on him. Based on their self-criticism, I gathered that they all felt Hsien was having a bad effect on our reformation and remolding. Hsien, who was present, clearly became worried about this and his face turned gray; he stuttered as he sought to deliver his own self-criticism.

I did not say a word during the session, but I continued to think about my own family. When someone suggested that I should say something, Hsien's face became ashen. "I don't have any opinion," I said in a low voice. "I blame my own lack of ability."

Everyone was taken by surprise at this and Hsien's mouth

fell open. Then, all of a sudden, I began to shout and my voice became strident. "I hate the place I was born and raised in! I hate that devilish system! It was designed to ruin a person when he was young. I hate it! I hate it!" Then my voice cracked as if my vocal cords had been seized by a sudden cramp. I could no longer speak or even hear what others said.

From the end of 1953 until early 1954, we were assigned the subject of imperialism to study intensively, and in March, our Center was moved to Fushun. Shortly thereafter a working group of specially trained investigation specialists arrived to commence processing the confessional material we had produced.

At our particular Center for the Manchukuo detainees, this processing was opened with a big meeting at which the responsible personnel of the investigating group addressed us.

"You people," they explained, "have gone through several years of study and re-education. Now, the time for admission of guilt has arrived. By this time you should have arrived at a very accurate understanding of your past conduct. You should be able to recognize what has been criminal in your past and be able to supply information on the criminal actions of the Japanese and of other Chinese traitors. The ultimate treatment you will receive from the Government will be based, on the one hand, on your own criminal conduct; and, on the other hand, on your attitude. The policy of the Government is to be lenient toward those who have confessed and sterner toward those who have resisted."

Our Center Chief then announced that he would not allow the prisoners to exchange information during the processing period and that notes and letters between the prisoners were henceforth prohibited. Thus, every day during recreation, each group would go to the courtyard separately and could not meet with the other groups.

After this meeting, all the groups returned to their respective cells to hold intra-cell discussion sessions. It was agreed among my cellmates that each and every one of us would be frank in our confessions in order to struggle for more lenient treatment; and, in order to gain the confidence of the newly arrived special investigating personnel, I decided to rewrite my reminiscences in greater detail and in a more systematic way.

But this did not prove to be so simple. When I came to the last days of the Manchukuo government and the Soviet Russian declaration of war against Japan, I recalled a particular incident. I had been worried that at this critical point the Japanese might become suspicious of me, so I had tried to curry favor with the Kwantung Army. On the night following the Soviet war declaration, I, acting without instructions, had asked the Premier, Chang Ching-hui, and a Japanese in charge of the General Affairs Bureau to come and see me and I gave them an oral decree asking the people of Manchukuo to support the Japanese Imperial Army in its resistance of the Soviet invasion.

Should I lie about this? If I did not confess it, it was unlikely that other people would know about it. Chang Ching-hui was clearly senile and the former head of the General Affairs Bureau had vanished. In this particular incident the Japanese had not prompted me to take action, and if I admitted it, wouldn't this arouse the suspicion of the investigators so that they would feel I was not always controlled by the Japanese? My final decision was that it was not important if I "forgot" one or two incidents like this. I could thus place the whole responsibility on the Japanese.

Previously, I had never paid attention to the suffering caused by the Japanese in the Northeast. Ten years had passed and I thought this was not my concern. As a consequence, I failed to appreciate the implications insofar as my confession was concerned, in the fact that the Japanese detainees themselves, who were in other Centers at Fushun, had undergone changes in their point of view during their ten-year "study" period.

At an important meeting, attended by my own Center inmates and cadre teams (organized by the Japanese "study committee," which had been formed after the majority of Japanese detainees had undergone enlightenment with respect to their own thoughts), several Japanese talked about their "studies" and frankly confessed many criminal actions, and even accused others.

During these confessions they discussed massacres, their opium policy, atrocities, etc., and these confessions and exposures of Japanese policy especially agitated the younger Manchukuo detainees. I was, as a result, thus denounced by my own nephews, brothers-in-law and Big Li, and was enmeshed in an atmosphere of hatred that came at me from all directions, even from my family clan. It was as if I were trapped in a hall of mirrors from each and every angle of which I could only see myself reflected in a hostile light.

This occurred at a subsequent meeting in our own Center. After we had returned from the conference organized by the Japanese "study committee," we were asked to talk about our feelings. Many people still felt agitated by the Japanese confessions and, one after another, stood up to talk. They voluntarily confessed their own actions and accused others. The accusations were for the most part concentrated on the former Manchukuo Minister of Justice, but I was afraid that I would also be accused by others who might not know that I had already confessed. Thus, I felt the need to talk at this conference in order to indicate my own attitude.

But after I had supplemented my pre-Japanese meeting confession with additional material, Little Ku unexpectedly stood up from the audience and questioned me. "You have said a lot, but how come you did not mention the note?" he asked.

I was shocked speechless.

"The note! The note Little Jui gave you," he continued.

Then Little Hsiu stood up and said, "A moment ago you mentioned that all of your jewels and treasure were surrendered voluntarily. Why didn't you mention that it was prompted by Little Jui?"

"Correct. Correct," I mumbled. "I was about to mention it, I was about to say that this action was actually initiated by Little Jui, but . . . but . . ." Fortunately the meeting was adjourned at this point.

Upon my return to my cell, I again took up my pen and wrote an additional self-exposure document for the Center authorities. When I thought how angry the Center Director would become when he found out these new details and how I had withheld them, I couldn't help but blame Little Jui.

Why should he have told the others about this incident? After all, we still belonged to the same family.

Each accusation had to be read by the accused person himself. Investigator Chiao showed me the file of material on me and asked me to examine it and initial the points on which I agreed and write a defense on the points with which I disagreed.

I first read the documents written by some of the former high Manchukuo officials and I signed my name to these. Subsequently, I read the documents written by my family clan. Before I had finished the first one, a cold sweat came out on the palms of my hands. For they contained even more denunciations than at the recent meeting that had followed the revelations by the Japanese. One of them was as follows:

On August 9, 1945, I entered the palace at night to see Pu Yi. Pu Yi was writing on a piece of paper. At that time, the Premier and a Japanese were waiting outside for a chance to see him. Pu Yi showed me the note he was writing. The contents were something like this: "Order all the military and civilian people in Manchukuo to join up with the Japanese Imperial Army to fight in order to crush the Soviet invaders." Pu Yi told me he would show this note to the Premier and the Japanese.

There was also the following:

At the movies in the palace, whenever the Japanese Emperor was shown on the screen, Pu Yi would stand at attention. Whenever there were scenes showing the Japanese occupation of new areas, he applauded because the movie projector operator was Japanese. In 1944, to save coal and charcoal, Pu Yi ordered that the heat should be turned off in his residence, but he kept an electric heater in his bedroom. When Pu Yi escaped to Talitzu-kou he put some Japanese gods and a picture of Hirohito's mother in the compartment of the train and each time he passed them, he made a 90-degree bow and also ordered others to do the same.

In Little Jui's accusation, he reported the following item:

He (Pu Yi) used about 20 orphans as servants. Some were eleven or twleve years old whose parents had been murdered by the Japanese invaders and who had been taken care of by a general relief association. They worked 17 to 18 hours a day and received only poor food to eat. He used all kinds of cruel punishment on them. Beating their palms was common and this was the lightest punishment they received. At times they were put in wooden cages. When they became eighteen or nineteen their height was only that of a child of twelve. An assistant of Pu Yi once beat an orphan to death and yet Pu Yi claims he is a Buddhist and vegetarian and has never even wanted to kill a fly or mosquito.

Big Li showed his hostility in another document:

Pu Yi is both cruel and afraid of death. He is suspicious, tricky and a hypocrite. When he beat or scolded his servants, it was not for mistakes they committed, but due to his own mood at the time. If he did not feel well, or was tired, then the servants would suffer all kinds of punishment, the lightest form of which was when he used his fists or kicked them. Yet when he met outsiders this hypocrite was the best of men.

There were wooden benches and horsewhips in Tientsin. In Manchukuo there were new forms of punishment added. He tried to train many accomplices to beat people and if they were slow at it, he would accuse them of siding with his victims and then they themselves would be beaten.

His nephews and attendants have all beaten others. On one occasion, a twelve- or thirteen-year-old orphan was so badly beaten he got a cut one foot long. It took a physician two or three months to cure him and, during the treatment, Pu Yi asked me to send the boy milk and other things and tell him that His Majesty was kind and ask him if he would have gotten such goodies in an orphanage.

After I had read all this material, even the arguments for my own defense, which I had just completed, seemed shaken to their roots. I had always found justification for my actions in the belief that someone else in my position would have done the same thing. Thus, when I had submitted to Japanese pressure and followed their directions, I had rationalized that I had to do it and had no other alternative. And when I made demands on family members or took away or gave them things, or punished them, I had felt that these actions were within my prerogatives. All this had seemed to me natural and reasonable. Now I understood that there were other people who were not like this, and that my family members were no longer interested in maintaining my reputation as the last Manchu Emperor.

The investigation material on conditions in the Northeast under the Japanese had demonstrated that there were common people who, even under extreme pressures, would not bend as I had done.

For example, there had been a common farmer named Hsiao Chen-fang who had helped his uncle send food to the Communist resistance movement and also acted as guide for the Communist army and undertook various resistance tasks. On April 21, 1943, in the middle of the night, six policemen suddenly entered his house. Since his uncle was absent, he was bound and taken to police headquarters for questioning. The police beat him nearly to death and later poured cold water into his nose to revive him and then beat him again. They did this four times, but he told them nothing. The last time they beat him they thought he was dead and had him taken to a common grave in a "sanitary cart."

While en route, this stubborn man revived and was saved by one of the cart drivers.

Also, in 1943, a teen-ager named Li Ying-hua sent some fresh eggs to the resistance army and was arrested by the police. At first they served him cigarettes, poured tea for him and invited him to eat. They told him, "You are only a child; we'll release you as soon as you tell us what you know about the resistance army." The boy, after he had smoked a cigarette, drunk the tea and eaten the food, said, "I'm only a farm boy. I don't know a thing!" The Secret Police then hung him upside down, gave him electric shocks, burned him with cigarettes and bumped his body against a nail board. But they found out nothing from him.

Thus, I learned that not all people in the world were soft-boned and that my own past illustrated that I was the type who would only jump on the weak, that I was afraid of the strong, that I treasured my life and was afraid of death.

In the past, however, I had had a fundamental reason to explain away these defects in character. I had believed that as the last Manchu Emperor my existence was more precious than others. But in the past few years, as a laundry worker and paper-box paster, and in the light of the investigations of conditions of the Northeast common people and in the attitude of my family, I could see that in this new light my life had a different value. Within this frame of reference, I was both guilty and inglorious. I thus had no more reason to defend my past deeds and so I signed my name on the last copy of the material the Center had given me.

31

Self-Pity

"A NEW YEAR HAS BEGUN. WHAT ARE YOUR RESOLUTIONS?" the Center Director asked me on New Year's Day, 1955.

I told him that I could only prepare myself for my punishment.

"Why be so pessimistic?" he asked as he shook his head. "You should take a more positive attitude toward your remolding and try to be a new man!"

I had heard these same words the previous month when I had put my signature on the last confession documents the investigators had presented to me. Although they had made me feel a bit more comfortable, they had not basically changed my pessimistic and passive attitude. I had fallen deep into a pit of self-pity.

In March a group of Liberation Army generals came to Fushun to inspect our Thought Control Center, which was under the Mukden Military District. The Director asked me and Pu Chieh to come and see them. When I first entered the room which was full of shiny gold epaulettes I thought it was a military tribunal; but later, I realized that the generals wanted to know about my studies and my remolding. Their attitude was friendly and they seemed very interested in what I had to say and asked me about my life as a child and also during my Manchukuo days. Later, a bearded general said, "Study well and remold. In the future you will be able to see for yourself the socialistic reconstruction of China."

On the way back to my cell, I decided that this man must have been a marshal, and Pu Chieh told me that he probably was not the only marshal among them.

Back in my cell, I related the marshal's remarks to my cellmates and Yuan, the former Manchukuo Ambassador to Japan, said, "Congratulations, Pu! Since the marshal said you will be able to see socialist reconstruction, this means you're safe!"

The others all became very excited over this since they decided that if the "number one" prisoner would be safe, they too would certainly be all right.

After the end of the period of accusations and acknowledgement of guilt, the ban on talking during the recreation period in the courtyard had been lifted, and also, our cell doors were no longer locked during the day. This good news was soon spread through the prison. At this time I thought of my nephews and Big Li who had been ignoring me since the period of accusations of guilt. I felt sure that this news would also make them very happy, and I used it as an excuse to look for them and tell them about it. I heard Little Ku's voice singing a new song and followed the sound until I found him with Little Hsiu standing beside a large tree in the corner of the yard. But before I got there they went away.

In April, the Center had us elect a Study Committee as the Japanese prisoners had done. This Committee, which was under the supervision of the Center authorities, enabled us to organize our own studies and daily life. It was responsible for reporting to the Center staff all problems that arose and for reporting on discussions and self-criticism meetings. It could also forward ideas on its own initiative. The Committee had five members who were chosen by election but had to be approved by the Center authorities; there was a chairman and four other members responsible respectively for study, daily life, sport and recreation. The study chief and the daily life chief in each cell had to report to the responsible committeeman every day.

Soon after its creation, the Committee decided that we should build a sports ground. Little Jui, who was the committeeman in charge of daily life, was in charge of this work. When I showed up for work the first time he scolded me in front of everyone. As I ran to my place in the line, I was buttoning my jacket. All of a sudden, I heard my name shouted.

"Pu Yi!"

"Coming, coming," I replied, running to the end of the line.

"Each time we assemble, you are always late. You keep all of us waiting just for you. You aren't even conscious of it," Little Jui shouted with a grim expression on his face. "Just look at yourself, you're a complete mess. You can't even button yourself properly."

As I looked down, I noticed that all my buttons were in the wrong holes. Everyone turned to look at me as I fumbled and fumbled, still unable to button my jacket properly.

One day my glasses broke again. After some hesitation, I asked for Big Li's help once more. "Please help me," I asked humbly in a low voice. "I've tried to do them myself several times, but I just can't. Nobody else can do it. I beg you to mend them for me."

"You still want me to serve you," he said, staring at me. "Haven't I waited on you long enough? Haven't I served you sufficiently?" When he finished speaking, he turned his back on me and walked off in the opposite direction. I stood helplessly, wishing that I could dash my head against the wall. But in a few minutes, Big Li came back and took the glasses from me.

"Very well," he said angrily. "I'll mend them for you. But let me tell you this; I'm only doing this to make it possible for you to reform. Otherwise, I wouldn't have the time."

Later, during the rest period, I went to the newly established library to relax by myself and I ran into Pu Chieh. I started talking about myself and told him that I was so disturbed by the attitude of my family members that I was unable to sleep at night. "Why don't you talk it over with the Center staff?" he suggested. "From what I hear, they have urged the prisoners to forget old grudges and help you."

One Sunday I was washing clothes as usual. When I finished it was about time for sports but since I wasn't in the mood, I went to the reading room by myself. As soon as I sat down, I heard people talking outside the window.

"Can you play tennis?"

"I don't know how to play. Ask Pu Yi, he knows how."

"He knows how, but he doesn't want to play. Anyway, goodness knows when he'll finish washing his clothes!"

"He's become much quicker at it lately."

"I don't believe you!"

This conversation infuriated me. I *had* finished my laundry and I'd washed just as many clothes as anyone else. Why couldn't they believe in me? It was as if by nature I was incapable of improvement. Thus I fetched my tennis racket and went out into the yard, not so much because I wanted to play, but because I wanted to show the others that I had finished my washing.

When I reached the tennis court, the people whom I had overheard were gone. There was someone else there and so I played with him. Lots of spectators gathered to watch, and I played happily and worked up a good sweat.

After I finished I washed my hands at the tap, and then ran into the Center Director who often spent Sundays at the Center.

"Pu Yi, you've made real progress today," he commented.

"Oh, I haven't played for a long time," I answered contentedly.

"I wasn't talking about your tennis," he said as he pointed toward my clothes drying on the line. "Since you can now do your washing as quickly as the others, you can enjoy the same amount of leisure and recreation as they do. Recreation is life's happiness."

I immediately nodded my head to indicate agreement and then accompanied him on his stroll around the yard.

"In the past, when others enjoyed their rest and recreation, you were still busy doing your work," he continued. "Thus you were not equal with the others and felt resentful. But now, you know how to wash clothes, and you have a status of equality and are thus much happier. As you can see, you yourself hold the key to the problem and you don't have to worry how others treat you."

A few days later, when our group returned to our cell after

having removed the garbage, our committee member in charge of daily life held a self-criticism session. "Someone left the water running after washing his hands," he said. "This was irresponsible and I hope it won't happen again."

As soon as Big Li heard this, he immediately turned toward me. "Pu Yi," he said, "weren't you the last to wash your hands?"

"Perhaps I forgot to turn off the faucet," I answered after a moment.

"Is there ever a time when you don't forget?"

"Yes, of course there are times I don't forget."

"The trouble with you is," Big Li continued, "you are not even ashamed. You still have the habits of an emperor. In the past, you never turned off faucets yourself; as a matter of fact you never even touched a doorknob. There were always others to open and close doors for you. Now, when you leave a room, you only open a door, but you never close one. You still cannot lay aside the pomp of emperorship."

"Now I come to think of it," Old Yuan interjected, "I notice that sometimes you often cover the door handle with a piece of newspaper. Why do you do that?"

"It's because you're afraid it's dirty, isn't it?" Big Li commented.

"Everyone touches a doorknob, so of course it's dirty," I said.

This remark produced an avalanche of attacks by my cellmates. "Why are you the only one to mind the dirt?" "Is it because you think you are above other people?" "Is it a dirty door you're worried about, or dirty people?" "In your heart you really look down on others, don't you?" And so on.

I did my best to protest that I entertained no such feelings, but basically I couldn't help but feel depressed. Did I really do this? Later, someone mentioned that whenever we went to take a bath, I was always the first to jump into the communal tub and always got out the moment anyone else got in. Someone else recalled that at the New Year parties in the Soviet Union, I had always been the first to help myself to a bowl of dumplings. After hearing all this, I had to admit to myself that Big Li's analysis was right and that I had not been able to cast off my emperor's airs.

Once, when we were washing, Big Li came up and reminded us not to splash water on the floor while we were brushing our teeth. He told us that if we did so, we should mop it up with a cloth because there was going to be a hygiene contest that day and failure to do so would mean that we would lose points. As I looked down at my feet, I noticed that I had spilled some tooth powder and water on the floor.

Big Li also noticed it and asked me to mop it up. Without thinking, I wiped it with the sole of my cloth shoe. He laid into me for this, accusing me of only thinking of myself. "The trouble with you is you can only think about your privileges, never about your duties." He was just at the point of taking a mop and doing it himself, when he changed his mind and told me to do it. I obediently carried out his orders.

Big Li brought in some new fly swatters one day and handed one to me. This was the first time I had ever handled a fly swatter and I felt awkward. I had never before killed a fly. Actually there were very few in the Center. I finally found one by an open window and waved my swatter to drive it out.

"What do you think you're doing," Big Li shouted from behind me. "Are you killing flies or saving lives?"

At the self-criticism meeting that night, no one mentioned the affair until Big Li told how I had forbidden the killing of flies in Changchun and had even organized a group of people to save a mouse from the mouth of a cat. Then, everyone had a good laugh and criticized me for my superstition. "Why should you call me superstitious?" I answered. "Didn't I kill flies last year?"

At this, Old Yuan couldn't help but burst into laughter. "Thanks for reminding me," he said. "If you hadn't mentioned it, I would have forgotten. You asked others to use the fly swatters while you used a newspaper to chase them away."

In the midst of the laughter, only Big Li kept a straight face. "I don't know what it means when other people save lives," he sneered, "but in your case I understand completely. It's pure selfishness so that you can get the blessing of Buddha. Others may all die so long as Buddha protects you. You think you are the most precious thing on earth."

"You're exaggerating," I protested.

"Pu Yi does sometimes seem humble," Old Yuan put in.

"Yes," I added. "That's true. I do not regard myself as superior to anyone else."

"Perhaps sometimes you do humble yourself," Big Li admitted. "But at other times you still think of yourself as higher and superior to others. I've no idea how you got this way."

32

Conditions Improve

SOON AFTER THE CHINESE NEW YEAR OF 1956, THE CEN-
ter Director gave us a talk on national construction. "You
have studied about the First Five Year Plan, agricultural
cooperation and the socialist transformation of the handi-
craft industry as well as privately owned industry and com-
merce," he explained. "You have also read in the newspapers about the development of joint public-private
enterprises in several of the big cities. But this is all book
knowledge. You now need to see with your own eyes the
present state of society. For this reason the government will
arrange for you to make observation trips. First you will go
to Fushun; then, later on, you will go to other cities."

The atmosphere in the Thought Control Center was very
happy that day. Many felt excited and encouraged by the
prospect of a trip to the outside world, and some regarded
this news as a sign that we would soon be released. But I did
not share this elation. I did not feel that I would be released
even if others were. Also, I was uncomfortable about the
prospect of public visits. That afternoon, near the garden
plots, I overheard some of the others talking about this same
problem.

"What do you think the people will do when they see
us?"

"Since we'll be conducted by government officials nothing
will happen to us. Otherwise they wouldn't let us go."

"I'm not too sure. What will happen if people get excited?

273

I used to be a government official and I've seen the masses when they get worked up.''

"Don't worry; the Government wouldn't let us go out if it wasn't sure of what it was doing.''

"Anyway, I don't think the Government will reveal who we are.''

"Whether they reveal it or not people will know. The people are bound to recognize one of us and then they'll know who the rest of us are.''

These conversations made me recall how the Northeast people had been compelled to bow to my pictures, and I didn't see how they could help but recognize me. If so, how could the Government suppose they wouldn't get excited when they saw me and demand a public trial?

At Taishanpao, a village on the outskirts of Fushun, everyone we met was kind to us and some even stopped work to stand up and greet us. In the house of an agricultural cooperative member I revealed my identity without disastrous results.

The house was occupied by a family of five named Liu. Only Mrs. Liu was at home when we arrived. She was cooking, and when she saw the Cooperative Communist cadre member lead us in, she immediately took off her apron and invited us into a new room that had been added on to her house. She treated us as real guests, and asked us to sit on the *kang*.

The cadre member who had brought us in explained that we had come for a visit and wanted to see life in a cooperative. Although Mrs. Liu was not very articulate, she was able to tell us that they had originally been a family of seven with about seven mou[1] of land to cultivate, and that during the Imperial Manchukuo regime they had been practically reduced to beggary. "Although we grew rice, we had to eat acorn flour,'' she explained. "We had to hand over all the rice we grew to the government and if they found a single grain of it in the house, we would be labeled 'economic criminials.' ''

Her son came in while she was speaking and answered many of our questions. Although crippled, he had become a

---

[1] A little over one acre.

bookkeeper for the cooperative storage pits. When he talked about the present, his voice and manner became cheerful and confident, just like his mother's. Subsequently, his mother showed us a large crock of rice in the corner.

"Who wants to look at rice?" her son asked with a laugh.

"Yes," the mother admitted. "There's nothing to it now. But how often did you see it during the reign of the Emperor?"

I had been frightened when we first went into the house lest they would ask me my name, but now I felt that it would be inexcusable of me if I did not tell them who I was. Thus I stood up and said to Mrs. Liu in a low tone: "The Emperor of whom you spoke was Pu Yi. I am he. I want to beg your pardon."

Before I had finished speaking, the former Manchukuo ministers who were with me all stood up and told her who they were. The old lady was dumfounded. Even if she had guessed that her visitors were prisoners being subject to thought remolding, she clearly had not known who we actually were or that I had been the Emperor and would ask her forgiveness.

How did she react? Did she revile me or weep or call in the neighbors or the families who had suffered during the war to vent their anger? On the contrary, she sighed and said, "All those events are past. Let's not talk about them. As long as you are willing to study and obey the instructions of Chairman Mao, and become regular men, it will do."

On March 10, three days after our trip to Taishanpao, a guard told me, Pu Chieh, my two brothers-in-law and my three nephews to go to the Center Chief's office. When we entered, to our astonishment we saw my uncle, Prince Tsai Tao, and my third and fifth sister from whom we had been separated for over ten years.

When I saw my uncle looking as healthy as ever and my sisters in their cotton-padded uniforms, I felt as if I were entering dreamland. Tsai Tao was the only surviving close relation of mine of the previous generation. In 1954 he had been elected to the National People's Congress as the representative of China's two million Manchus. He was concurrently a member of the National Committee of the Chinese

People's Political Consultative Conference. He told me that he had met Chairman Mao a few days previously at the second meeting of the Congress. Premier Chou En-lai had introduced him as Mr. Tsai Tao, the uncle of Pu Yi. Chairman Mao had shaken hands with him and said, "I have heard that Pu Yi's studies are going well; why don't you go visit him . . . ?"

As my uncle told us this, we had to wipe away our tears, and my nephew Little Jui sobbed out loud. From this meeting I learned the fate of the Manchu nation and my own Aisin-Gioro clan. As Tsai Tao explained it, before liberation there had been only 80,000 Manchus officially registered, but now the number was thirty times as high. After 1911, the Manchus had encountered increasing difficulty in surviving under the Peiyang war lords and the Kuomintang which had been anti-Manchu and thus they had assumed Han nationality and taken surnames like Chin, Chao and Lo. My father's family in Tientsin, for example, had taken the name of Chin. But after the Communists took over, more and more Manchus acknowledged their true minority nationality and, upon the proclamation of the new Constitution, all the Manchus had registered as actual Manchus and thus the number reached 2,400,000.

This change in government policy toward Manchus had not only affected the Aisin-Gioros and their careers, but also Prince Tsai Tao and the various royal princesses. My uncle was sixty-nine years old, and in such good health and physical vigor that I could see little of an old man about him. When he talked it was as he used to. He explained that after the Communist take-over, he had worked for a department of the Liberation Army that was in charge of horses (a field in which he was an expert) and had spent some time on the steppes of the Northwest. He also explained that he was planning to go back to the border area in order to inspect the work of the national minorities as part of his duties as a member of the National People's Congress.

Right after the entry of the Liberation Army into Peking many of the retired Manchu statesmen had felt very uncomfortable. Although the majority of them had not become members of the new Manchukuo nobility, they had not forgotten their status as descendants of the royal family and their respect for my person. When they learned I had been imprisoned they felt even more worried than before. The combination of this, the diminishing number of Manchus and their difficulties in earning a living all added to their uncertainty. Thus, when they learned of the opening of a special school for Manchu children, they were surprised. Later, when cadres from the People's Government visited many of them and invited them to be delegates to local consultative conferences and asked them to express opinions on Manchu problems they were even more surprised. It was clear that the new government was pursuing a different policy than the Kuomintang with the respect to the border peoples.

In Peking, all the descendants of my great-grandfather the Emperor Tao Kuang and of his brothers Prince Tun, Prince Kung and Prince Chun were over sixty except for a few cousins of mine who were a little younger. My second cousin Pu Chin (also known as Pu Hsueh-chai), an outstanding painter, calligrapher and player of the *ku chin* (an ancient Chinese stringed instrument), was over sixty and had never expected that he would once again be able to take his *ku chin* down from the wall and be allowed to carry it once a week to play on the banks of Peihai Lake in Peking. He had also been elected Vice-President of the *Ku Chin* Research Association and President of the Calligraphy Research Association and had become a teacher at the Academy of Chinese Painting. His cousin Pu Hsiu, who was Little Jui's uncle, had been at one time a "Companion of the Chien Ching Gate" in the Forbidden City and had looked after my property in Tientsin while I was in Manchukuo. Subsequently he had gone blind, but after the take-over, his experiences and the historical materials he carried in his mind were regarded as invaluable and he was employed as a member of the Institute for Classical and Historical Studies. Pu Hsiu recounted for others to write down what he remembered about Ch'ing history.

I once made a calculation on the basis of the "Jade Register" of the imperial family compiled in 1937 and the information provided by my younger brothers and sisters about the rate of infant mortality in my branch of the Aisin-Gioro clan. The death rate of children before reaching majority was 34 percent during the last part of the Ch'ing

Dynasty, 10 percent during the Republic, and none during the ten years since the take-over. The figures of the whole Aisin-Gioro clan were even more staggering and something like 45 percent of the boys and girls of my own and my father's generation dying before reaching majority, and most of the deaths occurring before reaching the age of two.

When I met my uncle and sisters I had not compiled these statistics, but when I listened to my sisters talking about their children, I couldn't help but think of all the children who had died in my own and my father's generation as well as the "Jade Register" which contained blank spaces for the children who had died before they had been given names. And in the previous generation, if they had reached maturity, besides airing their birds in cages early in the morning on the streets of Peking, they had nothing to do except to drink tea until lunchtime. They had no future under the Republic. Few of them learned anything and once they had used up their money they could not find employment or jobs since they were unskilled.

But now things had changed. In Peking, a younger brother and my six sisters had a total of twenty-seven children and, with the exception of those not yet of school age, the rest were in school or in college. My uncle Tsai Tao had sixteen grandchildren and great-grandchildren of whom the eldest was a technician at a hydroelectric plant, one granddaughter was a student at the Military Medical College, one had joined the People's Volunteers in Korea and had returned and was in college, another was an army literary and art worker, and others were, with the exception of the very young or those in school, all working. The past life of going to the races, hunting with eagles or strolling in the streets with lanterns was a joke.

From the time of this first visit of Tsai Tao, family members came to see me often at the Control Center.

The New Year of 1957 was celebrated with more festivity than the previous ones. The authorities told our Committee that if we thought we could manage a large-scale party, we could get the Number 3 and Number 4 Center Chiang Kai-shek detainees to fill the auditorium as an audience for our show.

The reason the Center authorities had given us their support was because they felt these shows enabled the detainees to educate themselves. In the past they had been very successfully used by the Japanese war prisoners, who wrote educational plays on the basis of what they read in the Japanese press. These had a great remolding effect on the writers, performers and audience alike. Our own Study Committee therefore decided to include plays of this sort in our own show. Two plays were decided upon: one was called *The Failure of the Aggressors* and dealt with the collapse of the British invasion of Egypt, and the other dealt with the transformation of a Manchukuo traitor and was titled *From Darkness to Glory*. These were written by my brother Pu Chieh and a former official of Wang Ching-wei's[2] government, named Mu.

As the work on the plays went ahead all kinds of other performances were also under preparation. Old Lung, our magician, whose tricks were always welcome, indicated that he would get up a large-scale act because he was tired of the small tricks he had previously performed of swallowing ping-pong balls and obtaining eggs from a hat. Old Cheng, two Mongol brothers and Old Kuo were busy preparing a Mongolian song-and-dance act. My cell chief who was fond of music was active rehearsing choral singing and others were busy with many of the traditional items. During these few days, the busiest man was Old Wan, the head of the study committee who was in charge of the program. Little Jui was responsible for the decorations since he was so skillful in making paper flowers and lanterns. Big Li was in charge of the lighting. Each and everyone of us were involved in the preparations.

In the past, I had not performed in the New Year shows and had not been asked to help out with the decorations. Even when I had offered to hold thumbtacks or paper streamers people had felt that I was so clumsy I would only be in their way. But this time, to my astonishment, Old Chu, our cell chief, discovered that my singing was passable and signed me up for the choir. I was grateful and practiced with

---

[2] A prominent Chinese revolutionary who set up a pro-Japanese regime in East China during World War II.

gusto. But just when I had learned my songs, Old Wan, my brother-in-law, who was chief of the Study Committee came to see me.

"Pu Yi," he said. "There's a part for you in the first show. It's not too difficult and there aren't any lines. Besides, you can make up your own lines as well. This is a significant task and part of your self-education. . . ."

"You don't need to persuade me," I interrupted. "As long as you think I'm all right, I'll do it."

"Of course, of course you will do it." Old Wan grinned. "You can do it; besides you have a loud voice and . . ."

"You flatter me! Tell me, what do you want me to play in?"

"The Failure of the Aggressors," Wan answered. "It's about the displeasure of heaven that the British incurred when they invaded Egypt. It's based on news items. Old Jun is playing the leading role—the Foreign Secretary, Selwyn Lloyd. You will be a left-wing Labour Member of Parliament."

I went to see Pu Chieh to read the script and to copy down my lines. Then I went to choose a costume. Since I was playing a foreigner, I, of course, had to wear Western-style clothing of which there was no shortage since many of the prisoners had arrived in them and they had been stored in the custodial section. I thus chose the suit I had worn at the International Tribunal in Tokyo, a shirt, a tie, etc., and then returned to my cell. Since nobody else was in the cell, I started dressing. As soon as I had put on a white Arrow shirt, Old Yuan happened to walk in and was dumfounded at what he saw.

"What are you doing?" he asked. Since I was excited and my shirt collar was too tight, I could not answer at first. "I'm going to take part in the play," I finally panted. "Please come here and help loosen the belt at the back of my vest."

Even though he did this, I still could not button it, and I thus realized I had put on weight. Even my leather shoes from England were too tight for me, and I asked Old Yuan in irritation if I would need to wear leather shoes to play a British M.P.

"Of course you must," Old Yuan answered. "The British

Labour Party M.P.s even wear perfume. So how could you think of not wearing shoes? Don't worry about it; your shoes won't be too tight after you wear them for a while and the vest can be altered. Go learn your lines. It's really a strange thing that you will be acting."

As I walked down the corridor I could still hear his laugh, but I was really very happy and, from that moment on, I used all my time to memorize my lines. What Old Wan had said was correct. They were very short; perhaps I was the actor with the fewest lines. According to the story of the play, at the very end Selwyn Lloyd made a speech in the House of Commons defending the invasion of Egypt and some of the opposition members started to question him and then joined in an attack on him. At this point, I was to stand up in their midst and challenge him and say: "Mr. Lloyd, please don't try to defend your actions. They are a shambles, a shambles, a shambles!" The Parliament was then supposed to be filled with a hubbub of angry shouting and demands for Lloyd's resignation, during which I was to shout "Get out." This play had a very simple plot in which the most important element was the parliamentary debate that only lasted fifteen minutes. But I spent dozens of fifteen minutes preparing my part fearful that I would forget my lines or make a mistake and thus disappoint the hopes that had been placed in me.

When New Year came and I went into the hall for the party, I was attracted by the atmosphere of festivity and the beautifully decorated stage and I forgot my nerves. The colorful decorations and the handmade paper flowers deserved the praise of all of us. It was all quite professional. Old Wan had written a beautiful sign in Sung Dynasty style calligraphy: *Evening Party to Celebrate the New Year*. When we saw how impressed the Chiang Kai-shek detainees were we couldn't help but feel happy.

The other acts went off successfully, drawing lots of applause. When our act got underway, Old Jun, who was dressed up to look just like Selwyn Lloyd, was very lively. Since he had a big nose, he was really the only M.P. who looked like an Englishman. His acting was outstanding in showing the anger, fear and desperation of a defeated Foreign Secretary. After the play had gone on for ten minutes,

Old Yuan, who was sitting next to me on the stage, and was playing the part of a member of Parliament, said to me (this was in the play), "Don't be so wooden, put some movement into it." At this point I looked forward and watched the audience and got the feeling that it was paying more attention to me, the left-wing M.P., than to the Foreign Secretary, Selwyn Lloyd. All of a sudden, I became very tense. No one had noticed me when I was singing in the choir, but now I had become the focal point of the audience. Before I could recover my composure, Old Yuan nudged me. "Say it, it's about time for you to refute him," he whispered. I stood up immediately, turned toward Old Jun who was still talking, and forgot my lines! Finally, inspiration came to me and, using English, I shouted at him, "No! No! No!" My shout interrupted Old Jun's speech and then I remembered my lines and continued, "Mr. Lloyd, please don't continue your tricky defense." Putting one hand on my waist, I pointed with the other, "In fact, this is a shambles, a shambles, a shambles!" Immediately, I heard a burst of applause from the audience, while on the stage we repeated in chorus, "SCRAM! SCRAM!" At this, the Foreign Secretary scuttled off the stage.

"You played very well." Old Yuan was the first to congratulate me as he descended from the stage. "Although you were a little excited, you were really good!" Later, others also indicated their approval and they laughed at the line I had improvised. Some even recalled the time when I had refused to meet a Swedish prince because he had his photo taken with a famous actor. I couldn't help but join in the laughter.

In 1958, the importance attached to labor and the enthusiasm for it made a deep impression on us. When we learned that Chairman Mao himself and Premier Chou had taken part in building the Ming Tombs Reservoir, we immediately asked the Center authorities and the study committee to organize us for productive labor.

The authorities met our request by allowing us to set up a workshop to manufacture miniature electric motors, but as we were short of manpower this task was given to Section 3 and Section 4 of the Chiang Kai-shek detainees and we were then organized into five specialized groups: animal raising, food processing, horticulture, hothouse vegetable raising and medicine. Four others and I were assigned to the medical group. Our job was to clean up the clinic daily and do various odd jobs and help with auxiliary medical work. We also spent two hours a day studying medicine under the direction of Dr. Wen of the Center staff, and also held group discussions. My four colleagues had all been doctors before; three of them reviewed their Western medicine and one his Chinese medicine. In addition we all took a course on acupuncture[3] and moxibustion.[4] This period of working and studying with a small group gave me new confidence.

When I first joined the medical group my proficiency was much below that of my associates. The surgical cotton pads I made looked like lumps of worn clothing padding and when I took blood pressure, I would either forget to listen to the stethoscope or else forget to look at my watch. When I was learning to use the electrical equipment for treating blood pressure, I was always in a state of confusion and could do nothing right. But I was determined to master my job and after the doctor or nurse had taught me something, I would ask my classmates for further explanation and then I would practice by myself. Thus I gradually learned to master my job as a medical assistant. At that time one of the Japanese detainees used to come for electrical treatment every day and he would always bow nearly to the ground afterward and say, "Thank you, Doctor," and I couldn't help but be delighted by this. I came to think that although my white coat and spectacles gave me the appearance of a doctor, the bowing also showed that my skillful technique had gained the patient's confidence. At the end of the first course, Dr. Wen gave us a test and I got full marks with the others. I thus became confident that I was not so stupid and had been able to master a trade so that I would no longer need my 468 pieces of jewelry to support myself.

---

[3] A form of medical treatment by which long metal needles are inserted into certain tissues in order to relieve nervous tension. If the acupuncture technician is expert, no blood is drawn.

[4] Application of burning licorice leaves and other herbs to the skin.

But I had rated myself too highly, as I found out when I was faced with a test. At the time when the Great Leap Forward was taking place throughout the country, the Center Director explained to us that in order to let our thoughts keep pace with the new situation we needed to step up our remolding studies and have thought reviews in order to eliminate ideological obstructions to our progress. The method used was for each of us to discuss in our study meetings the changes that had taken place in our thinking during the past few years and the issues which were not yet clarified.

When my turn came, a big problem developed. I talked about my past thinking and the changes in many of my thoughts. When I asked for comments, someone said: "People of your experience must have had deep and long emotional attachment to Japanese imperialism. Perhaps you still have links and connections with it. Your relationship with the Japanese was no less than ours, and since everyone else has talked about this, why is it that you have not even mentioned it? Do you mean to say that you don't have such feelings?"

"I only have hatred for the Japanese; I have no feeling or sentiment for them. I am different from you."

This provoked a storm of reaction. "Why aren't you more humble? Do you still think you are above us? What sort of feelings for them do you have now? Don't tell me you have made more progress than the rest of us."

I replied that in the past the Japanese and I had sought to utilize one another, but I had no feeling or sentiments for them. I did not look down on my fellow detainees. I was really telling the truth. But despite my explanations, no one chose to believe me and later, I was asked:

"When Manchukuo collapsed, the Japanese were going to send you to Tokyo and they gave you three hundred million yen for your expenses. Didn't that make you grateful to Japanese imperialism?"

"Three hundred million yen?" I was astounded. "I don't know anything about three hundred million yen!"

Actually, this was not a great mystery. When the Kwantung Army took the last gold reserves from the Manchukuo treasury, it was announced to the outside world that it was being transported to Japan for the Emperor of Manchukuo. But I had never seen a cent of this money, and everyone knew this. Had I thought back calmly I would have been able to remember the entire incident; but instead, I asserted with confidence that I knew nothing whatever about it.

"You don't know about it?" many of those who did know shouted. "This affair was handled by Chang Ching-hui and Rokuzo Takebe. Are you trying to deny it because Chang Ching-hui died recently? Didn't you write about it in your confession?" When I said I had not they were even more incredulous. "But everyone knows about it. This isn't a matter of three hundred, or three thousand, but of three hundred million."

That evening I cast my mind back and suddenly recalled that when I had been in Talitzukou someone had told me that the Kwantung Army had taken all the gold from the Bank of Manchukuo and said that it was to be used to support me in Japan. This must have been the 300 million they were talking about. But at that time I was too worried about my own safety to pay any attention to the matter. The following day I explained this to my study group.

"Why did you try to hide this?" several asked in a chorus.

"Who was hiding it? I absolutely forgot about it."

"Do you insist that you have forgotten it now?"

"Now, I recall it."

"Why didn't you recall it before?"

"What is forgotten is forgotten. It's only natural to forget sometimes, isn't it?"

The more I tried to argue the less they believed me. I became worried. Obviously they thought I was lying. If this was reported to the Center authorities, would they believe in me? As these thoughts rushed through my mind it was as if I were possessed by devils. I recalled incidents in the remote historic past of China when others had overwhelmed a person who had told the truth by their refusal to believe, and at the thought that my word was not likely to be taken against all the others, my courage melted away and I fell back into my old ways. I was prepared to forget my principles so long as I could weather this storm. I would be able to see my way through this crisis if I made a false confession. So I said that I had not dared to mention it before, since I was frightened that the government would punish me, but now they had all persuaded me to overcome my fears.

In the fall of that year, the former Center Director came to the prison and sent for me. When I opened the door of his office I saw the familiar gray-haired figure behind his desk reading a pile of papers. He asked me to sit down, and, after a while, put aside his papers and raised his head to talk to me.

"I've just finished reading the record of your group. How are you doing? Do you have any problems regarding ideology?"

At this moment I became hesitant. I looked at the pile of records of our cell and recalled the unanimous accusations against me and couldn't help wondering whether there was any point in telling the real truth about the 300 million yen incident, as it would be my word against all the others. Should I continue with the deception?

"Tell me what the meetings of your group are like," the Chief asked.

"Very good. You must have a systematic synthesis of our thoughts, and the conclusions are all accurate."

"Hm?" The Center Director raised his eyebrows. "Can you give me a more detailed description?" he asked.

It seemed to me that even my breathing had become unnatural. "What I said was true," I replied. "The report that I was too worried to mention certain things is quite true. But there were one or two items . . ."

"Continue. You know that I wish to understand better your ideology and thinking."

I felt that I could not hold back anymore and that I had to speak out. So I poured out the events of the last study meeting while my heart pounded like mad. The Chief listened to me very attentively and after I had finished speaking he said, "Why was it so difficult for you to say this? What were you thinking about?"

"I was afraid because they were all unanimous in believing that I was not telling the truth. . . ."

"So long as you tell the truth what are you frightened of?" The Chief spoke sternly and with dignity. "Do you think that the government cannot investigate the matter itself and reach its own verdict? You never seem to understand that you need courage to speak the truth."

33

A Special Pardon

ON SEPTEMBER 14, 1959, CHAIRMAN MAO TSE-TUNG, ON the occasion of the tenth anniversary of the founding of the People's Republic, forwarded a proposal to the Standing Committee of the National People's Congress providing for a special pardon for a number of war criminals, counterrevolutionaries and common criminals "who have really been reformed." According to Chairman Mao the majority of the prisoners under detention had been remolded and their pardon would help "change negative factors into positive ones" and enable the prisoners to realize that "under socialism their future lies in reform."

This proposal was passed by the Standing Committee on September 17 and the special pardon was proclaimed that same day. The scene created at the Reform Center by this proclamation was unforgettable. When the announcer had finished his last sentence there was a moment of silence followed by an explosion of cheers, slogans and applause. It was as if 10,000 strings of firecrackers had been ignited at one time, and the noise went on for a long time.

All sorts of views were expressed. Some felt the Party and Government were always true to their word and we now had a future and a place to go and it would not be long before we were out. Others said we would be pardoned in groups; some would go out first, others later. Some debated as to who would be included in the first group. Many came to understand that our pardon would depend on our reformation and remolding and thus some regretted their tendency to be slack with their studies. Meanwhile some who tried to be humble and modest about the degree of their reformation and the probability of their early release, nevertheless discreetly tidied up their things, destroyed their discarded notebooks and threw away their worn-out socks.

The courtyard was a babel of voices during the rest period. I heard Old Yuan ask Old Hsien, "Who will be in the first group?"

"Those who have received awards during the review of their study records probably won't have any problem. Possibly you will be one."

"No, I'm not good enough, but I'm sure you are."

"Me? If I should go out first I'll certainly send you some Peking delicacies. I really long to eat some Peking dates."

From another side of the courtyard, I heard another's voice: "If they want to release us they should release all at once, or not let anyone out."

"Don't you have any confidence in yourself?" someone answered him. "Are you afraid that you might be left behind?"

"Left behind? Unless they keep Pu Yi here they won't keep me."

What he said was really true. Even I felt he was right. On the following day the Deputy Chief asked me what I thought of the special pardon.

"I think that I am bound to be the very last one—that is, if I can ever remold myself. All the same, I shall try my best."

For most of the prisoners the special pardon and release meant reunion with their families, but this did not apply to me. My mother had died long ago, my father had died in 1951 and my last wife had divorced me in 1956.

We became more enthusiastic in our studies and work, and many of us waited impatiently for the next assessment of our progress. The food-processing team now made bean curd that was both soft and white, the stock-breeding team fattened up their pigs so that they were finer than ever, and my own medical team stopped making mistakes.

More than a month passed. One evening the Deputy Chief asked me to come and see him to discuss the special pardon. "What have you been thinking during the past two months?" he asked me.

I told him that some of us seemed to have been remolded very well. I mentioned several who had received special commendations and also the food-processing and pig-breeding teams.

"It is much easier now for you to think of other people's good points, isn't it?" the Deputy Chief asked with a smile. "If the special pardon should include you, what would you think?"

"But this is impossible," I replied.

Impossible! That was the thought I carried back with me to my cell. But if . . . if? Once this phrase came to my mind I suddenly became very tense. My hopes became greater and I couldn't help but entertain some dreams. I imagined myself, Old Wan, Little Jui and others taking our place among real people and doing the same things that real people did. Perhaps I might be given a job as a medical assistant in a hospital by the Labor Department, just as had happened to others who had been remolded. But this would require a long period of time. At the thought of the happiness that might be in store for me I was almost unable to sleep.

On the following day, we were told to assemble. As we walked into the great hall I saw hanging across the stage a broad crimson cloth that took my breath away. On it was written: *Special Pardon Meeting for the Fushun War Criminal Control Center.*

A representative of the Supreme People's Court, the two Center directors and others were sitting on the stage. Below, everyone was so quiet that I seemed to be able to hear my own heart beat.

After a few introductory words from the Center Chief, the representative of the Supreme People's Court went to the center of the stage, took out a piece of paper and read, "Aisin-Gioro Pu Yi."

My heart leapt. I walked toward the front of the stage and heard him read as follows:

Notice of a Special Pardon from the People's Court of the People's Republic of China

In accordance with the Special Pardon Order issued by the Chairman of the People's Republic of China on September 17, 1959, this Court has investigated the case of the "Manchukuo war criminal" Aisin-Gioro Pu Yi.

The war criminal Aisin-Gioro Pu Yi, male, 54 years old, of the Manchu nationality, and from Peking, has now served ten years' detention. As a result of remolding through labor and ideological education during his captivity he has shown that he has genuinely reformed. In accordance with the stipulations of Clause I of the Special Pardon Order he is therefore to be released.

SUPREME PEOPLE'S COURT OF THE
PEOPLE'S REPUBLIC OF CHINA

December 4, 1959

Before hearing the end of the pronouncement, I had already burst into tears.

VI

MY NEW LIFE

34

The Forbidden City—Revisited

On December 9, 1959, I arrived at Peking, my home town from which I had been absent for thirty-five years. On the station platform, I saw a younger sister whom I had not seen for more than ten years and a younger brother whom I had not seen for more than twenty years. I shook their hands very warmly and heard them call me "Elder Brother," a term they had never before used in addressing me. They thus made me feel that I had commenced a new type of life among my family members. I then bade good-bye to Li and Meng, both of whom had accompanied me all the way from Fushun. Li had been the cadre member in charge of our study section who had sought to quiet everyone after the dispute arose over my inadequacy at pasting labels on pencil boxes, and Meng had been one of the eight inmates from Chiang Kai-shek's organization who had received a special pardon at the same time I did.

As Meng left the platform with his wife, who had come to welcome him, my younger brother picked up my black leather suitcase and, with my sister, we walked out of the station together.

Once outside, I glanced at the station clock and took out my pocket watch to set it. When I had left Fushun the Center Director had taken this watch from among the things I had contributed to the Government and asked me to accept it. It was the same French gold pocket watch that I had bought at Wu Li Wen Company in 1924 on the day I had fled from my father's mansion to the Japanese Legation. Now I was using it to set the time for starting a new life.

My family were very amiable and kind to me and, early in the morning of the following day, I wanted to think of something I could do to help them. When I noticed that neighbors were using a broom to sweep the alley outside the house I joined them and swept all the way to the end. Unfortunately, when I finished I found that I could no longer locate the house where I was staying and, by mistake, walked into the home of total strangers.

These people were very considerate and kind about leading me to the correct house and said I did not need to thank them. "We are neighbors; but even if we were not," they explained, "you would not need to thank us for doing so little. It doesn't matter at all."

Later that day I saw my uncle Tsai Tao and his wife as well as some cousins and another sister and her husband. My uncle told me what had happened to the various members of my family clan. We also listened together to Pu Chin who played some music on the Chinese lute, and he showed me some of his calligraphy which was really so good that it had reached a new high standard. Later I saw some paintings of flowers and birds that another cousin had painted, and, after that, I went to call on a sister but found that she had already left for the street nursery where she worked. According to her husband who was an engineer for the Postal and Cable Department, she was now so busy that she no longer had time for the migraine headaches from which she used to suffer. I also saw an unmarried sister and three other married sisters and their husbands. One was active in political association study work, another was working on the archives of the Forbidden City and another, with her husband, were painters.

In this period of again getting to know my family, I was especially touched by all their children, and was taught, through their eyes, what the second generation regarded as honorable titles. For these growing youth in their ruby neckties, their idols were the champion Peking girl's motorcycle racer and a mountain-climbing chief. And the younger ones, still in middle school, were learning all kinds of specialized occupations. All, without exception, were proud to earn honorable titles.

During my first few days in Peking I also met many old friends including some who had once been eunuchs in the Forbidden City, and I learned of the present situation of many of them. They were spending a peaceful old age at a Center for the Aged that had been especially established by the Peking Civilian Administration Bureau.

Almost all the people I met said to me: "Now you have returned, you must go about the city and take a look and see the changes and improvements." And so I went for a walk with a younger sister and another young relative. In the square in front of the Gate of Heavenly Peace as we were walking slowly westward toward the Cultural Palace of Nationalities my sister said to me: "My brother, aren't you tired? Isn't this the first time you have walked so long?"

"I'm not tired," I answered. "It is because it *is* the first time, that I'm not tired!"

These words, "the first time," had become very much a part of the life I had just commenced. There had been two other "first times" that very morning; and in each case I had not felt uncomfortable, because it was the "first time"; only excited. That morning I had gone to a barbershop.

As soon as I sat on the barber chair, I heard a hair drier being used on the man next to me and did not know what it was or what to call it. I asked the barber what he called the device which made such a "woo . . . wooo . . . woo" sound.

"That's not a device," he replied joking, "that's the wind blowing."

"In that case," I said to him in all sincerity, "what do you do first; blow the wind or cut the hair?"

He looked stunned at this remark and for a moment obviously thought I was some odd creature from another world. "Have you never had a haircut before?" he asked, finally.

When I explained to him who I was and that it was indeed my first visit to a modern barbership we couldn't help laughing. Thus by the time I heard the woo . . . wooo . . . woo sound over my own head the novelty of it made me feel quite happy.

I had a similar experience the first time I rode on a public bus. I noticed that those waiting in line to board it let the older people and children go first and so I let a lady behind me go on ahead and didn't realize that she was the conductress who expected me to be quick about climbing aboard after her. Then, when she saw me standing motionless she shut the door and the bus left without me. One of my cousins who had seen what happened came back from the next bus stop up the street. We began to laugh when we saw one another and I said to him, "No need to worry. Nothing will happen to me."

The Civilian Administration Bureau of Peking, in order to help us become reoriented and to acquaint ourselves with life in the outside world, had organized all of us who had been pardoned and were residing in Peking into a special sight-seeing group. We were taken on guided tours of newly constructed factories, expanded public works enterprises, the Municipal People's Commune and other buildings. We spent about two months at this and, toward the end of the course, at the request of one of my companions, we took a tour of the Forbidden City. I was assigned as a special temporary guide for the group.

What surprised me the most was that the old and desolate atmosphere that had pervaded the palace by the time I had left it was now gone. It had been painted and even the door and window curtains, the draperies on the beds, the seat covers and tablecloths were new. Upon inquiry I found that all these had been made in a special weaving establishment near the palace to reproduce the original fabrics.

There were really not many jade pieces, porcelains, calligraphy, paintings and other ancient cultural relics left, but I did find some things that the Museum had purchased as well as others that had been contributed by private collectors. For instance, there was a famous painting of a river scene which Pu Chieh and I had taken and sold which had been repurchased. In the Imperial Garden I smelled the fragrance emitted by the old cypress trees and it brought back to me memories of my youth.

In March, 1960, I was assigned to work at the Peking Botanical Garden which was under the direction of the Chinese Scientific Botanical Research Center. I worked a half day and studied a half day. This was essentially a testing period for me during which my reformation and remolding could be observed by the authorities and was preparatory to my eventual assignment as a professional worker for the government. Under the direction of technicians I was taught in the hothouse how to plant seeds, how to care for the plants, how to transplant, and so on. When I was not on the job at the hothouse I either studied or worked on my autobiography. The people with whom I worked and lived at the Botanical Garden were friendly and kind from the top to the bottom.

One day, after I returned from a stroll outside, I discovered that my watch was missing. I couldn't help but feel upset. Also I believed that since I had gone for such a long walk I would never be able to find it again and that I might just as well give it up for lost. But when he learned about it, one of the Garden officials, who was also a roommate, insisted on hearing every detail of my walk and then immediately set out to retrace my steps. There were others, too, who instead of taking a rest went out to look for it. I was really very embarrassed. Later, Liu, the Garden official, found it in the Four Seasons Evergreen Dining Hall of the People's Commune. He was so happy to be able to give it back to me that I felt that what I had received from him was not a watch but a deep and genuine friendship.

In the summer of that year the Botanical Garden established a unit of the civilian militia. They drilled every day and I registered my desire to participate. When people said that I was too old, I answered that "as a member of the big family of my motherland, I should stand on duty to defend it."

Finally the officials were convinced and I was allowed to participate as a member of the overaged group and I dreamed of the time my Botanical Garden unit could participate in a parade by the Gate of Heavenly Peace. My wish was realized in a very short time and I joined in a demonstration of support of the Japanese people against the "Japanese-American Security Treaty." As we passed by the Gate, we shouted our slogan loudly: "Ten thousand years for the Chinese People's Republic! Long live the alliance of the people of the whole world!"

On November 26, 1960, I received my voter's certificate

with my name written on it: Aisin Gioro Pu Yi—and it seemed to me that nothing in my whole life was as valuable as this. When I placed my vote in the vermilion ballot box, I felt myself the richest man in the world. I was now a citizen of a country of 650,000,000 people and the gigantic hand that was extended by them to reach oppressed people and nationalities everywhere in the world was a reliable one.

In March, 1961, I concluded my testing stage and was assigned to a special job in the Literature and History Material Research Commission of the National Political Alliance. My assignment was to organize and arrange the literature and historical source material of the late Ch'ing Dynasty and the subsequent Peiyang clique war-lord governments. While working, I frequently ran into names that I was quite familiar with. Sometimes I even encountered historical events which had a relationship or connection with my own past.

After work, I continued to write my autobiography. I was supplied with valuable historical source material and some of it was copied down word for word by the hands of many friends whom I had never previously known. Part of this material was verified for me by my colleagues in the Publications Office and there were also elderly people who recalled their own experiences for me. The National Archives, the Historical Museum, the Peking Library and the Capital Library were especially helpful. I felt somewhat uneasy about receiving the assistance of so many strangers but this has become the regular way of doing things in China. Today, so long as you propagandize the truth, you receive aid from one and all including, needless to say, the Communist Party and the Government.

1962 was a special year of happiness for me. I was invited to attend the People's All China Political Consultative Conference, and I also audited the report of the National People's Congress regarding China's reconstruction. Also on May first of that year, my new wife, Li Shu-hsien, and I established our own little home. It wasn't much but to me it was something very special—a real family unit that represented the start of a new life for me. When I looked at my wife, my voter's certificate and the unlimited and broad future before me I knew I would never forget how I had obtained this life.

My thoughts thus went back to the summer of 1960, two years before, when Little Jui, who had also returned to Peking, and I went on a visit to Fragrance Hill Park in the Western Hills. We had talked about the various stages of change in our thought development and I told him that as far as I was concerned, at the beginning, I had been most preoccupied with the problem of life and death and whether or not the policy of leniency would be applicable to me. What had given me the first real feeling that I might be able to live was when I had surrendered the jewelry hidden in the double bottom of my suitcase and I had received such unexpectedly lenient treatment. "When I talk about it," I said to Little Jui, "I have you to thank for your assistance."

"My assistance?" he asked as he stared at me and opened his eyes. "Then you still don't know what really happened?"

"Of course," I answered. "Didn't the Center Chief ever tell you what happened? Due to the questioning of Little Ku, I admitted everything and later I had a self-criticism session with the Center Chief. I told him that when I had surrendered my things, I had not mentioned the note you had given me because I was afraid that you might receive punishment. The Chief explained that he had known all about the note and that it had been he who had asked you to write it in order to assist me in confessing of my own volition. That was the assistance to which I was referring."

"Judging from your description, I can see you still don't know what the real situation was," Little Jui replied. "You just don't know about it. When the Center Chief asked me to write the note to you, this was not what I had wanted. It was my idea to have you searched, to confiscate your things and then have you punished."

This was the first time that the detailed background of these motivations was revealed to me. As Little Jui related the sequence of events, the Center Chief had refused his request. "It will be easy to search him," the Chief had explained, "but this will not be helpful for his reform. Let's wait and see. Searching is never as good as a voluntary confession; it will be better if he reaches self-enlightenment by himself."

Later, Little Jui had again talked to the Center Chief and again asked him to search me, but the Director had explained that the speed of development of each man's thoughts was completely variable and that they should not be in a hurry. The Communist Party believed that a great majority of criminals could be reformed but that it was an individual process, requiring individual evaluation. The Chief had told Little Jui: "You should understand that it is hard for him because of his special status to believe in the policy of leniency for those who confess. If we search him, he will lose the opportunity to experience personally this policy. Let him surrender the things according to his own will. If you are in a hurry it would be better for you to think of some way to speed up his own self-enlightenment." As a result, it was decided that Little Jui should write the note to me.

After the note had been passed to me and there was no immediate reaction, Little Jui had become worried and again talked with the Center Chief. "Pu Yi will never understand until his death," Little Jui had explained. "Since he has no desire for self-enlightenment, why don't we search him?"

But the Center Chief had again urged patience. "From the beginning," he had argued, "I have felt that in this case we cannot hurry. It is more essential now than ever that we not get excited."

Later on, of course, I had become worried and had surrendered the jewelry and from this time on I had seen a way out. "It was at this juncture," I told Little Jui, "that I began to understand that the Government believed that a majority of the people could be reformed."

"But you yourself know," Little Jui answered, "that even after this you were still persistently resisting your reformation and cheating. Several of us had already told everything to the Government, even before the special investigators had arrived."

At that moment, I had been looking down on Peking in the distance, fading in the light of a glorious sunset behind us, and all the events of the past ten years had come to my mind one by one. I had recalled the grayish-white hair of the Center Chief, the queer speech and voice of the young

Deputy Chief of the Center; each and every one of the guards; each doctor and nurse; every single one of the Center personnel. While I had been trying to dupe them and while I was using all kinds of methods to resist them and exposing my own stupidity to the point where I no longer had felt like living, these Communist Party people had persisted in their belief that I could be remolded and had patiently guided me toward being a new man.

"Man" was the first word I had learned to read in *The Three Words Classic,*[1] my first primer, as a child. But in my previous life I had never appreciated the true meaning of its first four lines:

When a man is born (Jen chih chu),
His nature is basically good (hsing pen shan).
Human nature is similar (hsing hsiang chin);
Only environment makes it diverse (hsi hsiang yuan).

---

[1] A small book, written three words to each line, that Chinese children used to memorize. It was used in China for almost 700 years.

Epilogue
by Paul Kramer

THE MANCHURIAN MONARCHY OF HENRY PU YI WAS HELD by no binding force but Japanese military power. Although the dynasty was old, the Emperor, as evidenced by this autobiography, was neither personally imposing nor attractive. Furthermore, the original Manchu majority of Manchukuo had been overwhelmed numerically by a vast influx of Chinese and a minority immigration from both Russia and Japan. None of these newer residents had a motive to make sacrifices for the Crown—the Russians because it was yellow, the Japanese because it was alien, the Chinese (Hans) because it was foreign. It thus crashed, along with the Japanese Army that was its support, a few days after Russia's declaration of war on Japan, with no evidence of its being able to enlist popular backing against an invader of another color.

But to suppose that the ease with which Pu Yi's Manchu monarchy was overthrown is indicative of its political insignificance is to overlook the condition of the Sino-Soviet frontier. The border between the two countries has never in more recent times coincided with a clear delineation of the peoples who live near it. There are in China roughly two-and-a-half million Manchu people living largely north of the Great Wall and south of the Russian frontier. There are also one-and-a-half million Mongols along the frontier who have

305

been content since the eighteenth century to accept varying forms of Manchu leadership. In addition there are an undetermined number of Manchus within the borders of the Soviet Union since the Siberian territory north of the Amur River and the present Maritime Territory of Siberia were once part of the Manchu inheritance, until detached from China and ceded to Russia in 1858 and 1860.

Outer Mongolia, with a population of roughly a million Mongols and today a Soviet dependency, was under the Ch'ing Dynasty, a Chinese vassal. There are also Mongols living north of the frontier, in the USSR itself. The claim that China under Mao Tse-tung erased the insults in the form of territorial concessions that the imperial powers imposed upon China under the corrupt and feudal Ch'ings is belied by the dependency of Outer Mongolia on the Soviets and the existence of Vladivostok as the most important Russian naval base in the Far East.

The political history of the northeast (Manchuria) has never been sufficiently democratic to permit the emergence through elections of popular figures among the Manchus and the Mongols to replace fully the concept of leadership vested in the theory of dynastic succession. This was one reason why the Japanese made Pu Yi Emperor of Manchukuo and sought to perpetuate and develop control of the dynastic inheritance through the marriage of his brother and heir to a Japanese noblewoman. Another reason was his utility as a device for potential Japanese expansion into Siberia and Mongolia, the Oriental populations of which could be expected to respond to the dynastic claims of Pu Yi as opposed to the colonial claims of Moscow. Pu Yi thus owed his fourteen-year restoration not, as he hoped, to the desire of the Japanese to obtain through him control of China proper, but to the intent of Japan to use him as an instrument of psychological warfare and subversion in order to win from Russia what Russia had once won from China. The Black Dragon Society was used by the Japanese imperialists to assist in the restoration of Pu Yi. It was a sort of Japanese CIA. It had always an anti-Russian direction and its name in the languages of the Orient, by a play on words, suggested Japanese expansion north of the Amur River into Siberia, not expansion south of the Great Wall into China itself.

This identification with clandestine and subversive efforts along the Sino-Soviet frontier explains Pu Yi's importance as well as that of his heirs. His five-year imprisonment at the hands of the Soviets and more than nine-year detention by the Chinese Communists must be examined in the light of the relations between the two countries if the future is to be understood. The fact that Pu Yi has suggested that his "brainwashing" was something separate and personal, and divorced from outside events is unrealistic—an example of Maoist Communist policy of publicly emphasizing ideology as distinguished from practical politics in its effort to capture leadership of the international Communist movement.

The Yalta agreements of February 1945 created the opening pattern of Pu Yi's incarceration, which began six months later. By these arrangements among the Western powers, which were later translated into an agreement between Stalin and Chiang Kai-shek, Outer Mongolia became independent of China, Manchuria became a Soviet sphere of influence and Port Arthur a USSR naval base. The Northeast and Pu Yi's Manchu people reverted to the status they enjoyed before the Russo-Japanese war of 1905, when Russia rather than Japan enjoyed paramount interest over the area.

In view of this reversion of Manchurian suzerainty, it was only natural that when Japan was defeated in August 1945 and the monarchy crashed, Pu Yi passed from the "protection" of the Japanese to that of the USSR. This "protection" lasted from 1945 until July 31, 1950, when he was turned over to the Chinese Communists.

Meanwhile, the Northeast underwent a similar shift from Russia to China. October 1, 1949, marked the offical beginning of the People's Republic of China. Three months later Chairman Mao went to Moscow to confer with Stalin and brought home in February 1950 a treaty of friendship and alliance. Various concessions were made by the Soviets to their new ally, including the relinquishment of their special Manchurian rights. This was the heyday of Sino-Soviet cooperation and also the time when North Korea, at Moscow's instigation, invaded South Korea and was joined in the war by the Chinese Communists.

At the same time, in the Thought Control Center in Fushun to which Pu Yi was consigned as a result of this

Sino-Soviet accord, he experienced the most stringent "remolding." Separated from his family, denounced by his nephews, deprived of all prerogatives, he became a non-person. For if the Sino-Soviet frontier was to remain quiet, if there was to be no chicanery and subversion among the border peoples in the name of race, or nationality or color, then Pu Yi had no more utility than the curios and antiques he surrendered from time to time to his captors as a testimony of his devotion.

But on March 10, 1956, things began to improve for Pu Yi. His uncle, the former Prince Tsai Tao, was allowed to visit him in prison and give him news of the outside world and the status of the Manchu clans. Tsai Tao spoke of his election to the People's National Congress and adverted to visits he had made to the "Northwest" and of his work with "national minorities." These words from the lips of the former senior royal prince of China, the brother of the former Prince Regent, the uncle of the last emperor, could only mean that Chairman Mao had decided by the mid-1950s, just as the Japanese had decided in the mid-1930s, that the Manchu Aisin-Gioro clan (royal family of China) could be useful along the frontier.

And thus, soon after Tsai Tao's visit, Pu Yi's treatment and that of the other Manchu detainees improved. By September 1959, Pu Yi again acquired a personality of his own. This occurred despite the fact that shortly before his pardon, the Prison Governor found him guilty of lying in order to curry favor with the authorities.

Meanwhile, and parallel to Pu Yi's restoration as a person, Sino-Soviet relations deteriorated. In November 1957, the Soviet Union and Communist China signed the Moscow Declaration, which was an unsuccessful attempt to heal the ideological breach that was opening between the two countries. In 1960, shortly after Pu Yi's release from prison, Chinese students were called home from Russia and Russian technicians were withdrawn from China. Trade between the two countries slumped from $2 billion U.S. in 1959 to less than $1 billion in 1961.

In 1962, during the Cuban missile crisis, Communist China described Khrushchev's withdrawal of offensive weapons from Cuba as "100 percent appeasement, a Munich pure and simple." Subsequently, invective was hurled back and forth between the two countries and in 1965 negotiations for a new defensive alliance between Outer Mongolia and the USSR were opened. As relations between the two countries deteriorated, Pu Yi's status as a person in Peking attained new vigor. No longer a gardener working with his hands, he was allowed to do "research" and subsequently to write and have published a "best seller." Later he became a member of the Congress and a spokesman for the Manchu people.

This was Pu Yi until the Cultural Revolution of 1966. At that time, and once again as so often in the past, on the brink of the abyss, his life was saved by fellow patients and staff members of the hospital in which he was confined. They drove off the radical Red Guards who had come to take him away. He died of cancer the following year.

But the Manchu saga did not end with Pu Yi's death. His younger brother and heir, William Pu Chieh, was elected to the People's National Congress as the representative of the Manchu people in his place. This was the same Pu Chieh with whom Pu Yi had played hide-and-seek as a child within the walls of the Forbidden City, the Pu Chieh who had violated precedent by wearing sleeve linings of imperial yellow, who had lived in Manchukuo with him during the Japanese restoration and had been brainwashed with him at the War Prisoner Thought Control Center. Meanwhile, Pu Chieh had regained his father's house outside the Forbidden City and had it refurnished. Also, he was rejoined by his wife, Hiro Saga, cousin of the Empress of Japan, after an absence of sixteen years. Chou En-lai, the Premier of China, deliberately preserved the concept of the last Manchu. Why?

Auctioneers and dealers in Chinese antiquities throughout the West tell of how at significant sales of former imperial treasures that have found their way abroad, representatives of the Chinese government mysteriously appear to buy them so that they may be returned to the Forbidden City from which they were originally removed. They, like the Manchus who once possessed them, are regarded by the new China as valued symbols of the cultural heritage of the nation, useful for display and inspiration.

And if we were allowed to observe ranking Manchus closely and to see who visits them and to peruse their correspondence and reading matter, it is safe to assume that we would find them in touch with the peoples of the North-west and the Northeast. For these are the border peoples who, by virtue of their appearance and their language and their habits, can slip unnoticed through some remote mountain pass from China into Russia on the missions of violence and subversion and espionage that have become such an integral part of modern national rivalry. And how is Peking to know that its own border peoples are not being subject to similar nefarious infestations from Russia, unless it can count on their special loyalty by offering in the form of The Last Manchu a continuing public testimonial of their importance wholly beyond what their numbers would warrant in relation to the entire population of China?

P.K.